D0624673

THE URBAN

THE URBAN PICNIC

BY JOHN BURNS
& ELISABETH CATON

ARSENAL PULP PRESS

VANCOUVER

ARSENAL PULP PRESS
103 - 1014 Homer Street
Vancouver, B.C.
Canada V6B 2W9
arsenalpulp.com

The publisher gratefully acknowledges the support of the Government of Canada through the Book Publishing Industry Development Program for its publishing activities.

Design by Electra Design Group
Production assistance by Judy Yeung
Cover illustration by Jennifer Lyon
Cover design by Solo

Printed and bound in Canada

The authors and publisher assert that the information contained in this book is true and complete to the best of their knowledge. All recommendations are made without guarantee on the part of the authors and Arsenal Pulp Press. The authors and publisher disclaim any liability in connection with the use of this information. For more information, contact the publisher.

Efforts have been made to locate copyright holders of source material wherever possible. The publisher welcomes hearing from any copyright holders of material used in this book who have not been contacted.

National Library of Canada Cataloguing in Publication

Burns, John, 1968-
    The urban picnic : being an idiosyncratic and lyrically recollected account of menus, recipes, history, trivia, and admonitions on the subject of alfresco dining in cities both large and small / written by John Burns and Elisabeth Caton ; illustrations by Jennifer Lyon.

ISBN 1-55152-155-5

    1. Cookery. 2. Picnicking. 3. Menus. I. Caton, Elisabeth II. Title.

TX823.B87 2004   641.5   C2004-900679-7

CONTENTS

ACKNOWLEDGMENTS

T'aint no bloomin' picnic in those parts, I can tell you.
– Wee Willie Winkie

Openers: The notion of an urban picnic book, and the drive to bring it and us together, come thanks to the bright minds at Arsenal Pulp Press: Brian Lam, Blaine Kyllo, Kiran Gill Judge, Trish Kelly, and Robert Ballantyne. To them go all thanks but no blame.

Mains: Food is the product of community. To the contributing chefs – Nadine Abensur, Audrey Alsterberg and Wanda Urbanowicz, James Barber, Wanda Beaver, John Bishop, Mark Bittman, Bob Blumer, Regan Daley, Trish Deseine, Rob Feenie and Marnie Coldham, Joyce Goldstein, Krishna Jamal, Bill Jones, Nigella Lawson, Anne Lindsay, Barbara-jo McIntosh, James McNair, Umberto Menghi, Adrienne O'Callaghan, James Peterson, and the late David Veljacic – a big thank-you. To conspirators and mentors Jamie Broadhurst, Lorna Jackson, John Lekich, Barbara-jo McIntosh (again!), Angela Murrills, Beverley Sinclair and the editorial staff of the *Georgia Straight*, and Sarah Thring: a grateful tip o' the toque. To *The Urban Picnic*'s other contributors – Christina Burridge, Jurgen Gothe, and Jennifer Lyon – *slàinte*! And to Elisabeth Caton, mother-in-law, mentor, friend: love and thanks.

Sweets: Anything of value I've done here owes its soul to Catherine Kirkness, and to our children: Rowan Burns-Kirkness and Skye Burns-Kirkness. – JB

My first thanks must be to my beloved husband, Bob, who supported and encouraged me in all I ever undertook during our lives together, who was my most enthusiastic recipe tester and dining companion, who was so proud of me and John for writing this book and would have delighted in seeing it in print.

Thanks to my parents and sisters for sharing with me their gift for cooking, their love of good food, and a treasure trove of family recipes scribbled on bits of paper, and in an old notebook; my daughter Catherine, who first inspired me to try some vegetarian cooking and whose love of simple old favorites keeps me in touch with the essentials; my son-in-law and co-author John, ever patient and encouraging, who first suggested I write about food, and has been a helpful editor ever since. He convinced me we could create a book, and he made it happen; my grandchildren, Roger, Walter, and Harold in Ontario, and step-grandson Addison in Calgary, who are all Grandma-cookie connoisseurs, and Rowan and Skye in Vancouver, who share meals with me often, as well as cookies. (Rowan came up with the idea for Kid Kebabs, and they were a hit at our family picnic last summer.)

There are other people, too, who inspire me to cook and I can't thank them all here, but special thanks to my friend Joyce, whose mouth-watering descriptions of her vegetarian cooking as we stroll the seawall always make me rush home with more good ideas to try out.

I want to thank all the friends who assisted us by giving us family recipes, recently or in the long past, or helping us test new ones. Your input was invaluable: Jane and Simon, Mark and Victoria, Angela, James, Martin, Ann, Esmeralda, Patti, Zoe, Ian, CaraLynn, Sarah, Charlotte, Lucy, and Tia.

Barbara-jo McIntosh, your wisdom, knowledge, and generosity have saved our bacon more than a few times, and we thank you. — EC

INTRODUCTION

We reserve a whole type of eating experience for "out of doors," where for once we eat seated on the ground. We are very self-conscious about picnics, and the freedom we grant ourselves to lounge about on a blanket eating cold food with our hands. We travel long distances and put up with a thousand risks and inconveniences to reach this state.

— Margaret Visser, *The Rituals of Dinner*

Picnic. It's one of those evocative words. Go ahead, say it out loud. No one's watching. Picnic. There. An invocation, images rising up like clouds of mosquitoes: car blankets and wicker hampers, soft linen and Merchant Ivory films, buzzing summer meadows and springtime sylvan romance. That's a lot for six little letters to carry, especially with that perky nursery rhythm.

This book is not about those picnics. If you're entertaining fantasies about day trips and farmers' fields, browse on down the shelf. The forays these pages describe could happen by taxi as easily as SUV. (Or bicycle; we're big on bicycles.) And don't trek down to the outdoor outfitter's for a new Thermos with this collection of recipes and anecdotes for inspiration. You'll more likely be using takeout cups anyway. Forget *Howards End*. Think Howard Stern.

The idea of *The Urban Picnic* is to close the gap between country leisure and city chaos; to inject the possibility of those lazy rural afternoons into modern urban lives. After all, we could use a little balance. We insist on such all-or-nothing lifestyles: wage slaves spend forty-nine weeks at work, five days a week, year in year out. For too many of us, it's at the office before nine, lunch at the desk, stay till dinner, maybe bring a folder home at night. Families struggle to time-manage Junior's chock-a-block schedule, pencilling in play dates around Suzuki violin. All of us — singles, couples, families; workaholics and trust-funders alike — seem to have less time. Somewhere in the last thirty years, the whole notion of leisure disappeared (well, maybe not for the trust-funders), along with hobbies and Sunday drives. Remember those? We're lucky if we can squeeze in Tae Bo and the *New Yorker* each week.

A picnic is the Englishman's grand gesture, his final defiance flung in the face of fate. No climate in the world is less propitious to picnics than the climate of England, yet with a recklessness which is almost sublime, the English rush out of doors to eat a meal on every possible and impossible occasion.

— Georgina Battiscombe, *English Picnics* (1951)

Is this how it has to be? Who decided? The architects of the Industrial Revolution, that's who. The modern work week spelled the end of the natural cycles of labor and rest, which had for millennia been tied to the seasons. Social historian E. P. Thompson writes at length on this attitudinal shift in English history, and goes so far as to say that the rhythms of work that accompany the tasks that integrate into a rural lifestyle — farming, milking, burning turf fires — are, in a sense, "more humanly comprehensible than timed labor." Ironically, picnics came to symbolize the benefits of industrialization: paid holidays, proliferating technologies, the advent of leisure. Now, don't get me wrong; I'm not feeling misty-eyed for the joys of the 19th century. I *like* having three high-end gelaterias within six blocks of my condo. I *like* home delivery. I'm fine not having to burn

LACONIC, BUT EXPRESSIVE.
SCENE: NEIGHBORHOOD OF THE FIVE POINTS

First Ruffian. "WHERE TO NOW, SNOOTY?"
Second Ditto. "PICNIC."
First Ditto. "WOTTERYER GOT IN YER LUNCH WALLET?"
Second Ditto. "SLUNG SHOT."

turf. But we no longer live in an industrial age, so let's not act as though we did.

The technical era, this so-called information age of ours, does have its benefits. If we use our imaginations and commit ourselves to pleasure, we can start to engineer new models, to evolve beyond the Victorian law-clerk salaryman. If we work, we can telecommute from home, dressed in our PJs but networked into office and voicemail and the online beyond. And maybe we slip in a little time looking out the window or playing the piano. Hey, who's watching? Thanks to all our gizmos and gewgaws, we're portable now, too; we can carry our work with us, email with PalmPilots, spreadsheet on laptops, conference call by cellphone. No longer are we bound to our desks, our factories, our stores.

Or our class. Next time you're contemplating a tapenade along the river and someone gives you that "Shouldn't you be somewhere? What are you, a tourist?" look, give up a little smile and a shrug. Maybe you got out of the dot-com boom in time. Maybe this is just what you do.

For those of us still toiling among the fax machines and other detritus of this crazy, privileged, short-term-only-thanks, postindustrial society, there's still hope. Perhaps it's our tools and our creativity that can help us find balance and unfold a moment of leisure, even if it's only for the time it takes to eat a meal under that tree that grows in Brooklyn. These are some pretty massive forces at play, but for each of us, change starts with a single decision, even with a single meal rethought. As the song says: "Put down the knitting, the book, and the broom. Time for a holiday."

The picnic philosophy is one of flexibility, of leisure, of *carpe diem*. The sun is shining. Pack up, head out, give in. Heed the Slow Food manifesto: "savor suitable doses of guaranteed sensual pleasure." (For more on Slow Food, see page 13.)

And for goodness sake, enjoy. Picnics are process, or should be. This book is not about guilting you into flights of culinary fancy or keeping up with the Hamper Nazis. Recently, *Le Monde* and *The Economist* have been featuring articles about the urban picnic with headlines like "The rise of the picnic" and "Picnics are chic." What these trend stories stress is the informality of the new picnic. *Le Monde* quotes an employee of a Paris auditing firm: "We often share our baguettes and our booze with other groups. We feel as if we're on holiday. Paris, a city where people hardly speak to each other, then begins to take on a very different feel." (This could also have something to do with champagne king Veuve Clicquot's new sports-capped takeout bottles of bubbly. That sound you hear is James Beard spinning in his grave.) As a publicist for Alain Ducasse, one of France's leading chefs, explained to *The Economist*, it comes down to balance: "The big question in our lives is how to be at the same time a hedonist and in a hurry."

This book is here to help, to offer inspiration and practical tools to help you take to the streets with a new kind of picnic in mind. And none of it's difficult. Many of the recipes are dead simple. Pick up whatever's local and fresh one evening, prep it that night, and in the morning you're nine-tenths of the way to gourmet eating alfresco. Hedonism in a hurry.

As you saunter through *The Urban Picnic*, you'll see that the book is a picnic itself, making room on the blanket for history, quotations, advertisements, song lyrics, and related trivia. (I wish I could lay claim to this as an original thought, but there's nothing new under the sun. In 1825, Hariette Wilson wrote in her *Memoirs Written by Herself*: "I sate down to consider the plan of a book, in the style of the Spectator, a kind of pic nic, where every wiseacre might contribute his mite of knowledge.")

It's a picnic in another way as well. In its earliest sense, PICNIC suggested something we'd now recognize as a potluck; everyone contributed a dish, or paid to have a dish represent them. The whole requirement to head outdoors only arose later. So *The Urban Picnic* has opened its doors to a galley of guests, a wealth of wiseacres.

Skill without imagination is craftsmanship and gives us many useful objects such as wickerwork picnic baskets. Imagination without skill gives us modern art.

– Tom Stoppard, *Artist Descending a Staircase* (1972)

Chief among them is Elisabeth Caton, my mother-in-law and an outstanding cook in her own right. You'll find some 140 of her recipes, which we've put together into categories — sandwiches, mains, desserts, and so on — and also arranged into menus to help point (or at least suggest) the way. Sprinkled among her recipes, and featured in the menus, you'll find contributions from well-known cookbook authors and chefs from across North America and elsewhere. (You'll find a list of these stalwart friends of the picnic listed in the acknowledgments.) Remember that the menus are suggestions only; food is not like IKEA furniture parts. Your meal will not fall flatter than a three-legged chair if you improvise or substitute.

For the motor picnicker or camper, this handy little cook-book will solve all questions about food. Equipment necessary, supplies which have been proven practical, balanced menus, recipes—everything is given in the book to make delightful and delicious the meals of the amateur gypsy.

MAY E. SOUTHWORTH

HARPER & BROTHERS, PUBLISHERS
Established 1817

Along the way, you'll also notice that in the menus there are contributions from two more writers, experts in their fields — and hey, Hedonist in a Hurry could sit happily on both their business cards. Christina Burridge, executive director of the B.C. Seafood Alliance and a long-time food writer, suggests wine pairings for each menu. (Please check state or provincial laws covering the issue of alcohol in the great outdoors. If you get fingered by the law, I don't want you squandering your one phone call ringing me up to complain. I'll probably be down at the beach with Regan Daley's strawberry-banana layer cake anyway.) Jurgen Gothe, devotee of fine dining and drinking, is Canada's most widely heard broadcaster thanks to *DiscDrive*, the national weekday drive-home public-radio show; he collaborates with music to buoy the spirits. Illustrations by Jennifer Lyon keep the words from overrunning the page and remind us that grace and fun are the reasons we're here. These are all — food, menus, wines, music — starting points only, signposts to a richer, picnickier way of living.

Creativity is the key. The fare can be as simple as sushi to go or as complex as the Hipnic menu listed on page 72. Locations can vary wildly. Maybe you're just ducking around the corner with Umberto Menghi's Breast of Duck Rapido. Or maybe you're roaming with Joyce Goldstein's Roman Meat Loaf to one of those natural hideaways that exist in every city. Maybe you have picturesque shorelines or riverbanks where you live, or maybe only pocket parks and rooftop gardens. They all count. Ask around. Pretend you're a movie scout and carry a notebook at all times. With your urban picnic filters in place, the city begins to seem a greener, friendlier place.

And if your cellphone rings and it's work or the bank or your Tae Bo coach: don't answer. You're a new kind of busy. They'll leave a message. You can get back to them after a little something to eat. And maybe a nap.

— JB, Vancouver 2004

SLOW FOOD MANIFESTO

The Slow Food movement, which began in Paris in 1989, celebrates and promotes local, authentic cooking. Its resistance to the increasingly pervasive reach of multinational, corporate-driven, bland fast food has attracted over 75,000 members in forty-eight countries. The Internet can lead you to the closest chapter (called convivium) to your hometown. See slowfood.com. *Below is the organization's* cri de coeur, *which could be summed up as Tune In, Turn On, Eat Up.*

Our century, which began and has developed under the insignia of industrial civilization, first invented the machine and then took it as its life model.

We are enslaved by speed and have all succumbed to the same insidious virus: Fast Life, which disrupts our habits, pervades the privacy of our homes, and forces us to eat Fast Foods.

To be worthy of the name, *Homo Sapiens* should rid himself of speed before it reduces him to a species in danger of extinction.

A firm defense of quiet material pleasure is the only way to oppose the universal folly of Fast Life.

May suitable doses of guaranteed sensual pleasure and slow, long-lasting enjoyment preserve us from the contagion of the multitude who mistake frenzy for efficiency.

Our defense should begin at the table with Slow Food. Let us rediscover the flavors and savors of regional cooking and banish the degrading effects of Fast Food.

In the name of productivity, Fast Life has changed our way of being and threatens our environment and our landscapes. So Slow Food is now the only truly progressive answer.

That is what real culture is all about: developing taste rather than demeaning it. And what better way to set about this than an international exchange of experiences, knowledge, projects?

Slow Food guarantees a better future. Slow Food is an idea that needs plenty of qualified supporters who can help turn this (slow) motion into an international movement, with the little snail as its symbol.

— Endorsed and approved in 1989 by delegates from twenty countries

HISTORY

Yes, by all means let us take a picnic basket so that we can be independent of restaurants.
— Aldous Huxley, 1955

It wasn't until I had children of my own and became intimately familiar with the Magic School Bus that I actually started to understand electricity. I hadn't needed to before. When I plugged in the cord, good things happened. When I plugged in my tongue, bad things happened. I had it down. "Electron transfer." Pshaw. The lights went on, the lights went off — almost like electricity could carry on without me! The same is (depressingly) still true of countless other objects, processes, philosophies, taxonomies, entire nations, other galaxies.... When I stop and consider all the things I don't know, all the things that manage themselves without my understanding or my involvement, well, it's overwhelming.

We humans are a self-absorbed species. It's all about us. Take carburetors. (Please.) The only thing I know about them is how to spell them. And even there I'm only ninety percent sure. But their *purpose* I get: I put the key in the ignition, the car goes — somewhere in there, the carburetor is doing its bit. Until it needs fixing.

Then I get out the Yellow Pages and look up Carburetors — Broken.

Picnics are the same. (Yes, I'm getting to picnics.) With or without our understanding, they just keep on keeping on. How long have North Americans been picnicking? Europeans? Asians? Where does the word come from? Does it count as a picnic if it's not in the woods? Not on a blanket? Not packed in wicker?

Ignorant of their history, I've nonetheless managed to go on groaning-baskets excursions my whole life. Even though I had no idea of the etymology, the history, the cultural variations, the social ramifications, I was still able to throw together some food and do that thing we call picnicking. As a child, I may not have appreciated their cultural inheritance and their potential legacy, but intuitively I got their *purpose*, their "Calgon, take me away!" alternative to chairs and tables, indoor lights, and use your napkin, their snubbing their nose at the workaday routines and rules of the dining room. The way they function like keys, opening a doorway to freedom.

But now that I'm an adult with my own library card, I have this curiosity: how far can we push this notion of picnics? Where *did* they come from? Where are they going? If I have a picnic and no ants come, did it really happen?

The word PICNIC dates at least as far back as 1692 and Gilles Ménage's *Dictionnaire Etymologique, ou Origines de la Langue Françoise*. By the mid-18th century, it had found its way into the official lexicon: it appears in the 1740 edition of the almighty *Dictionnaire de l'Académie*. (In French, if a word has not been recognized by the Académie Française and is not entered into its dictionary, it's fair to say it doesn't exist.) It would be another fifty years before it entered common English, but the word is nonetheless believed to be an Anglicization (sometimes via Germany and/or Sweden) of the French verb PIQUER, meaning "to prick" or "to puncture." The NIQUE is often considered a meaningless alliterative suffix.

Seems neat and tidy. But packages can harbor surprises you discover only as you unpack them. It turns out that not everyone agrees. The *Oxford English Dictionary* — the closest the English-speaking world has to a linguistic rulebook — weighs in on the controversy thusly:

> The chronology of the word in French and English, with the fact that our earliest instances refer to the Continent, and are sometimes in the French form PIQUE-NIQUE, show that the word came from French (although some French scholars, in ignorance of these facts, have in view of the obscurity of its derivation, conjectured that the French word was from Eng.). Hatzfeld-Darmesteter merely say "Origin unknown: the Eng. PICNIC appears to be borrowed from French." Scheler mentions several conjectures, among others that of Boniface (18 ...) "*repas où chacun pique au plat pour sa nique* (NIQUE taken in the sense of 'small coin')." Others think it merely a riming combination formed on one of its elements.

It's all a bit huffy, in a cold-blooded academic way. (Remind me sometime to tell you why I never went on for my PhD.) French scholars "in ignorance of these facts" — at least, according to the English, who may have seen too many Monty Python skits — take a different tack. The following is my translation from the *Dictionnaire de la Langue Française*:

> The fact is that the spelling PIQUE-NIQUE, with its hyphen, is wrong [*vicieuse*], because the meaning is

The artist ... one day ... falls through a hole in the brambles, and from that moment he is following the dark rapids of an underground river which may sometimes flow so near to the surface that the laughing picnic parties are heard above.

— Cyril Connolly, quoted by Christopher Lehmann-Haupt, *New York Times* (March 15, 1984)

not *piquer la nique* (the word being English). It would be better to get rid of the hyphen, and write PIQUENIQUE or, better still, PIKENIKE. English etymology: PICK NICK, PIQUE-NIQUE, from "to pick," and NICK, meaning instant, moment. This etymology replaces all etymologies that have been made about PIQUE-NIQUE.

Hang on a nick. Or a nike. Is it a small coin or a moment seized? (Let's not even get into the fact that NIQUER can also mean an intimate act involving two people who.... Well, suffice to say it's considered rude to say "Nique ta mère.") No wonder your average food book glosses over with an "etymology unknown."

Anyway, how can we be squabbling about the origins of a word so overflowing with connotations of idyllic splendor? It all seems like a lot of nickpicking when you hold it up against egg-salad sandwiches and the rustling of the birch leaves.

A PICNIC POTLUCK

In *The Rituals of Dinner*, Canadian social historian Margaret Visser writes about what picnics have come to mean in western society, ducking out (sensibly) on the question of etymology ("aside from the probable connotation of 'picking' "). Across the centuries, she argues, the picnic has changed its specifics but has still managed to retain certain meanings, meanings that are with us today. She's worth quoting at length:

> People often think that "there is nothing like the out of doors" for lending one an appetite. Fresh air and natural beauty, adventure, no cooking, and no tables and chairs — a good picnic is a thrilling reversal of normal rules. Not very long ago, picnics were rather formal affairs to our way of thinking, with tables, chairs, and even servants. But everything is relative: what was formal then made a trestle-table in the open countryside seem exhilaratingly abandoned. The general feeling of relief from normal constraints might even lead to the kind of liberty depicted in Manet's painting *Le Déjeuner sur l'herbe*, a faint and distant echo of the shocking behavior of ancient Greek Bacchanals, who escaped the constraints of city living by going wild in the woods.

The Hungry Man's
OUTDOOR GRILL
Cookbook

Before we go wild ourselves, let's follow the picnic across the centuries.

In English, the earliest recorded use of the word comes in a letter from Lord Chesterfield to his son, Philip Stanhope, who was in Germany at the time. Beginning when his son was five, the hyperproductive Chesterfield had written, almost daily, to his son on questions of deportment and manners. (These days, he'd be the kind of person who forwards inspirational group emails. Every single day.) On October 29, 1748, Lord Chesterfield wrote: "I like the description of your *pic-nic*." In this early meaning, the word denoted a party, often fashionable, to which all guests brought a contribution; nowadays, we'd call this a potluck. (Chesterfield continued to write his son until Philip's death in 1768, at which point he switched to his godson, also called Philip, until Chesterfield himself died in 1773.)

Fifty years later, the word had landed definitively in England. Over the decades, its meaning had broadened to take in not just the *what* of the meal, but also the how and the who and the where. In 1802, the *Times* described a picnic this way: "A Pic-Nic Supper consists of a variety of dishes. The Subscribers to the entertainment have a bill of fare presented to them, with a number against each dish. The lot which he draws obliges him to furnish the dish marked against it, which he either takes with him in his carriage, or sends by a servant." Although it has the whiff of a hockey pool about it, the class implications of this description are nonetheless clear; equally evocative is a report from *The Annual Register* of the same year: "This season has been marked by a new species of entertainment, common to the fashionable world, called a Pic Nic supper. Of the derivation of the word, or who was the inventor, we profess ourselves ignorant." And elsewhere: "The rich have their sports, their balls, their parties of pleasure, and their *pic nics*."

This notion of potlucks and parties spread to encompass the entertainments that often accompanied the meals. By the beginning of the 1800s, a Picnic Society had sprung up in London to organize evenings in which every member — every wealthy member of the intelligentsia, that is — was both player and audience. From *The Spirit of the Public Journals* (1802): "One famous Pic-Nic indeed … came forward and said, they were 'a harmless and inoffensive society of persons of fashion.' … Nor was the public amazement lessened, when they were informed, that Pic-Nics were men who acted plays and wrote plays for their own amusement." Their *own* amusement is the key here; the *Times* goes on in a separate article to complain about the incomprehensibility of these entertainments: "We are induced to contend against any thing so contemptible as the pick-nickery and nick-nackery — the pert affectation, and subaltern vanity of rehearsing to an audience that cannot understand, in a language one cannot pronounce." (Debate raged to such a degree that a W. Cutspear felt

It is not only our fate but our business to lose innocence, and once we have lost that it is futile to attempt a picnic in Eden.

— Elizabeth Bowen (1899–1973), British novelist, story writer, essayist, and memoirist; born in Ireland. As quoted in *Elizabeth Bowen*, by Victoria Glendinning (1979).

moved to write that year *Dramatic Rights; Or, Private Theatricals and Picnic Suppers Justified by Fair Argument.*)

Members met in the Pantheon on Oxford Street (a theatre, then bazaar, then demolished by Marks & Spencer in 1937). Interest in the society waned as the founders and the century wound down, but picnics had by this time outgrown their original purpose and their social class. In both England and North America, they continued to rise in popularity throughout the 1800s, and were increasingly enjoyed outdoors, particularly as the railway spread across the United Kingdom and the United States. (Oddly, a catering company in Mayfair, London, claims the Picnic Society "has been reborn and organizes outings to places like Henley, Ascot, Glynbourne [sic] and to many other privately run prestigious events where picnics are required." If you'd like to know more, visit *www.paxuk.com.*)

The modern, alfresco meaning is pinned down in A *Dictionary of the English Language* (1868): "open air party, in which a meal, to which each guest contributes a portion of the viands, is the essential characteristic." Lest this all seem too innocent and rustic, know that the moral perils of just sitting around were noted even at the time. In the July 1848 edition of *The Ladies' Repository: A Monthly Periodical Devoted to Literature, Arts, and Religion,* "Florence" wrote the following warning to the lax, cross-dressing, singing-and-storytelling slackers of the day:

SPOFFORD PICNIC

EXCURSION

— VIA —

STR. CITY OF HAVERHILL,   CAPT. JOHN OSGOOD.

TO OLD OCEAN, BLACK ROCKS, SALISBURY & PLUM ISLAND BEACHES.

Thursday, Aug. 30 th. 1888.

Leave Haverhill 10 A. M.   Return in season for Trains E. & W.

Remember this is the SPOFFORD Excursion and is via this beautiful route, acknowledged by everybody to excel in every particular.   Cheapest and easiest, 44 miles on the beautiful Merrimac River.

Seven hundred thousand people in the past eight years and not a single accident of any kind.   (A great record.)

The scenery cannot be equalled in this country, passing through Groveland, East Haverhill, West Newbury, Merrimac, Merrimacport, Amesbury, Salisbury, Newburyport, through five Bridges, under the Historical Chain Bridge, (built in 1801 by Lord Timothy Dexter.) one end of which rests on the picturesque Deer Island, in full view of the residence of our cousin, the late Hon. R. S. Spofford.

The many attractions at the Beaches makes this one of the most enjoyable excursions in the country.   Don't fail to take it in, steamer is large enough for 1.000 persons.

Refreshment Saloon on the steamer.   Tickets will be for sale at the Picnic Wednesday, and at wharf in Haverhill, ·Thursday morning.   Positively Limited.

ROUND TRIP, 50 CTS.   CHILDREN, 25

DANIEL HOOKE, Gen. Pass. Agt.

HOOKE'S ELECTRIC PRINTING HOUSE.

PICNICS & PARTIES

By Florence – July 1848

My discrimination is rather dull, and this, in connection with other points in my character, not worthy of recital, is the reason why I never understood the propriety of attending picnics and social parties. My cousin Caroline, at my elbow, who has been to school some, and has studied geography, says the country is a great place for fun, and that she not only goes out occasionally, but whenever it is possible to obtain company, or whenever an invitation is sent her to take a stroll through the woods, over the hills, and far away. She thinks, moreover, that there is not only no harm in a picnic, but that it tends most wonderfully to the development of the social principle and the improvement of the heart.

Unfortunately for my weak mind, I never could, and cannot now, appreciate the force of her logic. Here the picture is: some twenty-five, or thirty, or forty young persons, of both sexes, conclude that they must spend a day in the woods. Ordinary affairs are pitched aside, and, with appropriate paraphernalia, they leave for the wished-for place. Mischief and merriment are the first things demanding attention. Repartees and brainless jokes pass round to kill time, and make the hours run merrily. Now this, and now that, indiscretion is committed. Some gentleman puts off his hat, and hoods his head with some lady's vail or sun-bonnet, and some lady, with equal wisdom, throws off her bonnet, and puts on some gentleman's hat. Another pilfers a neighbor's kerchief, and throws it up in the branches of a tree; a third tells the wonderful story of some such character as Robin Hood, or William Gulliver, and a fourth sings the affectingly edifying song of "Miss Lucy Neal." So the day wears off, and at night the question puts itself, "What profit to me has been this day's work?" And, seriously, may I not reiterate, where has been the profit? How much better is any one for all the follies he or she has committed through the day? What more heavenly feelings have been inspired? What better state of heart is produced, and what better prayer can any one offer up to her Father in heaven? Answers to these questions may be evaded, and conscience may be hushed to quiet, but there is an hour coming, when conscience will start from her long, deep sleep, and when every trifle and every misspent moment of life will fall like a dagger upon the heart, and cause its victim to writhe in an agony to which no power on earth or in heaven will bring mitigation.

STRAWBERRIES IN THE GARDEN

In England, anyway, this notion of an outdoor feast was nothing new. As far back as the Middle Ages, outdoor feasts and banquets accompanied hunts. As *The Good Huswifes Jewell* (c. 1596) narrates, a hunting breakfast, eaten alfresco, was no mere croissant and a coffee; you'd be protein-loading with "colde loynes of Veale, cold Capon, Beefe and Goose, With Pigeon Pyes, and Mutton Colde." It would be over three centuries before the first Frigidaire appears in a private kitchen. Many leftovers are hurriedly consumed.

In the late 16th century, it became customary to roast meat at the end of the hunt, furnishing a second round of picnicking. Among the royalty, Elizabeth I included, a predilection for outdoors banqueting arose, in pavilions or marquees decorated "with all manners of flowers." These were the salad days — so to speak — for big eaters. As super-foodie M.F.K. Fisher wrote in her first book, *Serve It Forth* (1937), the English hunger would never again be so healthy. With her trademark asperity and wit, Fisher conjured up an Elizabethan age that had already turned its back on Rabelaisian excess and taken its first mincing steps toward our own sorry Age of Calista Flockhart. Already, the ladies breakfasted like babies, thinking they could start the day decently on a pot of ale and but one meager pound of bacon. The Queen, God be thanked, paid no attention to the new-style finicking, and made her first meal of the day light but sustaining: butter, bread (brown, to stay in the stomach longer and more wholesomely than white), a stew of mutton, a joint of beef, one of veal, some rabbits in a pie, chickens, and fruits, with beef and wine to wash all down in really hygienic fashion.

After some waggish tsk-tsking, Fisher concluded: "We cannot but be thankful ... as we sit down to our balanced lunches of orange juice and salad, free perhaps from the gout and dropsy that stood like evil fiends behind every dining-bench in old England. But are we so thankful that we are free also from fine furious Elizabethan life?"

Vaulting ahead to the Georgian age, we find picnics well-established for all social classes, and it is here that modern eyes can find the appearance of picnics as we might imagine them: sumptuous, sun-dappled affairs calling for cold chickens and warm linens. As James Beard writes in his *James Beard's Treasury of Outdoor Cooking* (1960): "At the turn of the [20th] century, the landed gentry thought nothing of sending servants on ahead to the picnic site to establish an outdoor drawing room. By the time the picnickers arrived, rugs had been spread, tables set, flowers arranged in vases, the gramophone was playing, and the food was ready. And what food! Caviar, foie gras, quenelles, larks, grouse, pheasant, several salads, red and white wines, molded desserts, coffee, cognac, and champagne were the least the well-to-do picnicker could expect." These Victorians and Edwardians, forcing their indoors onto the natural world all around, would have in mind the characters of Jane Austen's *Emma* (1815), who variously struggle to wed, or to prevent the wedding, of each other. Notice the opposition of home and heath in this exchange between Mrs Elton, quoted here first, and Mr Knightley:

"It is to be a morning scheme, you know, Knightley; quite a simple thing. I shall wear a large bonnet, and bring one of my little baskets hanging on my arm. Here, – probably this basket with pink ribbon. Nothing can be more simple, you see. And Jane will have such another. There is to be no form or parade – a sort of gipsy party. We are to walk about your gardens, and gather the strawberries ourselves, and sit under trees; – and whatever else you may like to provide, it is to be all out of doors – a table spread in the shade, you know. Every thing as natural and simple as possible. Is not that your idea?"

"Not quite. My idea of the simple and the natural will be to have the table spread in the dining-room. The nature and the simplicity of gentlemen and ladies, with their servants and furniture, I think is best observed by meals within doors. When you are tired of eating strawberries in the garden, there shall be cold meat in the house."

An article in *Appleton's Journal of Literature, Science, and Art* (1869) considers the same city/country dichotomy, with happier results:

The great charm of this social device is undoubtedly the freedom it affords. It is to eat, to chat, to lie, to sit, to talk, to walk, with some thing of the unconstraint of primitive life. We find a fascination in carrying back our civilization to the wilderness. To eat cold chicken, and drink iced claret under trees, amid the grass and the flowers; to have the sunlight dancing down through the branches, and sparkling in our wine, while we inhale a bouquet from the aromatic forest, and beflowered earth, more fragrant and delicious than Seating themselves on the greensward, they eat while the corks fly and there is talk, laughter and merriment, and perfect freedom, for the universe is their drawing room and the sun their lamp. Besides, they have appetite, Nature's special gift, which lends to such a meal a vivacity unknown indoors, however beautiful the surroundings.

– Jean Anthelme Brillat-Savarin

that of the ripest Falernian; to gather from the fresh and exhilarating air zest and appetite; to enjoy all these things in delightful company (there must be both youth and beauty, in the latter, to give the picnic the proper seasoning) affords a charm that is subtly enjoyable, and which defies our clumsy analysis. The eagerness with which we enter upon picnics, the keenness with Which we relish them, are proofs of the supremacy of out-of-doors. Nature is still dear to us, notwithstanding all the veneering of civilization; and it is pleasant to reflect how, at this moment, on the sides of innumerable hills, on mountain tops, in wooded valleys, by many a lake and rivulet, on little wooded islands, in the far-off prairies, in southern savannas, are countless picnic parties, all of which, let us hope, are finding full realization of the true ideal of a picnic.

At home or abroad, though, certain considerations were weighed with great seriousness. Ladies were considered nervous anywhere near clifftops, ants, or unshaded ground. After the extensive menu (from lobster tails to trifle and tea), guests entertained the group with music, and took part in games such as croquet, tag, and blind man's bluff — the Picnic Society having bestowed this one legacy, at least. Natural history being all the rage, scientific sorties might follow, the better to trap and preserve tattered nature for future scrutiny. Needless to say, men and women would observe the frantic array of etiquettery in their wanderings.

Learning and courting aside, it was the food that distinguished the 19th-century picnic. In *Mrs Beeton's Book of Household Management: A Guide to Cookery in All Branches* (first published 1861), the diva of type-A entertaining enthused that "Provided care has been taken in choosing congenial guests, and that in a mixed party one sex does not preponderate, a well arranged picnic is one of the pleasantest forms of entertainment." In terms of victuals, she warned, "It is advisable to estimate quantities extravagantly, for nothing is more annoying than to find everything exhausted and guests hungry." And, let's remember, there were the servants for the washing-up. For a picnic lunch for twenty, Mrs Beeton advised:

4 lobsters	10 pounds Wing rib of beef
4 roast chickens	1 small ham
2 chaudfroid of chicken	1 veal and ham pie
salad and dressing	2 fruit tarts
cream	2 dozen Balmoral tartlets
2 creams	2 jellies
4 loaves of bread	2 pounds of biscuits
1½ pounds of cheese	½ pound of butter
1 dozen pears	1 dozen bananas
1 dozen apples	

A century ago, she estimated that would cost £3, 19 shillings, and 8 pence ($19.40 at the time; about $382 now), plus "wines, mineral waters, lemon juice; plates, dishes, knives, forks, spoons, glasses, tablecloths, servietts, glass cloths, corkscrews, champagne-opener, castor sugar, oil, vinegar, mustard, pepper, cayenne, salt and pickles." And a chafing dish. And accessories.

It was at this time that the word PICNIC came to suggest a relaxed meal, and, by extension, any easy thing. In "The Drums of the Fore and Aft" (1888), Rudyard Kipling's Wee Willie Winkie says, "T'aint no bloomin' picnic in those parts, I can tell you." It's a tribute to the much-admired Victorian capacity for denial that anyone of that age could come up with such a metaphor; clearly it wasn't the housekeepers and cooks who were consulted. But then, remember Margaret Visser: "Everything is relative: what was formal then made a trestle-table in the open countryside seem exhilaratingly abandoned." Even if that trestle-top was groaning with the rich, excessive fare of which the Victorians were so very, very fond.

THE CONDUCT OF THE PARTY

At the dawn of the 19th century, a picnic may have been a holiday from responsibility and civilization, the sort of (watered-down) Woodstock letting-down of hair that lets all the lovers go wild in Shakespeare comedies. But whether in cities or woods, there were still strong social laws in play, laws that could be bent, but not broken.

The dauntingly titled *Social Etiquette or, Manners and Customs of Polite Society: Contemporary Rules and Etiquette for All Occasions* (1896), by the formidable Maud C. Cooke, makes it clear there are limits to just how lax behavior should become: "Picnics and excursions," the Canadian rulebook warns, "are delightful summer entertainments. But it is essential that whoever goes on a picnic should possess the power to find 'sermons in stones, books in the running brooks, and good in everything;' know how to dress, know where to go, and above all, know what to carry to eat."

It continues: "A very great variety of food should be avoided, also soft puddings and creamy mixtures of any sort, which persistently 'leak out.'" What should be packed instead then, according to Cooke? "Plain, substantial food, simple and well-cooked, should ever be chosen, with a few sweet and simple dainties to top off with." And who does this packing? "This can be divided up among the party by the one who is most executive, with the ladies to furnish the substantials and the gentlemen the beverages. The men assume the expenses of the boats or other conveyances."

For the ideal picnic there has to be water, and from that point of view, France is wonderful picnic country, so rich in magnificent rivers, waterfalls, reservoirs, that it is rare not to be able to find some delicious spot where you can sit by the water, watch dragonflies and listen to the birds or to the beguiling sound of a fast-flowing stream. As you drink wine from a tumbler, sprinkle your bread with olive oil and salt, and eat it with ripe tomatoes or rough country sausage you feel better off than in even the most perfect restaurant.

– Elizabeth David, *An Omelette and a Glass of Wine*

My favorite advice: "A rubber coat or mackintosh is also a necessity, for no matter how warm the day, there is a risk of sitting out in the woods on the bare ground." Oh, so *that's* where babies come from.

"There are several important items which must not be forgotten, and among them are hand-towels and soap, combs, hand-mirror, thread, needle and thimble, a corkscrew and a can opener." Makes sense.

More peculiar — to modern sensibilities, anyway — is the advice concerning chaperones. Clearly, all this fresh air and sunshine can only lead to one thing, hence:

It might seem needless to say that there should always be a chaperon on picnic parties if it were not that even in this day there appears, in some places, to be a lack of proper understanding on this subject. Dwellers in large cities see matters in a clearer light, and a young man who is thoroughly versed in points of etiquette will not think of inviting a young lady to accompany him to the theater without also requesting her mother or a married friend to join them.... When a number of young people get off together, they are apt, without the least intention of impropriety, to let their spirits carry them away and lead them into absurdities they would never commit in a graver moment.... Most young men and women will feel a security and sense of comfort from having some one along to take the responsibility of the conduct of the party that they could never know were there no chaperon present.

Bear in mind the latest fashion for a young lady picnicker: "Light-weight wool goods, or heavy cotton or linen material that will wash and not tear easily, is most suitable for these occasions. Linen or cotton duck is very serviceable."

What planet the author of *Social Etiquette* inhabited at this time is perhaps questionable, for the rest of the continent was exploding with the turn of the century. America was still recovering from its civil war, at which, perhaps, America's last truly innocent picnic was held. On July 21, 1861, a sunny Sunday near the town of Manassas, Virginia, 13,000 federal troops advanced on rebel defenders, driving them across the river that lent the first significant engagement of the war its name: the First Battle of Bull Run. As J. Matthew Gallman's *The Civil War Chronicle* (2000) details:

What began as an orderly Union retreat soon turned into a full scale riot, with terrified, inexperienced troops running headlong into bewildered civilians (including many congressmen) who had ridden out for the day from Washington. A panicked swarm of wagons, artillery pieces, horses, and men quickly choked the few fords and bridges leading back to the Union camp of Centerville, but the Confederates were simply too exhausted and inexperienced to mount much of a pursuit.

Nearly 5,000 soldiers died that day, not exactly the spectacle the Northern Brahmins had anticipated when they set out that dawn, with packed lunches, to watch the disgrace of Johnny Reb. Again from *Chronicle*:

> Many of the civilian spectators at Bull Run had considered the impending battle something of an entertainment and therefore brought along picnic baskets to appease their appetites as the fighting unfolded. The flight of the Union troops, however, unpleasantly interrupted their lunches.

According to eyewitness accounts quoted in Richard Wheeler's *A Rising Thunder* (1964), these affluent alfrescans travelled in "carriages and [other] vehicles drawn up as if they were attending a small country race.... In one was a lady with an opera-glass." And later: "Hacks containing unlucky spectators of the late affray were smashed like glass, and the occupants were lost sight of in the debris."

As the 19th century lumbered to its conclusion, massive internal migration was adding to the influx of immigrants from Eastern and Southern Europe to bring huge numbers of people into cities already swollen with the poor, who were — sound familiar? — struggling to keep body and soul together. In 1900, sixty percent of Americans lived in rural areas; by 1920, the split was even. (Today, that number is below twenty-five percent.) For the veterans of the Civil War and immigrants alike, contemporary etiquette "and rules for all occasions" were increasingly beside the point. In cities, workers were little more than prisoners, with long days in factories or at home with piecework; they were no longer able to enjoy the outdoors as they and their ancestors had. It was in this period that the socialist New York Central Labor Union organized a parade and picnic to raise funds for a labor newspaper. In September 1882, more than 10,000 workers attended; within twenty-five years, Labor Day was recognized in all the states but one.

Picnics continued, but their sylvan innocence was smirched. The satirical American magazine *Punchinello* frequently expressed a viperous disdain for everything that the remaining chaperoned, wool-wearing, bourgeois, culturally pretentious Pollyannas stood for.

> Once if I remember well,
> my life was a feast
> where all hearts opened
> and all wines flowed
>
> — Arthur Rimbaud, 1873

ADVICE TO PICNIC PARTIES

Punchinello – August 20, 1870

In this culminating period of the summer season, it is natural that the civic mind should turn itself to the Contemplation of sweet rural things, including shady groves, lunch-baskets, wild flowers, sandwiches, bird songs, and bottled lager-bier.

The skies are at their bluest, now; the woods and fields are at their greenest; flowers are blooming their yellowest, and purplest, and scarletest. All Nature is smiling, in fact, with one large, comprehensive smile, exactly like a first-class Prang chromo with a fresh coat of varnish upon it.

Things being thus, what can be more charming than a rural excursion to some tangled thicket, the very brambles, and poison-ivy, and possible copperhead snakes of which are points of unspeakable value to a picnic party, because they are sensational, and one cannot have them in the city without rushing into fabulous extra expense. It is good, then, that neighbors should club together for the festive purposes of the picnic, and a few words of advice regarding the arrangement of such parties may be seasonable.

If your excursion includes a steamboat trip, always select a boat that is likely to be crowded to its utmost capacity, more especially one of which a majority of the passengers are babies in arms. There will probably be some roughs on board, who will be certain to get up a row, in which case you can make the babies in arms very effective as "buffers" for warding off blows, while the crowd will save you from being knocked down.

Should there be a bar on board the steamer, it will be the duty of the gentlemen of the party to keep serving the ladies with cool beverages from it at brief intervals during the trip. This will promote cheerfulness, and, at the same time, save for picnic duty proper the contents of the stone jars that are slumbering sweetly among the pork-pies and apple-dumplings by which the lunch-baskets are occupied.

Never take more than one knife and fork with you to a picnic, no matter how large the party may be. The probability is that you may be attacked by a gang of rowdies, and it is no part of your business to furnish them with weapons.

Avoid taking up your ground near a swamp or stagnant water of any kind. This is not so much on account of mosquitoes as because of the small saurian reptiles that abound in such places. If your party is a large one, there will certainly be one lady in it, at least, who has had a lizard in her stomach for several years, and the struggles of the confined reptile to join its congeners in the swamp might induce convulsions, and so mar the hilarity of the party.

To provide against an attack by the city brigands who are always prowling in the vicinity of picnic parties, it will be judicious to attend to the following rules:

Select all the fat women of the party, and seat them in a ring outside the rest of the picnickers, and with their faces toward the centre of the circle. In the event of a discharge of missiles this will be found a very effective corden — quite as effective, in fact, as the feather beds used in the making up of barricades.

Let the babies of the party be so distributed that each, or as many as possible of the gentlemen present, can have one at hand to snatch up and use for a fender should an attack at close quarters be made.

If any dark, designful strangers should intrude themselves upon the party, unbidden, the gentlemen present should by no means exhibit the slightest disposition to resent the intrusion, or to show fight, as the strangers are sure to be professional thieves, and, as such, ready to commit murder, if necessary. Treat the strangers with every consideration possible under the circumstances. Should there be no champagne, apologize for the absence of it, and offer the next best vintage you happen to have. Of course, having lunched, the strangers will be eager to acquire possession of all valuables belonging to the party. The gentlemen, therefore, will make a point of promptly handing over to them their own watches and jewelry, as well as those of their lady friends.

Having arrived home, (we assume the possibility of this,) refrain carefully, from communicating with the police on the subject of the events of the day. The publicity that would follow would render you an object of derision, and no possible good could result to you from disclosure of the facts. But you should at once make up your mind never to participate in another picnic.

Despite the sarcasm, even the sharp-penned urbanites had a store of patience for the weary picnicker. An unsigned story in the *Brooklyn Eagle* from July 23, 1875, has the grace to record that:

> The writer didn't feel at all ugly last evening when a fat lady with a fat boy baby sat down on him and his new clothes in a [street] car, and the only reason that he didn't was simply because this body was coming home from a picnic, and she had danced and drank lager beer and was quite happy, and she had beside such a winning way about her when she turned, and in apologetic tones, said: "You pegs my pardon, sir." And of course the writer did accept her backhanded excuse for mistaking him for a cushion.

There's something about that lager beer.

Which brings us to the temperance movement, and the depravity of alcohol. Eight years later, the *Brooklyn Eagle* ran a page two story headlined "DANGEROUS. The Evils That Spring From Moonlight Picnics. A Growing Source of Crime – Children Ruined and Homes Destroyed – Scathing Condemnation of the Practice by Officials and the Catholic Clergy." In a lengthy jeremiad, the unsigned story decries again and again the evil outcome of these night-time annual get-togethers of societies with (granted, suspicious) names such as the Growlers, the Select Five, Merry Few, Dock Rats, the Finest, County Longfords, Violets, the Langtrys, and the Jolly Boys.

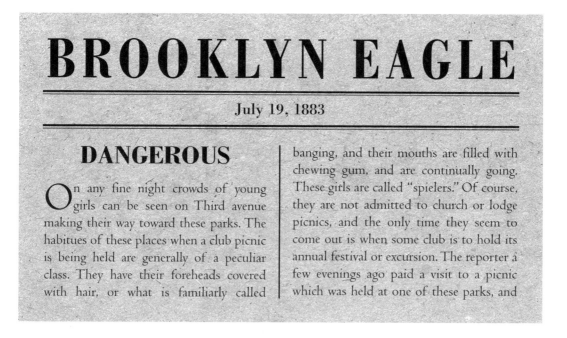

BROOKLYN EAGLE

July 19, 1883

DANGEROUS

On any fine night crowds of young girls can be seen on Third avenue making their way toward these parks. The habitues of these places when a club picnic is being held are generally of a peculiar class. They have their foreheads covered with hair, or what is familiarly called banging, and their mouths are filled with chewing gum, and are continually going. These girls are called "spielers." Of course, they are not admitted to church or lodge picnics, and the only time they seem to come out is when some club is to hold its annual festival or excursion. The reporter a few evenings ago paid a visit to a picnic which was held at one of these parks, and there witnessed scenes which all true temperance advocates would be shocked at. Seated under the trees and behind large tables were young girls drinking beer with men twice their ages. When a dance was announced they would go on the platform and make themselves conspicuous by dancing in a very loud and unladylike manner.

... After the reporter had explained his mission Mr Wilkin [superintendent of the Society for the Prevention of Cruelty to Children] said: "These moonlight picnics have a bad influence on young girls. They tend to swell the criminal class not only among the girls, but among the boys. More girls have been ruined at these picnics than respectable people realize. One day last week a worthy man called at this office and told me that his daughter, barely 14 years of age, was in the habit of attending these picnics with a companion, and would not come home until late hours of the night, or early in the morning. Fearing that she would get beyond his control he had her committed to the House of the Good Shepherd. Last week we also sent another girl to that institution who was in the habit of attending picnics of the same class."

... "There is no other source of crime which has a tendency to ruin girls like moonlight picnics. I have been in this society for seven years and have given this subject my closest attention. It is generally the case that young girls go with companions who are somewhat depraved,

having been constant attendants at these affairs, and the ruin of the former is soon accomplished. ... The consequence is that they become lower and lower every time they attend these affairs. When we receive complaints here we generally find that the stray sheep has been a constant attendant at moonlight picnics."

... "When these cases of mothers complaining of their daughters come before us we find out first if they have been in the habit of visiting the resorts alluded to, and, if such is the case, we have them sent away at once, because that is the only remedy for their salvation. The parents are to blame in most of these cases. It is generally with these girls from soda water to beer and then to a depraved life."

... "Young girls are now being ruined by the wholesale, and you can rest assured that moonlight picnics constitute a prolific source in creating depraved women and bold and brazen faced young men. There are very few young girls who are not injured by attending these picnics, and after visiting them they become so low that they are sent to prison and jails as habitual drunkards and disorderly characters."

... The Rev. Father Fransioli was next visited, and was found at his pastoral residence in Warren street. In answer to several questions he said: "I denounced from the pulpit of St Peter's Church moonlight picnics and promenades eight years ago, when they had just started. I have always considered them the most dangerous and immoral amusement ever devised."

STAR-SPANGLED BANQUETS

Next to the invention of the Thermos, the automobile has been the greatest friend to the picnic, and, for that reason, two men can rightly claim to be godfathers to the picnic: Henry Ford and Alfred Sloan. In 1912, a Ford car took just over twelve hours on an assembly line; two years later, that number had been reduced to one and a half. To retain employees and increase their productivity, Ford also shortened working hours, cutting days from nine hours to eight and weeks from six days to five. Along the way, with the success of the Ford automobile, he reduced the price of the average Ford car so that by 1925, a car cost only $290 (approximately $3,000 today).

Over at General Motors, president Alfred Sloan pioneered the dark magic of automobile marketing, introducing the yearly model change and the notion of vertical niche: the era of a model for every level of earner — Chevrolet, Buick, or Cadillac — had arrived. Keen!

These titans had a powerful effect on the American consumer and the American landscape. In 1919, there were 6.7 million cars on American roads; ten years later, that number had quadrupled, nearly one for every household in the U.S. or one car for every five Americans (compared to one car for every thirty-seven English and one car for every forty French). That sixty percent bought on credit would spell a major speed bump come the end of the decade and the advent of the Great Depression.

In those same ten years, American roads and highway systems doubled. By 1929, there were 852,000 miles of roads, compared to just 369,000 in 1920. And where were those Americans going on all their roads? Mostly out of the city and into the country, for weekend excursions, evening drives, and afternoon picnics. Where *weren't* they going? To Sunday service, or anywhere else where watchful chaperones could have their say.

A 1923 article in the trade magazine *Playground* characterizes the effect of the automobile this way:

The farmers' picnic is returning to its oldtime glory. There was a day when 25,000 gathered at Sylvan Beach for the Hop Growers' picnic, and many of them were hop growers. The Old and Original at Long Branch drew its 10,000 and the Six-Town at Davis grove nearly as many. Farmers came in buggies from miles around to make a day of it; and as many came by train where there was a railroad communication.... Then came the Chautauqua and the automobile. The Chautauqua brought the farmer to the village for several days, where he got wholesome entertainment for a small sum, with Bryan occasionally added for a little more. The automobile made it easy for the

Park it!

One of the great pleasures in life is a Picnic in the Park. Now **Waldo's** is going to make it possible for you to enjoy the delightful spring weather and have a Picnic in the Park, within just a few feet from our doors. **Waldo's** special Picnic in the Park luncheons will be carefully selected and prepared to satisfy both gourmet and healthfood tastes. Plan to take your (check one) –

Boss___ Self___ Secretary___ Husband___ Wife___ Lover___ Other___

to a Picnic in the Park on **Waldo's** picnic day –Thursdays –or the day of your choice! Our specially prepared picnic luncheons will have,..... along with great food, a king-size napkin, salt, pepper, toothpick, wetwipe and mint. *Perhaps the best thing of all is the price* $1.00, tax inc. To make certain there's a picnic luncheon for you, why not call **Waldo's** and tell them to reserve as many as you might need. All parks are complete with ground, trees, grass (perhaps) birds, smog-free air (keep your fingers crossed), and no ants. **Waldo's** picnic parks are in these locations – Equitable Plaza-On the Plaza Level above us & outside our front doors. Beverly Hills –Right behind our building. Century City-On the Plaza, right outside our door.

Waldo's EQUITABLE PLAZA · 3435 WILSHIRE BLVD. · (213) 381-6405
CENTURY CITY · 2070 CENTURY PARK EAST-(213) 553-5263/ BEVERLY HILLS-9410 WILSHIRE-(213) 275-5311

city man to go picnicking with his family at this own convenience and it gave the farmer an easy exit to the movie. The picnic with a name and a reputation dwindled in attendance, against the competition of these new forms of entertainment.

Alongside these technological shifts, the great bloom of capitalism was on the rose in North America. Refrigerators, washing machines, vacuum cleaners, and toasters sprouted like mushrooms after a spring rain. By 1930, two-thirds of all American households had electricity, much of it running the "labor-saving" devices that increasingly held women to new standards of cleanliness. Advertisers became savvy, hiring psychologists such as John B. Watson (founder of behaviorism) and Edward Bernays (nephew of Sigmund Freud) to design campaigns. America's first million-dollar campaign? The National Biscuit Company's Uneeda Biscuit, in the waterproof box ("take a box with you on your travels; splendid for sandwiches; perfect for picnics").

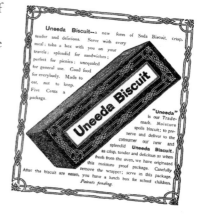

By the 1920s, the New Woman was voting, taking a job outside the home, and getting behind the wheel of the family car. Domestic inventions — electric washing machines, irons, vacuum cleaners; electric ranges, refrigerators, and toasters — were changing dietary habits, as was a trend toward simpler and lighter food. The turn-of-the-century Ruebens-like beauty was skinnying down to the war-time flapper, and low-cal food was following suit. According to the U.S. Department of Agriculture, "Surveys showed that, by the mid-1920's, the time spent by women in meal preparation and cleanup had fallen from forty-four hours per week to under thirty hours."

Women were *happening*.

One New Woman, Emily Post, made a career out of walking the tightrope between convention and modernity. To today's ears, she sounds fusty, humorous even, but hers was the dominant voice for an emerging middle class — triumphant after the War to End All Wars, cushioned by a generation of labor laws — eager to fit in. Her thoughts on picnics are too delicious to ignore.

- People who picnic along the public highway leaving a clutter of greasy paper and swill (not a pretty name, but neither is it a pretty object!) for other people to walk or drive past, and to make a breeding place for flies, and furnish nourishment

I do not like to eat al fresco. No sane person does, I feel. When it is nice enough for people to eat outside, it is also nice enough for mosquitoes, horse and deer flies, as well as wasps and yellowjackets. I don't much like sand in my food and thus while I will endure a beach picnic I never look forward to them. My idea of bliss is a screened-in porch from which you can watch the sun go down, or come up. You can sit in temperate shade and not fry your brains while you eat. You are protected from flying critters, sandstorms and rain and you can still enjoy a nice cool breeze.

— Laurie Colwin, *Home Cooking*

for rats, choose a disgusting way to repay the land-owner for the liberty they took in temporarily occupying his property.

- Some people have the gift of hospitality; others whose intentions are just as kind and whose houses are perfection in luxury of appointments, seem to petrify every approach. Such people appearing at a picnic color the entire scene with the blue light of their austerity. Such people are usually not masters, but slaves, of etiquette. Their chief concern is whether this is correct, or whether that is properly done, or is this person or that such an one as they care to know? They seem, like Hermione (Don Marquis's heroine), to be anxiously asking themselves, "Have I failed to-day, or have I not?"

- There is no more excuse for rude or careless or selfish behavior at a picnic than at a ball.

- A hostess should never speak of annoyances of any kind — no matter what happens! Unless she is actually unable to stand up, she should not mention physical ills any more than mental ones.... If the cook leaves, then a picnic must be made of the situation as though a picnic were the most delightful thing that could happen.

- Courtesy demands that you, when you are a guest, shall show neither annoyance nor disappointment — no matter what happens. Before you can hope to become even a passable guest, let alone a perfect one, you must learn as it were not to notice if hot soup is poured down your back. If you neither understand nor care for dogs or children, and both insist on climbing all over you, you must seemingly like it; just as you must be amiable and polite to your fellow guests, even though they be of all the people on earth the most detestable to you. You must with the very best dissimulation at your command, appear to find the food delicious though they offer you all of the viands that are especially distasteful to your palate, or antagonistic to your digestion. You must disguise your hatred of red ants and scrambled food, if everyone else is bent on a picnic.... If a plan is made to picnic, she likes picnics above everything and proves her liking by enthusiastically making the sandwiches or the salad dressing or whatever she thinks she makes best.

Are You a Picnic Pest?

asks
Grace P. Smith

Picnickers forgot
Part of their fire—
The trees in remembrance
Are making a pyre!

This wild deer is caught
In a rusty tin can
Carelessly left
By a "civilized" man!

Bottles broken on the beach
Cause a lot of gashes.

- Needless to say a bad loser is about as welcome at a card table as rain at a picnic.

— Emily Post, *Etiquette* (1922)

In July 1936, *Parents' Magazine* ran a breathless piece called "Picnicking With a Baby" for just the sort of woman who would be an American version of Mrs Beeton's most loyal readers. She would undoubtedly have received a copy of *Joy of Cooking*, first published in 1931, and would take to heart Gladys H. Murray's article, which began: "If you really love picnics but think that this year you must stay home 'on account of the baby' take my advice and take the baby on a picnic. If he's a chip off the old block he will enjoy it, too, and a day in the open will be good for him. Really, it isn't as much trouble as you would suppose."

Technology continued to drive the evolution of the picnic, as the private automobile followed its manifest destiny, opening the countryside to marauding tribes of what would come to be called nuclear families. By 1940, on the eve of America's entry into the Second World War, those families were already beginning to turn inward, circling the wagons against the hotheads in Europe.

"Men on Picnics," Lydia Hewes's delightfully wry *Good Housekeeping* article (August 1940), begins: " 'A picnic,' said one man, 'is dozens of olives, no bottle opener, a few sandwiches completely surrounded by ants — immediately followed by an attack of poison ivy or hay fever.' I believe this is the historic male attitude toward outdoor eating.... This would indicate there is very little left of the vigorous pioneer spirit." Hewes pokes good-natured fun at the male stick-in-the-mud ("what are you gonna do?" she seems to be saying), listing the various impediments to fun alfresco: "There is the person who insists on wading in the brook. She always manages to fall in with her clothes on. There is the one who has come all dressed up, as for a garden party, and who sits in a nest of wet tomato sandwiches. She spends the rest of the time worrying about whether the spots will come out. And there is the bore who isn't afraid of bugs; he'll drop one in your lap and get a hearty laugh out of it.... And the eternally feminine soul who is afraid of the curious cow in the bushes."

I knew that a picnic worth doing at all was worth doing with a hell of a lot of care, and this belief has remained with me ever since. Even when I have carside picnics in Europe and in America, there are good glasses along, good forks and knives, and if possible, china plates. I would rather smuggle a few dirty plates into my hotel to wash, wherever I happen to be, than eat food on paper plates.

— James Beard, *Delights and Prejudices*

For all her mockery, Hewes sounds a note of concern that would prove prophetic:

> In latter years, I have noted that the highway-and-byway style of picnicking has waned in favor of the back-yard variety. This is due partly to the great increase in good roads, which are now so overpopulated that it is almost impossible to find any spot, let alone a better one, offering seclusion. Also to the fact that along the roadside today are such marvelous temples, dedicated to the hot dog and hamburger, that a picnic is no longer the only answer to a traveler's prayer.

> Above all, there has been the growth in the popularity of outdoor cookery, the result of which has been a nationwide wave of outdoor fireplaces. Hardly a country or suburban home now that doesn't boast of one, whether it is merely a portable stove or one of those elaborate stone or brick structures.... Wherever it is, it is as definite a part of the American scene as the playroom or the trailer.

And see how familiar this sounds, ringing across sixty-odd years:

> The next advantage of back-yard cookery is that it gives the man of the house a chance to flaunt his culinary ability. Most men actually fancy themselves much better cooks than women. "Name at least one famous woman chef," they taunt you, and of course you can't. There is no doubt about its being a fine sight to see a man standing before the fire, with an important Oscar-of-the-Waldorf air, turning the steaks, while the rest of the company try to keep the smoke out of their eyes, slap mosquitoes, and say admiringly, "There's nobody can cook a steak like John!" His wife, if she is tactful, sits in the background and lets people rave, while she wonders what John would have done if she hadn't provided him with not only the steaks, but all the properties that go toward the culmination of this impressive business.

By 1946, *House Beautiful* announced, "There's a New Era in Picnicking." Splayed across a double-page spread were eight photos of the miracles of modern technology: "Off the market during the war years, Thermos jugs are reappearing in stores." And Ther-Mo-Paks. And Therm-a-Jugs. And Porta-Barbecues. And: "Picnics needn't be makeshifts any more. There's equipment to keep hot foods hot, cold foods cold; and it's all designed for easy carrying, whether you travel by car or canoe, or just stay at home."

The era of the space-age gadgets had begun.

1900	Hershey's chocolate bar
1900–10	George Washington Carver finds new uses for peanuts, sweet potatoes, and soybeans
1901	A&P incorporates with 200 stores (in 1912, expands with cash and carry format)
1903	Dole canned pineapple
1903	Kellogg adds sugar to corn flakes, boosting popularity
1903	Pepsi Cola
1904	Quaker markets first puffed cereal
1906	Pure Food and Drug Act prohibits food adulteration and misbranding
1906	Meat Inspection Act requires Federal inspection of slaughterhouses
1910	Double-crimped can reduces costs for processors
1910	Aunt Jemima Pancake Flour
1911	First vitamin, vitamin B1, discovered
1912	Oreos
1912	Hellman's mayonnaise
1914	USDA establishes National Extension Service, which employs home economists
1914–18	First World War
1916	USDA prints its first food guide: "Food for Young Children"
1916	Piggly Wiggly opens first self-service food store
1917	Food Administration under Herbert Hoover conserves food for war effort
1920	Charles Birdseye deep-freezes food
1921	White Castle chain of hamburger shops opens
1923	Welch's grape jelly
1925	First home mechanical refrigerator, Frigidaire, sold

Tea to the English is really a picnic indoors.

— Alice Walker, *The Color Purple*

1926	General Mills creates "Betty Crocker," symbolizing growing importance of advertising
1928	Peter Pan peanut butter
1928	Velveeta
1929	Great Depression begins with stock market crash
1930	Vitamins synthesized in the laboratory
1930	Wonder Bread markets first automatically sliced bread
1932	Fritos corn chips
1933–40	New Deal legislation, Great Depression relief and reform
1935	Howard Johnson begins as franchised restaurant
1935	Rural Electrification Administration extends electricity to countryside
1937	Kraft Macaroni and Cheese Dinner
1937	Spam
1937	McDonald brothers open first drive-in
1939–45	Second World War
1941	National Victory Garden Program launched
1941	Recommended Daily Allowances published
1942–46	Food price controls and food rationing during Second World War
1942	Dannon yogurt
1942	La Choy canned Chinese foods
1943	Bread flour fortified with vitamin B1
1946	National School Lunch Act requires school-provided meals to be nutritionally balanced and have minimum amounts of specific food groups
1946	Maxwell House instant coffee
1950–56	Korean War and postwar readjustment
1951	Swanson produces first frozen meals, pot pies
1952	Campbell's Cooking With Condensed Soup greatly expands use of soups in casseroles

1954	Swanson makes first frozen TV dinner
1954	Ray Kroc buys McDonald's, starts building national chain
1954	Butterball turkey
1956	USDA publishes "Basic Four" food guide
1958	Delaney Clause added to the Pure Food and Drug Act, banned food additives shown to cause cancer in laboratory animals
1958	Rice-a-Roni
1961–75	US involvement in Vietnam
1963	Julia Child's *The French Chef* debuts on television
1964	Carnation Instant Breakfast
1964	Food Stamp Act establishes a national food stamp program
1965	Cool Whip
1965	Shake 'n' Bake
1966	Child Nutrition Act begins the school breakfast program
1969, 1971	White House Conferences on Food, Nutrition, and Health
1970	Hamburger Helper
1970	Quaker Oats 100% Natural granola
1972	Snapple fruit juices
1973	Voluntary nutrition labeling appears on food packages
1973	McDonald's introduces Egg McMuffin
1974	Special Supplemental Food Program for Women, Infants, and Children (WIC) begins
1976	Perrier
1977	US Senate Committee releases "Dietary Goals for the United States"
1980, 1985	USDA and DHHS publish "Dietary Guidelines for Americans"

1981	Stouffer's Lean Cuisine frozen dinners
1982	Diet, Nutrition, and Cancer published by National Cancer Institute
1982	Bud Light
1985	Aspartame, a low-calorie intensive sweetener, approved
1986	Pop Secret Microwave Popcorn
1987	Campbell's Special Request soups
1989	Berlin Wall falls
1990s	Stock market hits historic highs, longest peacetime expansion
1990	USDA and DHHS publish third edition of "Dietary Guidelines"
1990	Nutrition Education and Labeling Act makes nutrition labeling mandatory
1991	Stouffer's Homestyle entrees
1992	USDA/DHHS release Food Guide Pyramid
1993	SnackWell's cookies and crackers
1990s	USDA modernizes meat and poultry inspection in response to food safety concerns
1998	Frito-Lay Wow! chips (made with the fat substitute, olestra); 47 percent of US food dollar is spent away from home

— *FoodReview;* "A Taste of the 20th Century"

In Britain, meanwhile, the picnic – like everything else – remained in thrall to the notion of class; the moneyed meal reached its apotheosis in the annual opera festival of Glyndebourne, fifty miles from London on the estate of John Christie. Glyndebourne's first season was in May 1934 with two weeks' performances of Mozart operas. The pattern of fine dining during the production's long interval, followed by a walk in the beautiful gardens, was struck from that first year. By 1953, Vita Sackville-West had this to say about the event: "The Graciousness of civilisation here surely touches a peak where the arts of music, architecture and gardening combine for the delight of man." To that we might add gourmanding. The Glyndebourne season continues to this day, and with it the sumptuous picnics that complement the rich music. Ingrid Sutton, an Englishwoman related to a friend of ours, recently emailed us this description:

This IS a Picnic!
Zu Zu the new ginger snap for 5 cents a package!
A merry-go-round of pleasure from the time the package is opened 'till the last snap is gone. Everybody is invited. The fare is 5 cent If you want to go 'long with the rest
SAY
Zu Zu

When my husband and I and two friends last went to Glyndebourne we started with Champagne and smoked salmon sandwiches. This was followed by sliced stuffed loin of pork, mixed bean salad, and potato salad. For dessert we had baked sliced nectarines covered with almond pastry and whipped cream on the side. We always seem to start with fish. Sometimes smoked fillets of trout or salmon mousse with thin slices of buttered brown bread. Cold chicken in various forms: coriander and lime casseroled breasts of chicken are a favorite, accompanied by rice mixed with cooked peas or corn kernels and a tomato salad, to be followed by chocolate or strawberry mousse. We have white or red wine available to suit our guests' preferences. Sometimes we have a cheese board, but there is usually not enough time during the interval to add that to the feast. We always have coffee and some form of chocolate to finish.

This is a far cry from the labor-saving gadgets and time-saving burgers that besmirched the '50s in North America. Although every Ward Cleaver was building clever portable dining contraptions with plans straight out of *Popular Science* ("Building an Insulated Picnic Box") and *Popular Mechanics* ("Plan of the Month: Suitcase Picnic Bench"), the goal, like the decade, had little to do with sensual abandon. By the 1970s, the first stirrings of the corporate wage slave were felt and it was only a matter of time before the birth of that most dreaded of affairs: the company picnic. Pity help the reader of *Glamour* magazine coming across a story like "What to Wear to the Company Outing" (July 1988).

But this sounds too much like handwringing. There's no real problem. Picnics have survived – picnics will *always* survive – and will adapt themselves to the prevailing culture and economy. This book is another step in its evolution, a tiny nudge to rediscover what our ancestors always knew: when the going gets tough....

The final words belong to Blake Edwards, co-author of the 1970 movie *Darling Lili*. In the film, Bill (Rock Hudson) talks to Lili (Julie Andrews) after he had a band of gypsies serenade her outside her window.

Bill: I have champagne, caviar, marinated truffles, brilliant foie gras, and half-a-dozen assorted Hungarian gypsies.

Lili: Sounds delicious.

Bill: I thought we'd go on a picnic.

Lili: At three in the morning?

Bill: It's the best time – no ants.

FOOD SAFETY

Now, this will just take a moment. Think of it like stretching at the gym before you start doing bench presses: an ounce of prevention and all that.... Poorly prepared and stored foods can make us sick. This is true whether we're eating indoors or out, but the warm temperatures and relaxed attitudes associated with alfresco eating have made some folks associate picnics with food poisoning. Not to downplay the severity of the issue, but this is clearly not reasonable. Food-borne illnesses — caused by contamination from bacteria (or their toxins) or other pathogens — are serious, but there's no reason you can't eat an urban picnic with complete safety, just as you assume safety in your home or at a restaurant. It all comes down to treating your food and yourself sensibly and well. Use your common sense and get informed when it comes to buying, storing, prepping, and keeping food.

Think ahead. Plan your picnic preparation carefully so that the foods that most need to be well-chilled are prepared first and refrigerated, and those that need to be eaten hot are prepared last or refrigerated then thoroughly reheated just before you leave. Cooked foods should not be left standing on the table or kitchen counter, or in a picnic box or basket without ice or insulation, for more than two hours. Disease-causing bacteria grow in temperatures between 40°F and 140°F (4°C and 60°C), and foods that have been in this temperature range — which public-health officials refer to as the Danger Zone — for more than two hours should not be eaten. It comes down to this: keep cold food cold and hot food hot.

Got that?

An insulated picnic cooler is a wise investment, and there are so many styles and sizes available that you can find one to fit any picnic occasion. Some require a bag of ice cubes or a large block of ice to provide the cooling, while others use freezer packs. The latter need to be well frozen beforehand to be effective. If you are traveling in a vehicle, pack the cooler in the coolest part of it, and once you are at your destination, place the cooler in a shady location and replenish the ice if necessary.

On very hot days, you can add extra cold power to your cooler by packing frozen tetra packs of juice or frozen plastic bottles of water in with the food, as long as they have some time to thaw out before they are to be consumed. There may be other foods you are taking to the picnic that could be frozen ahead of time and used in the same way en route to the picnic. If you are short of space in your cooler, a large bowl of ice cubes can be used as a container for a smaller sealed bowl in order to keep a small quantity of food chilled. Aluminum foil also helps keep cold in and warmth out (or vice versa), and if cold food is well-wrapped in foil, then in wet newspaper layers, it will stay very cold for some hours.

To keep hot foods hot for your picnic, wrap them well in foil, then an outer layer of something dense, such as layers of newspaper or a thick blanket. A box filled with straw is another excellent insulator and a covered casserole, with piping-hot contents, can be foil-wrapped and buried in straw and will stay very hot for several hours. Okay, few of us have a box of straw at our disposal, but a box lined thickly with newspaper is also quite effective.

Your cooler should always be kept immaculately clean, and, during the picnic, drained as necessary to prevent water from sitting in the bottom. When packing food in coolers, make sure that there is no cross-contamination from one food to another (particularly involving uncooked meats) by wrapping foods well and ensuring lids are fitted properly.

If you are barbecuing meat in the course of a picnic, use a food thermometer on larger pieces to make sure it has reached a safe internal temperature. Beef, lamb, and veal chops should be cooked to at least 145°F (63°C); pork, ground veal, and ground beef to 160°F (71°C); whole poultry and thighs to 180°F (82°C); poultry breasts to 170°F (77°C); ground chicken or turkey to 165°F (74°C). Seafood should be thoroughly cooked to an internal temperature of at least 145°F (63°C). If you don't have a thermometer, look for other signs of doneness. Fish, for example, is cooked when the thickest part becomes opaque and the fish flakes easily when poked with a fork.

FOR MORE INFORMATION

IN THE UNITED STATES

The FDA's food information line: 1-888-723-3366; *cfsan.fda.gov*
The FDA, through its National Food Safety Information Network: *foodsafety.gov*
USDA Meat and Poultry Hotline: 1-800-535-4555; *fsis.usda.gov*

IN CANADA

Health Canada: (613) 957-2991; *hc-sc.gc.ca*
The Canadian Food Inspection Agency monitors and reports on food safety: 1-800-442-2342; *inspection.gc.ca/english/index/fssae.shtml*

The University of Guelph maintains the website *eatwelleatsafe.ca*, which is chock full of news items and informed opinion. It's part of the Food Safety Network (*foodsafetynetwork.ca*), whose motto is Safe Food: From Farm to Fork

PICNIC TIPS

Planning your picnic well will save you a great deal of aggravation and ensure a successful outing. Guest lists, menus, and lists of things to take can be compiled early, and the necessary shopping completed before you start preparing food. Even a simple plan for what food will fit into which container and whether you have enough lids will save stress on picnic day.

We can't do the guest list for you, but we've done our best with the menus, and here's our list of things to take. You can adapt it to your own circumstances, depending on how many people you are planning for, where you're going, how light you want to travel, and so on.

To pack your food you may need:
Cooler or insulated pack, ice cubes or block ice, pre-frozen freezer packs, frozen plastic bottles of water, insulated jugs, vacuum flasks, aluminum stack pails or tiffin boxes, collapsible pails, plastic tubes of condiments, foil, plastic food wrap, plastic bags, large and small lidded containers, rubber bands

To carry your picnic to the perfect site you may need:
A long pole which can be used to carry bags and baskets, anything with a handle, carried by one person at each end of the pole, or a light-weight folding cot that can be used to tote your hamper or cooler and can also be used as a picnic table when it's set up

For comfortable lounging you may need:
Picnic blankets, Japanese mats, collapsible chairs or stools, sun umbrella

To serve and eat your food and drinks you may need:
Plastic or washable table cloth, knives, forks, spoons, plates, napkins, cups, glasses, corkscrew, can opener, paring knife, cutting board

To clean up after the picnic you may need:
Paper towels, large bags or cartons so you can separate the recyclables from the garbage, wet-wipes or damp cloths

In the spirit of silliness, we reprint here the suggested games from *Picnic Time*, a promotional publication (c. 1920) of the Lydia E. Pinkham Medicine Company of Lynn, Massachusetts – makers of Lydia E. Pinkham's Vegetable Compound and Sanative Wash.

Peanut Race

Place four empty saucers in a row. Opposite them and ten feet away, place four saucers each containing twelve peanuts. The four players are to carry the peanuts on a knife and put them in the empty saucers. More than one may be carried at once. Peanuts dropped may be picked up with the knife at any time but to win, a player must have every peanut in his saucer.

Thirty Inch Dash

Give each player a string thirty inches long with a marshmallow tied at the end. After placing the free end in their mouths, they must not touch the string. The winner is the one who first gets the marshmallow into his mouth.

Forward Pass

Form two lines. Give the last player in each line a silver spoon. Pass it down the line by the handle using only the left hand. Every player must pass it. No skipping. When the player at the front receives the spoon he runs to the rear and passes it forward again. Anyone who drops the spoon must run to the end of the line and start it over. The line which first gets back into its original position wins.

Riding the Cow

Place a quart milk bottle on its side. Sit on it lengthwise, holding a needle and thread. Put your feet out straight, left heel on the ground, right heel on left toe. Balance yourself and thread the needle. (It can be done!)

Walking the Tightrope

Stretch a length of white twine on the floor or ground. Watch your steps thru the small end of an opera glass. (Harder than you think!)

Balloon Race

Race against the wind in an open field. Balloons must be steered with the hands, not kicked.

Clothespin Race

Stretch rope or heavy twine between trees. Provide each pair of players with twenty clothespins in a paper bag. At a signal the player holding the bag opens it and puts his clothespins on the line, one at a time. When he has finished, his partner removes them one by one and puts them back in the bag. If a clothespin is dropped, it must be picked up before proceeding with the others.

Pie Eating Contest

Give each girl one-quarter of a pie. (Blueberry is the most fun.) Blindfold an equal number of men and have the girls feed them. Every bit of pie must be eaten.

Needle and Thread Race

Form the girls in line, each with a needle. Twenty feet away form the men in line, each with a thread. At a signal the couples rush toward each other and see who can thread their needle first.

A Trip to Toonerville

Give each player a suitcase and an umbrella. They race to a given point, open the suitcase, put on the sweater, hat, gloves, glasses, scarf, etc. it contains, open the umbrella and, carrying the suitcase, race back to the starting point. The more there is in the suitcase the more fun, but to be fair be sure to put an equal amount in each case.

A NOTE ON INGREDIENTS AND QUANTITIES

We are committed to eating and cooking with organic foods, in the belief that they are healthier for everyone. Organically produced ingredients are not specified in the recipes in this book but would be our first choice.

The recipes written by Elisabeth express all quantities either by volume, in cups, tablespoons, teaspoons, or by weight, both pounds and ounces, standard for the U.S. and Canada, and metric (Canada, the U.K., and Australia). British volume measures have the same name as the North American ones in many cases, but not all are the exact equivalent. For example, U.S. and Canadian teaspoon, tablespoon, and cup measures are slightly smaller than British ones.

When ingredients are measured in cups, tablespoons, teaspoons etc, all measurements are assumed to be level. A rounded or heaped teaspoon can hold twice as much or more as a level one and change a recipe quite drastically! If you are doubling or halving recipes it is useful to know that three teaspoons fill one tablespoon, and four tablespoons fill one quarter cup.

Most of the recipes indicate how many servings, although it is only a guide for the cook, not a prescription. One person's idea of a serving is not necessarily the same as another's. Furthermore, a serving of a highly spiced or dense food might, by choice, be much smaller than that of a lighter, bulkier food. A third reason why it is difficult to indicate portion sizes for some recipes is that some of the ingredients will vary in size. Exactly how big is a large onion or a medium potato or half a medium cabbage?

As for our menus, except for the Romantic and Hotel Room picnics (which we have designed for two people), the recipes are not all intended for the same number of people, nor should they be. They are suggestions to inspire you, not a set of rules to follow! Once you know how many people will need to be served, you can figure out how much food to prepare, and double, halve, or otherwise alter the recipes in any given menu to suit. You will quickly note, also, that we have created vegetarian and non-vegetarian alternatives for every menu, except the last one. Although a Shakespearean menu could be produced without meat, it probably shouldn't be.

Our guest contributors have each expressed their recipes in their own style, some with very detailed instructions, others more elliptically, but all with clarity and elegance, and we feel that they give our menus the star quality they need. We hope you will enjoy preparing your picnics as much as we have enjoyed preparing our recipes for you.

MENUS

TRADITIONAL

The masses have gathered and they're clamoring for something retro. Go all out: wicker baskets, checkered tablecloths, hamburgers on the barbecue ... do they still make those bottles of Chianti with the bulbous bottom? Wear gingham, make like Mickey Rooney and Judy Garland, and after the meal you can put on a sheee-ow!

vegetable sticks, assorted pickles

Devilled Eggs, p. 105

Traditional Potato Salad, p. 182

Tomato and Cucumber Salad, p. 179

Coleslaw, p. 149

barbecued hamburgers *or* barbecued hotdogs

corn on the cob, steamed on the barbecue

Rhubarb and Strawberry Pie, p. 314

Lemon Cheesecake with Sour Cream Topping (Mark Bittman), p. 302

sliced watermelon

Iced Tea, p. 328

Wine Suggestion:

Chianti in a wicker flask, so 1960s, can still be found to go with the red checkerboard tablecloth, as can the equally retro pink Mateus Rosé from Portugal.

TRADITIONAL (VEGGIE)

vegetable sticks, assorted pickles

Devilled Eggs, p. 105

Traditional Potato Salad, p. 182

Tomato and Cucumber Salad, p. 179

Coleslaw, p. 149

barbecued veggie burgers *or* barbecued tofu dogs

corn on the cob, steamed on the barbecue

Rhubarb and Strawberry Pie, p. 314

Lemon Cheesecake with Sour Cream Topping (Mark Bittman), p. 302

sliced watermelon

Iced Tea, p. 328

Music:

For the wickerware and the plastic plates and the cute little tablecloths you bought in Portugal — and yes, they still make those Chianti bottles with the straw (fiasco is what they're called, putting me in mind of a few picnics of the past …) — and you want a hint of southern-fried blues and something slippery with the watermelon and the iced tea and the white Zinfandel …

The Los Angeles Guitar Quartet (crackerjack covers of Count Basie and Pachelbel's *Canon* and even John Philip Sousa on one of its discs)

Les Paul & Mary Ford reissues

Carlos del Junco's blues harmonica (especially *Up & at 'Em*, where Jane Siberry sings along on one song)

The Marsalis Family, together on one CD for the first time

Bruce Cockburn's *Deluxe Edition* (all the True North discs remastered, repackaged, looking — and sounding! — good; 9 or 10 CDs to date)

Carmen Miranda (the best performer to sing — or talk — through her hat since Joanne Kates; Naxos has reissues)

Properbox boxed sets (these are 4-CD sets from Britain of some major blasts from the past; try Jo Stafford, Nat King Cole Trio, Basie Band)

Some easy acoustics blues, not too far back, maybe made in the '60s or '70s

A little Sarah McLachlan … awww …

BARBECUE

According to industry statistics, Americans bought over 15 million barbecues and grills in 2002. That's a lot of smoke getting in our eyes! There's not much you can't cook on a grill, if you really put your mind to it. We take up the challenge with a menu for the barbie, from appetizers to dessert. (Probably a good idea to clean the racks between the meat and the fruit.)

Prunes in Bacon, p. 260

Beef Tikka with Raita (Krishna Jamal), p. 256 and p. 118

Lamb Kebabs with Green Herbs and Garlic, p. 259

Tomato and Potato Salad, p. 180

Napa Cabbage Slaw, p. 167

s'mores

Barbecued Desserts (Adrienne O'Callaghan), p. 278

Wine Suggestion:

What else with a barbie but a big, juicy, peppery Australian Shiraz? Lindemans, Penfolds, and the other big brands turn out consistently rich, spicy examples, whether Shiraz on its own or blended with Cabernet Sauvignon.

BARBECUE (VEGGIE)

Barbecued Mushroom Caps with Sun-Dried Tomato and Herb Dressing, p. 251

Barbecued Tofu Kebabs with Peanut-Chili Sauce, p. 254

Salmon Grilled Between Romaine Leaves (Bob Blumer), p. 261

Tomato and Potato Salad, p. 180

Napa Cabbage Slaw, p. 167

s'mores

Barbecued Desserts (Adrienne O'Callaghan), p. 278

Music:

"Smoke Gets in Your Eyes" being one of the obvious, but only if you can find the fabulous chamber version by the Paganini Ensemble (worth searching for), and yes, "Smoke on the Water" (but only if you get the Rolf Harris version, on his delirious album of rock covers called King Rolf*).*

Mid-career Louis Armstrong (there are literally dozens of reissues out)

Lyle Lovett (the *Large Band* album or *My Baby Don't Tolerate*, the one with the gospel shouting on it)

Red Priest, who prove that early music is anything but dull

The Dances From Terpsichore by the 15th-century German composer Michael Praetorius

The Klezmatics (state-of-the-art klezmer riotousness, and does it ever go with alfresco dining)

Alison Brown Quartet (the American banjo hipnified to the highest)

Pearl Django, Hot Club of San Francisco, Bill Hilly Band (tongue-in-cheek swing based on the Django Reinhardt traditions)

Giuliano Carmignola (is he the James Brown of the baroque violin?)

CELEBRATION

You could carry the whole meal yourself, but hey, life is short. Why not delegate some of the following among a group? Whether you're putting together an informal wedding or a surprise birthday, marking a bar mitzvah or a promotion, an outdoor setting will make your celebration the talk of the town. Scale the number of salads and desserts to suit your occasion.

Guacamole (Bob Blumer), p. 108

Maryland Crab Dip, p. 123

baguette slices

Tomato Herb Tarts, p. 129

Barbecued Lemon Chicken (Anne Lindsay), p. 250

Barbecued Butterflied Lamb Leg, p. 249

Tabouleh Salad, p. 177

Grilled Asparagus Salad with Prosciutto, Parmigiano-Reggiano,

and Balsamic Vinaigrette (Rob Feenie), p. 158

Five Bean Salad, p. 154

Banana-Strawberry Layer Cake (Regan Daley), p. 275

watermelon boat with Fresh Fruit Salad, p. 296

Fruit Punch, p. 324

Wine Suggestion:

Nothing makes a celebration sparkle like champagne, but West Coast winemakers from California to British Columbia turn out first-rate bubbly for a more local flavor at half the price.

CELEBRATION (VEGGIE)

Guacamole (Bob Blumer), p. 108

Artichoke and Sun-Dried Tomato Dip, p. 97

baguette slices

Tomato Herb Tarts, p. 129

Vegetable Anise Pie, p. 245

Peppers Stuffed with Corn, Potato, Egg, and Violet Salad (James Barber), p. 233

Tabouleh Salad, p. 177

Carrot, Raisin, and Sesame Salad, p. 147

Sunflower Tofu Salad, p. 175

Banana-Strawberry Layer Cake (Regan Daley), p. 275

watermelon boat with Fresh Fruit Salad, p. 296

Fruit Punch, p. 324

Music:

The surprise element, so why not dig out something really old: Harry Lauder 78s, Johnny and the Hurricanes 45s, Wilf Carter mono LPs, the Sex Pistols? But seriously, trumpet voluntaries, brass galore, anything and anyone doing some shouting and noisemaking (Properbox #2, mentioned earlier, is a four-CD history of jazz drumming . . .) We need exuberance here.

The Canadian Brass (about the most eclectic brass band in the land)

Ukulele Orchestra of Great Britain (catch their cover of "Johnny B. Goode")

76 Trombones Play 76 Trombones (honest!)

Il Giardino Armonico (a baroque band that's shot from guns; in fact, one of their covers has a bullet splintering a violin; great noise)

Clara Ward Gospel Singers (they were the best; check for reissues)

Montreal Jubilation Gospel Choir

Dixieland jam sessions by just about anybody

Simon Fraser University Pipe Band (rated best in the world four years running)

Fontella Bass (Yep, "Rescue Me," but also her newer, gospel-tinged work)

Renée Fleming's best-of disc — heavenly

KIDS

Come on, admit it. You think your kids are pickier than my kids. Well, I double-dog-dare you, kangaroo court, to come up with two kids with more food "issues" than mine. The trick, at least according to me, is to rethink nutrition. Here's a menu long on protein, fruits, and fresh vegetables. So what if there are two desserts? Run them ragged, then eat early.

carrot and celery sticks, cucumber slices

Sliced Meat Rolls, p. 241

Apple-Marinated Chicken Drumsticks, p. 213

Mousetraps, p. 266

Butterfly Cupcakes, p. 283

Chocolate-Chip Seed Cookies, p. 288

Lemonade, p. 329

Wine Suggestion:

If the adults aren't happy watching the kids over a beer, try them on a snappy Sauvignon Blanc from the Loire Valley or a Pinot Blanc from Alsace. Grown-up wines that are light on alcohol.

KIDS (VEGGIE)

carrot and celery sticks, cucumber slices

Stuffed Celery Sticks, p. 124

Kid Kebabs, p. 224

Mousetraps, p. 266

Butterfly Cupcakes, p. 283

Chocolate-Chip Seed Cookies, p. 288

Lemonade, p. 329

Music:

We are blessed, in Canada and the U.S., with some of the best kids' music anywhere — entire labels devoted to the stuff — and while there is the requisite cute quotient in ample evidence, there's so much that isn't that you can pick and choose forever.

Kirk Elliott and Norm Hacking's *Orange Cats Make the Very Best Friends*

Dean Jones (*Dog on Fleas*)

Rick Scott (the *Yo Mo Concerto* and "The Wild Bunnies of Kitsilano" for sure)

Music for Little People — the label's entire catalog!

Valdy's *Kids' Record*

Kirk & Magoo's *Mars Rocks*

Tickle Tune Typhoon

Some kinda Raffi

Lots of Maria Muldaur

Judy and David Gershon

The Wombles

BEACH

There's no setting with more Wow! factor. If you're lucky enough to live by the sea, you also know that not just any food will suit the surroundings — not to mention survive all the flying sand. The soup in particular won't benefit from grit, so try to choose a spot with a little shelter. Later, while you're working off those squares, remember: the rest of the world pays good money for this view. Enjoy!

Gazpacho Soup, p. 137

Croque-Monsieur Sandwiches, p. 203

Coleslaw with Curried Peanut Dressing (Bill Jones), p. 150

Sesame Potatoes, p. 122

Apple Cake with Ginger and Cardamom, p. 272

Lemonade, p. 329

Wine Suggestion:

Thirst-quenching light whites from Portugal (Vinho Verde) or North Italy (Pinot Grigio) are just right with the salt and the sand.

BEACH (VEGGIE)

Gazpacho Soup, p. 137

Salad Rolls, p. 238

Coleslaw with Curried Peanut Dressing (Bill Jones), p. 150

Sesame Potatoes, p. 122

Blueberry Cake, p. 281

Lemonade, p. 329

Music:

The natural, maybe even more so than the backyard. The Beach Boys, obviously, but don't forget Brian Wilson's amazing performance in The Queen's Jubilee Concert *(the DVD is best).*

The Ventures reissues; Johnny and the Hurricanes too, if you can find any

Katrina & the Waves (the '83/'84 originals are just out)

Buckwheat Zydeco

Brave Combo (Denton, Texas's most amazing polka band)

Queen's four-CD *Platinum Collection* (everyone knows all the words to "Bohemian Rhapsody", right?)

Desert Blues Volumes 1 & 2 (German issue, 2 CDs per set of Arab-influenced "blues" music; fascinating)

Inti-Illimani (expat Chilean band, alive and well and living in Paris)

Nelly (no, no, not the guy; I mean Nelly Furtado)

Jah Wobble (spacey, trancey, dancey; even on the sand)

Bonzo Dog Band (many times reissued, sounding better every time)

Cecilia Bartoli (because she rocks, especially on Vivaldi and Gluck)

Juanes (*People* magazine recently put the Colombian hottie on their sexiest-man-alive list; imagine him with his shirt off. Never mind imagine, go to the website ...)

BACKPACK

Here are two menus for the Great Explorer. The first maxes calories with minimum weight. Prep, pack, and tote: you and your backpack are ready to roam! The second is designed for anyone in urgent need of recovery: after a hike, a game of softball, or even a strenuous day of shopping.

cheese chunks and vegetable sticks

Loin of Pork with Prunes, p. 227

Peanut Butter Squares, p. 310

fresh fruit (non-squashable)

Iced Tea p. 328 or Lemonade p. 329

EXTREME

vegetable sticks with Sun-Dried Tomato Hummus, p. 109

Edamame Bean Salad with Green Peas, p. 153

Bacon and Egg Pie, p. 214

Sherry Balls, p. 317

fresh fruit

Iced Tea p. 328 or Lemonade p. 329

Wine Suggestion:

Australian bag-in-a-box wines will reduce the weight load and deliver decent flavor when you're ready to relax.

BACKPACK (VEGGIE)

cheese chunks and vegetable sticks

baguette sandwiches, (see Salad Sandwiches, p. 208)

egg salad/tuna/tofu salad

Peanut Butter Squares, p. 310

fresh fruit (non-squashable)

Iced Tea p. 328 or Lemonade p. 329

EXTREME (VEGGIE)

vegetable sticks with Sun-Dried Tomato Hummus, p. 109

Edamame Bean Salad with Green Peas, p. 153

Millet Pie, p. 228

Sherry Balls, p. 317

fresh fruit

Iced Tea p. 328 or Lemonade p. 329

Music:

What? You want to schlepp a Walkman along, too? Okay … how about the Wagner Ring Cycle? It's only 14 CDs. Or how about some music for alphorn? There are four or five discs out there and it's way easier than bringing the instrument. If you do encounter one — an alphorn — in the wild, stay perfectly still and make a noise like an edelweiss. It'll pass.

Nigel Kennedy's new *Four Seasons* by Vivaldi: delicious and all open-airy

Mark Knopfler (*Sailing to Philadelphia* or *The Ragpicker's Dream*, or both)

Anouar Brahem: the art of the eastern *oud*, quietly breathtaking

Travelin' Light with Sam Pilafian on tuba and Frank Vignola on guitar; if they can do it, so can you. *You're* not packing the tuba …

Tubular Bells 2003 (Mike Oldfield's still at it)

Brainwashed, the last one from George Harrison

The Traveling Wilburys: still sound fine

Franz Schubert's *Wanderer Fantasy*

Max Bruch's *Scottish Fantasy*

Acoustic folk guitar (like, *Six Strings North of the Border, Vols 1 & 2*)

Everything But the Girl

SPECTATOR SPORTS

Did you know that even watching sports burns calories? It's true, and you read it here first. (You're welcome.) Spread out a blanket, snap some photos of loved ones at play — it's exhausting even thinking about it. But when the ravenous descend on this high-protein pick-me-up, you'll be a shoo-in for MVP.

Pecan Salmon Roll (Barbara-jo McIntosh), p. 114

Baba Ganoush with Baguette Chunks, p. 111

Grilled Tandoori Chicken (Anne Lindsay), p. 257

Salade Niçoise, p. 174

Apple Polenta Flan, p. 273

Wine Suggestion:

*Unwooded Australian Chardonnay like Banrock Station, Chilean Pinot Noir,
and plenty of a local microbrew.*

SPECTATOR SPORTS (VEGGIE)

Cheese Nut Slices, p. 102

Baba Ganoush with Baguette Chunks, p. 111

Lentil, Apple, and Almond Salad, p. 162

Kidney Bean Salad with White Wine, Corn, and Peppers, p. 161

Carrot Coconut Cake (Rebar), p. 286

Music:

Being a person who neither spectates nor participates, this one is tough. What about the people beside you? Will they make you turn it down? So, I'm thinking . . .

Willie Nelson's studio recordings, don't bring any of the recent live stuff — uggh!

John Philip Sousa marches (Keith Brion's band)

Louis Moreau Gottschalk piano pieces: lots of cakewalks and tarantellas)

John Williams's movie themes: lots of bombast and cymbals)

Jase Maxwell, either as himself or as Zoox Coby: brilliant and off-the-wall)

Sam Cook & the Soul Stirrers (there's a 3-CD box out there, has some great gospel tunes in the mix)

Joan Baez's "Elvis Presley Blues": start a disturbance, why don't you?

Bond: that's the glam-girl string quartet, not the James (come to think of it, get him too — the James Bond soundtracks!)

The *Latin Grammy Nominees* annual issue

WINTER

Maybe it's because we live in a coastal rainforest, but winter picnicking doesn't seem all that strange a notion. Think of it as the off-season, and you've got the great outdoors to yourself. After all, how many summer days will your city's finest spot be waiting just for you? Bundle up, pack a sense of adventure, and experience outdoor eating from a whole new perspective. (Snowball fights are an excellent way to build appetites.)

Pea Soup with Ham, p. 139

Halibut and Potato Salad, p. 159

Thai Beef and Cucumber Salad, p. 178

Traditional Covered Apple Pie (Wanda Beaver), p. 320

Hot Cocoa, p. 326

Wine Suggestion:

Hot apple cider spiked with Calvados, the Normandy apple brandy, to keep out the cold.

WINTER (VEGGIE)

Bulgarian Bean Soup, p. 134

Marinated Roast Vegetables, p. 164

Red Cabbage Salad with Pistachios (James Peterson), p. 173

Traditional Covered Apple Pie (Wanda Beaver), p. 320

Hot Cocoa, p. 326

Music:

I once had a picnic on a glacier. It was catered, they flew us in, plied us with wine, fed us well, flew us out. I loved it. I've no idea what it cost, but I do know it's probably more than my Visa limit. I use my barbecue all winter, but it's only a short, mostly covered dash from the back door. Oh, you mean like a real picnic, somewhere cold?

Lori Cullen and Ron Davis, because she is the epitome of vocal cool

Mel Tormé, 'cause who's mellower or warmer, eh?

Ognjen Popovic and *Baltic Rumba*: gets you real warm, real fast

Paris to Kyiv Ensemble

The Electric V, a fantastic "expansion" on Vivaldi's *Four Seasons* made by Thomas Wilbrandt about 20 years ago, reissued two or three times since; find it and keep it close, it's brilliant stuff, especially the "Winter" section.

John Coltrane *Legacy*: some of his greatest solos, reissued

Johnny Cash: the last three recordings on American Records; what the legend is all about

The Rockin' Highliners

Philippe Boesmans's *Wintermaerchen*, a marvelously challenging modern work based on *A Winter's Tale*, with classical orchestra and jazz-rock ensemble and a real head-bender. For when you come back inside …

BRUNCH

Yes, you could go the eggs Benny and hash browns route, but isn't that a little obvious? Whether you're recovering from the night before or easing into a day off, brunch is a chance to dawdle, to graze, to enjoy a mini holiday. And by the time you've meandered from soup to fruit, doesn't it feel like maybe a little lunch is in order?

Vichyssoise, p. 141

Applesauce Bran Muffins, p. 263

Feta and Sun-Blushed Tomato Scones (Nadine Abensur), p. 265

Quiche Lorraine, p. 235

Potato Pizza (James Barber), p. 234

Mushroom Medley, p. 166

Pineapple Celery Salad, p. 169

Strawberry Shortcake, p. 319

Marinated Peaches, p. 306

Wine Suggestion:

*Champagne with fresh-squeezed orange juice is classic,
but whizzed-up peach or raspberries are even better.*

BRUNCH (VEGGIE)

Vichyssoise, p. 141

Banana Bread, p. 274

Feta and Sun-Blushed Tomato Scones (Nadine Abensur), p. 265

Frittata, p. 220

Potato Pizza (James Barber), p. 234

Mushroom Medley, p. 166

Celeriac Salad with Lime-Coconut Dressing, p. 148

Strawberry Shortcake, p. 319

Marinated Peaches, p. 306

Music:

These have to be among the best picnics. You tuck in, drink up, and then get to spend the balance of the day working on a brisk nap; come dinner and you rustle up a little something . . . a truly trashy movie on the tube and then to bed. Now you can face Monday. I like lutes a lot, and guitars, from the classical to Adrian Legg, and easy songs . . .

Morgana King (anything you can find, but the double disc of her three Reprise albums is a gem)

Scott Joplin piano rags

Adi Braun (a terrific singer who's carving a big rep in Europe. Opera star Russell Braun's little sister, taking a different route. Get him, too, while you're out shopping)

John Mayall, the early American albums, just for fun

The King's Consort

Norbert Kraft's *Naxos Guitar Collection* (plenty of variety)

Tosca (the one with Angela Gheorghiu and Roberto Alagna, for when there's a lull in the conversation or everyone's too stuffed to move)

AFTERNOON TEA

And here we said we weren't going to make like Merchant Ivory. There's no clotted cream here, but otherwise, it's everything a high tea should be. Wear your linens.

Layered Sandwiches, p. 204

Selection might include: pâté, pickles, and lettuce; roast beef, cucumber, and tomato; scrambled egg, bacon, and salsa

Rolled Sandwiches, p. 206

Selection might include: cream cheese with smoked salmon and capers; devilled ham and asparagus spears; cream cheese with blue cheese and celery; cream cheese with hot fruit chutney

Buttermilk Scallion scones, p. 264

Butterscotch Almond Cookies, p. 284

Devil's Food Cake, p. 290, with Ganache Filling (James McNair), p. 291

Iced Tea, p. 328, or hot tea

Wine Suggestion:

Seaview sparkling wine from Australia has the right baked-bread flavors. German Riesling from Lingenfelder or Dr. Loosen delivers the seductive hint of sweetness that goes well with afternoon drinking.

AFTERNOON TEA (VEGGIE)

Layered Sandwiches, p. 204

Selection might include: veggie pâté, pickles, and lettuce; egg salad, alfalfa sprouts, and tomato slices; asparagus with lemon juice, Parmesan, and cucumber slices

Rolled Sandwiches, p. 206

Selection might include: cream cheese with blue cheese and celery; cream cheese with hot fruit chutney; cream cheese with sun-dried tomatoes and black olives; cream cheese with marinated beets

Buttermilk Scallion Scones, p. 264

Butterscotch Almond Cookies, p. 284

Devil's Food Cake, p. 290, with Ganache Filling (James McNair), p. 291

Iced Tea, p. 328, or hot tea

Music:

Just find me the harpist from the cosmetics department at Harrods and I'm happy. Or Yolanda Kondonassis. And just one sugar …

Suitable soundtracks, like *Keep the Aspidistra Flying* or even *Captain Corelli's Mandolin*

Palm Court Orchestra

I Salonisti

Further out, let's hear some Valerie Smith & Liberty Pike (really good, really clean, lighter-than-air bluegrass)

The Rosenberg Trio (latter-day European gypsy jazz)

Symphony #2 for Dot Matrix Printers by The User (would I make this up? throw this in the afternoon mix and wake everybody up …)

Lara St. John's *re: Bach*

SUNSET

There's something about a sunset that makes flavors more intense. Maybe it's the way the minutes seems to slow, then rush forward just as the sun slips below the horizon. Maybe it's that feeling that the day's obligations are over: everything left is a bonus. Dessert time!

Potted Shrimp Infused with Savory Herbs and Garlic (John Bishop), p. 116, with crackers

Rolled Sandwiches, p. 206

Selection might include: cream cheese with tomato and bacon; cream cheese with black olives; cream cheese with smoked salmon and capers

Lemon Chocolate Fudge Squares, p. 304

Meringues with Whipped Cream, p. 307

Mint Julep Peaches (Nigella Lawson), p. 308

Iced coffee

Wine Suggestion:

A ripe, spicy Chardonnay from Australia, Chile, or California or a sunny, generous red from the South of France.

SUNSET (VEGGIE)

Veggie Pâté with crackers, p. 132

Rolled Sandwiches, p. 206

Selection might include: cream cheese with black olives; cream cheese with sunflower seeds and bitter-orange marmalade; cream cheese with blue cheese and celery

Lemon Chocolate Fudge Squares, p. 304

Meringues with Whipped Cream, p. 307

Mint Julep Peaches (Nigella Lawson), p. 308

Iced coffee

Music:

Red sails galore, and where's Webley Edwards when you need him to call? I think we need piano barcarolles by Felix Mendelssohn, mazurkas by Frédéric Chopin, rags by William Bolcom, stride by Willie "The Lion" Smith. Or Andy Fielding.

"The Graceful Ghost Rag" (Bolcom)

Cesaria Evora *Anthology*

Angela Hewitt's Bach albums

Marc-André Hamelin's anything albums

John Tavener is nice, maybe a little heavy

Dexter Gordon ballads

Pat Metheny & Charlie Haden (the *Missouri Sky* album in particular)

Yo-Yo Ma's last three recordings

Rob Wasserman's solo bass recordings

Vince Guaraldi's *Linus and Lucy* music

LATE NIGHT

We've designed this illicit feast for a night-owl twosome (prepare ahead and pull — ta da! — from the fridge at the last moment), but any number or location could work: outdoors, on the balcony, in the living room. If you are choosing an intimate liaison, all you're missing is some kind of late-night aerobic workout. Hmm. . . .

Chicken Liver Crostini (Umberto Menghi), p. 104

Chèvre Spread with crackers, p. 103

Rustic Apricot Galette (Regan Daley), p. 315

Double Chocolate Raspberry Tarts (Trish Deseine), p. 293

Prunes in Port, p. 311

Coffee

Wine Suggestion:

A midnight feast needs something sweet: a perfumey Muscat from southern France or Italy goes well with both chicken livers and goat cheese and the tarts. The sparkling Asti Spumante would be especially good.

LATE NIGHT (VEGGIE)

Jumbo Shrimp Sautéed in Lemon Butter, p. 223 or Asparagus Quiche Tartelettes, p. 99

Chèvre Spread with crackers, p. 103

Rustic Apricot Galette (Regan Daley), p. 315

Double Chocolate Raspberry Tarts (Trish Deseine), p. 293

Prunes in Port, p. 311

Coffee

Music:

Three dots cover a lot of ground, and a multitude of sins ...

Shirley Horn

Diana Krall *Live in Paris*

The 12 Cellists of the Berlin Philharmonic's 'Round Midnight album

Satie: The Complete Solo Piano Music by Jean-Yves Thibaudet; at five CDs, enough to last you till the morning ...

Rodney Crowell, the more recent "story" albums

Gregorio Allegri's *Miserere*

Ben Webster (the king of the air-brakes saxophone)

Arnold Schoenberg's *Verklaerte Nacht* (the full orchestra version)

Samuel Barber's *Adagio for Strings*

Johnny Hartman and John Coltrane (the two LPs are now on one CD)

John Fahey reissues from the '70s

HIPNIC

In case you're still thinking picnics are your Aunt Matilda's ambrosia salad, here's a menu that showcases all the flash you could ever need from an outdoor meal. Maybe this decadent lineup is the reward to promise yourself or a loved one; maybe it's just because. Everybody deserves to end at least one meal in their lives with Nigella Lawson's caramelized oranges.

Shrimp in Rosy Agar Agar Aspic with Wasabi Cream, p. 123

Gravlax, p. 106, with marbled rye, sour cream, and dill

Penne, Arugula, Prosciutto, and Olives with Lemon Vinaigrette (Bill Jones), p. 168

Tomato Bocconcini Salad with Basil, p. 181

Caramelized Oranges with Greek Yogurt (Nigella Lawson), p. 285

Wine Suggestion:

Riesling is ready for revival. Sales are up across North America, suggesting it's finally broken through the style barrier. A gorgeous German or an aromatic Alsatian will please all the guests.

HIPNIC (VEGGIE)

Jalapeños Stuffed with Chèvre, p. 110

Cool Cucumber Avocado Soup, p. 136

Gravlax, p. 106, with marbled rye, sour cream, and dill

Mesclun Greens with Toasted Pecans, Nectarine Slices, and Sherry Vinaigrette, p. 165

Tomato Bocconcini Salad with Basil, p. 181

Caramelized Oranges with Greek Yogurt (Nigella Lawson), p. 285

Music:

Don't ask me, just pick up whatever's on this week's Billboard Top Ten. All right, we'll add a few to that predictably monochromatic mix.

Phish

Elvis Costello (the two that came out in 2002 and the "through-composed" major works he's done since. When will the Diana Krall collaborative album appear?)

Tuvan throat singers. (Are they *it* or what?)

Mose Allison (spot-on hip for 50 years, and how does he *do* that?)

Shooglenifty (especially *The Arms Dealer's Daughter* album)

Horace X

Les Saqueboutiers de Toulouse

Nexus Percussion Ensemble

Bill Frisell with Petra Haden

Bill Frisell with the Intercontinentals

Bill Frisell with anybody

Rani Arbo & Daisy Mayhem

Les Tambours du Bronx

The Tiger Lilies & Kronos Quartet *The Gorey End*

Ani diFranco

ON THE WATER

It seemed appropriate, somehow, to give some choices for this menu, something to do with the notion of floating free, away from all the constraints of dry land. Whether you're on your own yacht or the local ferry, this is a menu that will blossom in a marine setting. Just add wind and water, and savor.

Marinated Mushrooms, p. 111
breads with Anchovy Butter (Barbara-jo McIntosh), p. 96
Swedish Pickled Cucumber, p. 176
Ahi Tuna Sashimi and Green Papaya Salad with Chili-Lime Dressing (Rob Feenie), p. 143
Roman Meatloaf (Joyce Goldstein), p. 237
Gingerbread Butterfly Cupcakes, p. 298

Wine Suggestion:

Sauvignon Blanc from New Zealand and Albariño from Spain have the sharp, refreshing tang of salt sea air to match the occasion.

ON THE WATER (VEGGIE)

Marinated Mushrooms, p. 111

breads with Veggie Butter, p. 131

Swedish Pickled Cucumber, p. 176

Couscous Vegetable Salad with Orange-Miso Dressing, p. 151

Waldorf Salad, p. 185

Gingerbread Butterfly Cupcakes, p. 298

Music:

Almost as good as being on the beach is messing about in boats. Water Music by Handel is so obvious, but truth to tell, it is a good tune, or twenty. So start with that and then mix and match from the following:

Freddie Cannon's "Sea Cruise" (I mean, you gotta)

Anything with cascading harps in it

Maybe one of those "environmental discs" of sea sounds, just to enhance the ambiance

Penguin Café Orchestra

Harry Manx & Kevin Breit

"The Flying Theme" from *E.T.* (especially if you're on the bridge)

Nigel Kennedy and the Kroke Band's *East Meets East*

Some remastered Stan Kenton, really loud

The Orlando Consort and Perfect Houseplants (medieval and modern music mixed, remarkably)

ROMANTIC

A loaf of bread, a jug of wine.... Still a plan, but allow us to introduce John Bishop's pear-chèvre pastries. Whether you choose the cheese platter or Umberto Menghi's succulent duck breast, things are going to do nothing but heat up. Plenty of kir royales will help quench the fires. Really. Oh, and if you can't figure out why we suggest linguine salad for a romantic picnic, you haven't watched The Lady and the Tramp *recently enough.*

Roasted Pear and Goat Cheese Phyllo Pastries (John Bishop), p. 120
Artichokes with Vinaigrette, p. 98
Linguine Salad with Cherry Tomatoes and Avocado Dressing, p. 163
Breast of Duck Rapido (Umberto Menghi), p. 216
Chocolate-Dipped Strawberries, p. 289

Wine Suggestion:

Rosé champagne is pure romance in a bottle. Moët et Chandon and Veuve Clicquot both do good ones. Pink Spanish cava from Freixenet or Cordoníu is full of frothy frivolity for far less money. Or blend blackcurrant Cassis with any sparkling wine for a kir royale.

ROMANTIC (VEGGIE)

Roasted Pear and Goat Cheese Phyllo Pastries (John Bishop), p. 120

Artichokes with Vinaigrette, p. 98

Linguine Salad with Cherry Tomatoes and Avocado Dressing, p. 163

cheese plate with Summer Fruit Relish, p. 125 and baguette

Chocolate-Dipped Strawberries, p. 289

Music:

Loaf of bread, jug of wine music being so subjective, I offer only a few that please me.

André Previn and Anne-Sophie Mutter (I mean, how romantic is that personal and musical partnership?)

Scheherazade (especially the recent Kirov Orchestra recording, except don't put anything breakable in front of the speakers!)

Philip Glass piano pieces

Angela Gheorghiu and Roberto Alagna; any of the big opera duets

The Albinoni *Adagio*? (A lot of people find it majorly romantic; it just tends to put me to sleep ...)

Lute music of Sylvius Leopold Weiss

The slow movements from Alan Hovhaness's symphonies

HOTEL ROOM

A luxurious hotel room, sun streaming in, the murmur of traffic. A vase of flowers, music low, and on the bed ... the food of love. Nadine Abensur's caramelized figs keep well, so make ahead and have on hand for when desire strikes. The rest you can either make or buy; it's your choice: this one's all about the host having as much pleasure as the guest.

crudités (dressing optional)

Sushi with Japanese pickled ginger, p. 126

Dried Figs Caramelized with Kumquats, Mascarpone, and Ginger (Nadine Abensur), p. 295

liqueur-filled chocolates

Wine Suggestion:

Empty the minibar to chill a bottle of great California Chardonnay from Rodney Strong, Byron Estate, or Signorello. Good red Burgundy would also give lots of pleasure.

HOTEL ROOM (VEGGIE)

crudités

Sushi with Japanese pickled ginger, p. 126

Dried Figs Caramelized with Kumquats, Mascarpone, and Ginger (Nadine Abensur), p. 295

liqueur-filled chocolates

Music:

Some of the best picnics of my acquaintance have occurred in this setting: you hit the delis and bakeries, dump the bags on the bed, find a corkscrew and a couple of knives, and bingo. So the problem is, what's for music on the tiny tableside radio, or worse, the TV. Bring those MP3s.

Laura Nyro's live sessions (*The Loom's Desire*)

Jane Siberry's "Twelve Days of Christmas" (if it happens to be December, or even if it isn't)

Jimmy Giuffre, Jim Hall, Bob Brookmeyer (the Atlantic reissues of The Jimmy Giuffre 3 sessions)

Juanes (see the Kids menu, and depending on who you're with)

Charles Mingus, the earlier albums on Atlantic and Impulse

Hampton Grease Band *Music to Eat* (if you can find it and if you have a bizarre sense of time, place, humor, whatever)

Ravel String Quartet (there's only one)

Eine Kleine Nachtmusik (Mozart, straight or fiddled with)

FILM FESTIVAL

With over 800 film and video festivals in North America each year, you're going to have to work pretty hard to avoid attending one. Whether you're spending a day in the dark or only two hours, however, you cannot live on popcorn alone. You can try, of course, but why bother when you could be savoring — quietly! — roast chicken with tarragon. When concessions start serving food like this (and why don't they?), we'll stop smuggling. Until then, at least buy your drink from the theater (to ease my conscience). Of course, this menu works for any lights-out, eat-with-your-fingers marathon. Don't forget the napkins!

Tomato, Bocconcini, and Basil on Toothpicks, p. 128

Cold Roast Chicken with Tarragon, p. 236

Brownies, p. 282

purchased drink from theatre concession

Wine Suggestion:

Individual bottles of champagne complete with their own straw.
Piper Heidsieck and Pommery are the pioneers.

FILM FESTIVAL (VEGGIE)

Tomato, Bocconcini, and Basil on Toothpicks, p. 128

Nori Nut Rolls, p. 230

Ginger Crunch Squares, p. 297

purchased drink from theatre concession

Music:

Well, movie soundtracks, methinks — from Modesty Blaise *to* Veronica Guerin,
Elmer Gantry *to* The Swimmer, Phaedra *to* Six Feet Under *(all right, that's not a
movie but it's cool, especially the theme).*

Oscar Peterson & Glenn Gould, solo and back-to-back

Anything by John Williams, especially his treatment of other people's movie music

Delos has a couple of CDs of TV and film music "in the style of" the great composers; lots of fun

Erich Wolfgang Korngold: music from his Hollywood films

Michael Nyman: some of the music from his films (love *The Piano*)

All and any of Philip Glass's movie music

MUSIC FESTIVAL

Everywhere you look, there's a music festival springing up. If you're planning to spend a weekend helicopter dancing, plan nutrition carefully. Short of reprinting the Moosewood cookbook, here is some delectable fare to fuel body and soul.

Sardine Spread, p. 121, with Baked Pita Triangles, p. 101

Broiled Chicken Legs, p. 217

Tuna and Rice Salad (Joyce Goldstein), p. 183

Fruit with Yogurt-Honey Dip, p. 322

Hokey Pokey Biscuits, p. 300

Iced Mint Syrup, p. 327

Wine Suggestion:

A big flask of chilled sangria based on a tasty Spanish red like Sangre de Toro from Torres. Or the wine all by itself. It still comes with a little plastic bull round the neck of the bottle.

MUSIC FESTIVAL (VEGGIE)

Hummus, p. 109, with Baked Pita Triangles, p. 101

Cheese and Onion Tart, p. 219

Quinoa Corn Salad (Rebar), p. 172

Fruit with Yogurt-Honey Dip, p. 322

Hokey Pokey Biscuits, p. 300

Iced Mint Syrup, p. 327

Music:

Whatever you just bought at the front of the stage for ten bucks, no tax, from the players who just finished a set . . .

Zubot & Dawson

Stephan Micus

Tom Russell

The The's *Hanky Panky* (Hank Williams covers, still in print and still brilliant)

Kirk Elliott

Celtic with backbone (don't like the wispy, mushy stuff), so Loretto Reid Band, The McDade's, Sharon Shannon, Micheal O Suilleabhain

Doug Cox

Joni Mitchell (then, not now)

Art Turner

Oliver Schroer

RAINBOW

Food as décor? There can be no contest for Hostess with the Mostest if you color-coordinate your picnic to the theme of the day. We've included two — one in celebration of Gay Pride; the other for either Fourth of July or Canada Day (bonus points if you know which one gets blue). But don't stop there. St Patrick's Day, Bastille Day, Valentine's Day, Diwali ... you could become quite unbalanced.

Red

Raspberry Mousse, p. 313; Macerated Strawberries, p. 318; Ratatouille, p. 119; rare roast beef slices; Tomato Herb Tarts, p. 129; Beet, Noodle, and Jicama Salad, p. 146; Chilled Borscht, p. 135; Gazpacho, p. 137; watermelon slices; Wine Fruit Punch, p. 333

Orange

Carrot, Raisin, and Sesame Salad, p. 147; Golden Yam Salad, p. 155; orange pepper sticks; Gravlax, p. 106; Rustic Apricot Galette, p. 315; Bulgarian Bean Soup, p. 134; Sautéed Jumbo Shrimp, p. 223; Salmon Chowder, p. 140; Potted Shrimp Infused with Savory Herbs and Garlic, p. 116

Yellow

Curried Cauliflower Salad, p. 152; Bean Salad (yellow beans only), p. 154; corn on the cob; yellow pepper sticks; Pineapple Celery Salad, p. 169; Asparagus Quiche Tartelettes, p. 99; Cheese and Onion Tart, p. 219; Frittata, p. 220; Devilled Eggs, p. 105; Apple Polenta Flan, p. 273; Marinated Peaches, p. 306; Fruit Punch, p. 324

Green

Cool Cucumber Avocado Soup, p. 136; Japanese Spinach Salad, p. 160; tossed green salad; Swedish Pickled Cucumber, p. 176; asparagus; Artichokes with Vinaigrette, p. 98; Guacamole, p. 108; Veggie Butter, p. 131; Coleslaw, p. 149; Napa Cabbage Slaw, p. 167; Spinach Hummus, p. 109

Blue

Blue martinis; blue cheese; blue corn chips

Purple

Blueberry Cake, p. 281; Purple Grape Jelly, p. 312; Sushi Rolls, p. 126, made with laver (jee choy – a purple seaweed); purple asparagus; Japanese eggplant; purple broccoli; plums

Wine Suggestion:

Wine comes white, pink, or red in almost every shade from greeny white to inky purple. You can find blue bottles, red bottles, and white and black ones, as well as the traditional green and brown. Anything French would suit the red, white, and blue.

Music:

Color music? Composer Madeleine Dring built a whole philosophy and career on the premise, but the recordings are tough to find; fascinating, though, if you do. Scriabin did, too; some big-scale, typically Russian works with lots of bombast (if not as much fun). Meanwhile: the blues, Red Norvo, Bill Evans's On Green Dolphin Street, Peggy Lee and Black Coffee, Jimmy Ponder's White Room (or the Moody Blues and Nights in White Satin), Mellow Yellow, Orange Colored Sky, Les Brown and his Band of Renown, Deep Purple, Mood Indigo, Blue Velvet, Red Sails in the Sunset, nor is it easy being green. I'm done here.

RED/WHITE/BLUE

Red and White

Tomatoes Stuffed with Ricotta, p. 130; Kidney Bean Salad, p. 161; Jalapeños Stuffed with Chèvre, p. 110; Tomato and Potato Salad, p. 180; Potato and Bacon Salad, p. 170; Linguine Salad with Cherry Tomatoes, p. 163; Rhubarb Strawberry Pie, p. 314; Strawberry Shortcake, p. 319; radishes; Feta and Sun-Blushed Tomato Scones, p. 265

Red (see Rainbow)

White

Soused Fish, p. 242; Celeriac Salad with Coconut-Lime Dressing, p. 148; Waldorf Salad, p. 185; Sesame Potatoes, p. 122; sour cream; Salad Rolls, p. 238; Halibut and Potato Salad, p. 159; Meringues with Whipped Cream, p. 307

Blue (see Rainbow)

SHAKESPEARE

Although a 21st-century urban picnic would bear little resemblance to anything the great bard might have dreamed up, the food, at least, could be reassuringly familiar to him. Our recipes, developed from research done on centuries-old recipe collections, are updated for modern equipment, supermarkets, and digestive systems. Whether you dance a gavotte in doublet and hose is up to you. Vegetarians: Run for the hills!

Pickled Mustles, p. 115

Grand Mixed Sallet with Roast Capon, p. 156

Pease Porrage, p. 113

Souced Fish, p. 242

Oxford Kates Sausages with Mustard, p. 232

Jellied Salmon, p. 221

Gooseberry or Apple Creame, p. 299

Mackroons, p. 305

Hippocras, p. 325

Wine Suggestion:

Shakespeare would have enjoyed beer, sherris-sack (the ancestor of sherry), or claret. So go with a glass of Tío Pepe or a bottle of red Bordeaux.

Music:

Exiting stage left, pursued by a bear . . .

Cleo Laine's *The Complete Works* (which she does in a minute; a must)

Philip Pickett's *Alchemist*

Philip Pickett and the New London Consort's music for The Globe Theatre

Guy Woolfenden's music for the Royal Shakespeare Company

Romeo & Juliet by Sergei Prokofiev of course (and anyone else's, for comparison)

David Frishberg's original songs (sung by himself or others – Blossom Dearie, Diana Krall); many of them as clever as any Shakespearians.

RECIPES

RECIPES

RECIPES

RECIPES

RECEIPES

RECURVED

RECIPES

STARTERS
& SIDES

ANCHOVY BUTTER

Created by Barbara-jo McIntosh, owner of the incomparable Barbara-Jo's Books to Cooks in Vancouver, this delicious butter can be kept in the freezer and used in many ways, tossed on pasta or with a broiled steak, chicken, or fish. To serve it with baguette slices, allow it to come to room temperature, but do not let it get any warmer.

MAKES ABOUT 2 CUPS

1 1.75-oz (50-g) can anchovy fillets

1 lb (455 g) butter

2 shallots, finely chopped

½ cup flat leaf parsley, chopped

½ cup pimento, diced

In a food processor with steel blade, combine all ingredients and pulse until all ingredients are uniformly distributed throughout the butter.

Lay 16 inches (40 cm) of waxed paper lengthwise on a clean work surface. Place all the anchovy butter ⅓ of the way up the wax paper. Fold the end nearest you up over the butter and roll to form a uniform 2-inch (5-cm) cylinder. Tightly wrap the ends. Wrap again with plastic wrap and place in freezer.

ARTICHOKE AND SUN-DRIED TOMATO DIP

The complex flavor of this tasty dip comes not from a long list of ingredients, but from the jar of commercially prepared marinated artichokes that you buy to make it with! So be excessive! Buy the best you can find, with a marinade of high quality olive oil and herbs. The dip can be made the day before the picnic.

MAKES 1½ CUPS

10 oz (300 g) drained marinated artichoke hearts (set the liquid aside)

3 oz (90 g) oil-packed sun-dried tomatoes, plus 2 or 3 pieces for garnish

¼ tsp or more of lemon pepper, or

¼ tsp black pepper plus a small amount of lemon zest and a squeeze of lemon juice

In a food processor or blender, purée the artichokes and sun-dried tomatoes, adding as much of the reserved marinade as you need to make a soft purée.

Coarsely chop the pieces of sun-dried tomato set aside for garnish and stir them into the purée along with the lemon pepper, or pepper, lemon zest and juice.

Take the dip out of the fridge or cooler about an hour or so before serving, so that it has time to warm up a little.

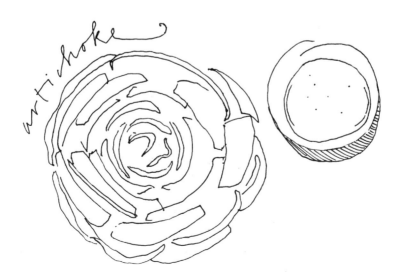

ARTICHOKES WITH VINAIGRETTE

Large artichokes need washing, and then the lowest of the outer leaves removed. Those higher up need their prickly ends trimmed (kitchen shears work well), and to prevent browning of the cut surfaces in the air, dip cut ends in a solution of half lemon juice and half water. Steam the artichokes in a deep stainless steel pot, so that they can sit upright, and throughout the 40 minutes of cooking time, keep the level of water in the pot at about 1½ inches (3.8 cm). The water should be simmering, not boiling. Keep the lid on the pot so that the artichokes can steam.

SERVES 2

2 large artichokes, steamed as above
　　and drained

Vinaigrette

3 tbsp lemon juice

1 tsp freshly crushed garlic (optional)

¼ tsp Dijon mustard

¼ – ½ tsp salt

dash black pepper or pepper sauce

¼ tsp honey (optional)

3 tbsp olive oil

In a bowl, mix all the vinaigrette ingredients except for the oil. Whisk in the oil, and adjust for seasoning. Shake the vinaigrette well just before serving, and pour it into a small wide dish so that you can both dip your artichoke leaves into it.

ASPARAGUS QUICHE TARTELETTES

These are crustless mini-quiches rather than tarts, baked in muffin pans to produce a moist interior and a firmer, chewier outside. They are easy to make and to pack for a picnic. The substitution of more asparagus for the carrot in the recipe is a delicious way to celebrate the advent of fresh asparagus in the markets or your own garden.

MAKES 16

4 eggs

2 tbsp melted butter

½ tsp salt

½ tsp pepper or hot sauce

1 cup flour

1 tsp baking powder

1 cup milk

1 cup onions or leeks, chopped

1 cup carrot, grated (or omit the carrot and use 2 cups of asparagus instead of one)

1 cup asparagus, chopped, slender young stalks only

1 cup sharp cheese, grated, divided into 2

Preheat oven to 350°F (175°C).

In a bowl, beat the eggs with the butter, salt and pepper, and add the milk.

In another bowl, place the flour and baking powder, mix well, then add the egg mixture, stirring to break down the lumps. Add the milk and the vegetables, and lastly, ½ cup of the cheese.

Spoon mixture into well-greased muffin pans, and sprinkle the rest of the cheese over the top of each one. Bake in oven for 30 minutes or until a tester inserted in the middle of one piece comes out clean.

BABA GANOUSH

It may be tricky to spell but it's delicious to eat with warm pita bread, or crackers, vegetable sticks or big chunks of fresh whole-grain bread.

SERVES 4 TO 6

1 medium eggplant

¼ cup tahini paste

2 tbsp lemon juice (juice of half a lemon)

2 tbsp olive oil

2 tsp balsamic vinegar

garlic to taste (begin with a small clove, crushed; add more if desired)

salt and pepper to taste

Pierce the eggplant before cooking to let steam out. Cook the eggplant under a hot broiler until it is soft and the skin is somewhat charred, turning it from time to time.

When it is cooked, and cool enough to handle, peel off the skin and place the soft interior in a bowl with the other ingredients. Mash and mix them together thoroughly. The dip should be chilled if you make it the day before the picnic, but serve it at room temperature.

BAKED PITA TRIANGLES

Just right for dipping into something tasty, but very more-ish all by themselves.

SERVES 6

6 whole wheat pita breads

2 tbsp olive oil

1 tsp paprika

Preheat oven to 325°F (160°C).

Cut each circle of pita bread into eight triangles, and place them on a generously oiled baking sheet. If you have an oil spray pump, spray them lightly, but otherwise, toss them very gently so that they absorb some of the oil from the tray. Dust them with paprika using a shaker.

Bake in oven for 15 to 20 minutes, turning them once during this time. Allow them to cool completely before packing. When cool they will be crisp.

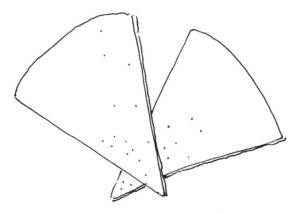

CHEESE NUT SLICES

Cheese and nuts, an age-old combo that never goes out of style!

SERVES 4 TO 6

2 cups cheese, grated (Swiss or medium cheddar)

½ cup soft butter

milk (see directions)

½ cup same cheese as above, cubed

½ cup nuts, chopped (pistachios, pecans, or toasted almonds)

4 buns, or 4 pieces baguette about 6 inches (15 cm) long

In a bowl, blend the grated cheese, butter, and just enough milk to make a thick paste. Mix in the cheese cubes and nuts. Divide this mixture into four portions.

Cut the ends off the buns or baguette pieces and hollow them out enough to spoon in the cheese mixture from both ends. When the pieces are stuffed, wrap them firmly in foil or plastic wrap and chill for a couple of hours, then slice them thinly for serving.

CHÈVRE SPREAD

The soft creamy goat cheese has an assertive flavor that perfectly complements the fresh herbs.

MAKES ¾ CUP

4 – 5 oz (130 g) chèvre

2 tbsp parsley, finely chopped

1 green onion, chopped small

1 tsp fresh thyme leaves

2 tbsp buttermilk or yogurt

black pepper to taste

In a bowl, combine all the ingredients and mix thoroughly, adding a little more buttermilk or yogurt to obtain a spreading consistency. Adjust for seasoning. This spread is intensely flavored and good with crackers or bread.

CHICKEN LIVER CROSTINI

Umberto Menghi owns Italian restaurants in British Columbia and a prestigious cooking school in Tuscany, and is a renowned chef, food writer, teacher, and TV personality. His chicken liver pâté sets the mood for our late-night picnic, sensual, richly complex in flavor, and oh, so smooth. You can prepare it the night before too.

SERVES 6

11 oz (300 g) chicken livers, membranes removed

1 medium onion, coarsely chopped

1 stalk celery with leaves, coarsely chopped

2 cloves garlic, coarsely chopped

½ cup 2-day-old bread, broken up

1 branch rosemary, leaves removed

small handful of sage leaves

small handful of parsley

½ cup meat broth

4 tbsp dry white wine

2 tbsp butter

2 tbsp extra virgin olive oil

3 tbsp capers

3 anchovy fillets

black pepper to taste

12 – 16 slices Tuscan loaf or baguette, crisped but not toasted

In a heavy-bottomed pot over medium heat, combine chicken livers, onion, celery, garlic, bread chunks, rosemary, sage, and parsley, and cook covered for 10 minutes, stirring occasionally.

Add the broth and cook covered for another 30 minutes. Add the wine and leave the pot uncovered until the liquid has evaporated.

Remove from heat and put the mixture in a food processor or blender with the butter, oil, capers, and anchovies. Purée until it becomes a smooth, moist spread. Stir in pepper to taste.

Spread on crisped bread and serve warm or cold. This spread keeps well in the refrigerator or freezer.

DEVILLED EGGS

A picnic classic and still as good as ever. Devilled eggs can be made spicy hot with lots of pepper sauce or a teaspoon or two of curry paste or powder.

MAKES 8 PIECES

4 large eggs

2 tbsp buttermilk or plain yogurt or
  whipping cream

1 tbsp parsley, finely chopped

1 tbsp chives, finely chopped

1 green onion, white part only,
  chopped

¼ – ½ tsp salt

pepper or hot sauce to taste

In a pot over medium heat, bring the eggs slowly to a boil in water to cover them. Reduce heat to low and simmer for 7 minutes, then remove from the water and cool in cold water.

Shell the eggs when cool, cut them in half, and remove the yolks carefully.

Place the yolks in a bowl with the buttermilk and blend until smooth. Add the remaining ingredients and mix well. Check for seasoning before dividing the mixture into 8 portions and spooning it into the egg-white cups.

GRAVLAX

Home-made gravlax is not as much work as it sounds, and well worth the effort. Whereas smoked salmon is cured in brine and wood-smoked, gravlax is salted and pressed; either way you are eating raw salmon (although the texture of some smoked salmon suggests it's close to being cooked). That's why I start off with pre-frozen sockeye, caught wild at sea, to make my gravlax. (No farm antibiotics, and none of the lively and destructive little parasites which may lurk in any raw fish, because freezing, as well as cooking, kills them!) But the fish must smell and look completely fresh when you buy it.

SERVES DOZENS

3 – 3½ lb (1.3 – 1.5 kg) piece of sockeye salmon

2 tbsp rock salt

2 tbsp peppercorns

2 tbsp sugar

large bunch of fresh dill

Select a chunk from the widest section of a good-sized sockeye salmon. Ask the cutter to remove the bone and cut the piece in two along its length, so you have two thick fillets, almost square in shape, with the skin on. Use a pair of tweezers to pull out any bones remaining in the fillets.

Grind salt, peppercorns, and sugar into a coarse powder. Wash and dry the dill, cutting off any hard thick stalk ends.

Select a glass or china bowl with a flat bottom, and sides deep enough to accommodate the thickness of the two fillets.

Lay a quarter of the dill sprigs in the bottom, use the salt mixture to completely coat the two fillets, then place one on the dill, skin side down. Put half of the dill on top of it, and any remaining loose salt mixture. Lay the second fillet on top, skin side up, placing the two fillets thick side to thin side, with the remaining dill on top. Cover the surface loosely with plastic food wrap.

The challenge, before you refrigerate your salmon to cure, is to place enough weight on top of it to compress it. I use a piece of thin plywood, cut to fit inside my chosen bowl, and a heavy rock. A container of water or a dish of pebbles makes a good weight too, and to distribute it evenly across the fish you can use a flat plate or a book (wrapped in foil). The gravlax needs to cure for 48 hours, and to be turned every 12 hours by removing the weight and the plastic wrap and flipping the entire "sandwich" over. Make sure the dill sprigs remain in place, and increase the weight if there's no liquid collecting in the bowl after 24 hours. After 2 days, discard both dill and liquid, and the gravlax is ready to use.

Remove some of its peppery coating before you serve it sliced very thinly, on crackers or pumpernickel, with a dab of sour cream, or in any other way you might serve smoked salmon.

Our suggested presentation for the Hipnic menu is thinly sliced gravlax on small squares of marbled rye bread, topped with a tiny dab of sour cream and a wisp of fresh dill weed.

Note: I set aside as much as we want to eat fresh-cured, then wrap small chunks in plastic wrap and foil, and freeze them for later use. (Yes, you are freezing previously frozen fish but it isn't a problem here, assuming you practice good food-handling hygiene and are working with a healthy product — see recipe introduction.) Once the gravlax has been frozen, use it within a couple of months, and it will have retained all its good flavor and texture. Partially thawed and skin side down, it slides off the skin in paper-thin slices, with the help of a very sharp knife.

An interesting variation:
Prepare gravlax using Szechuan peppercorns instead of regular, and substituting 2 tbsp of Lapsang Souchong tea leaves for the dill, grinding the dry leaves in with the salt mixture. The tea gives it a lovely smoky flavor, but make sure to scrape it all off before you slice and serve or freeze the gravlax.

GUACAMOLE

The Surreal Gourmet, *expat Canadian Bob Blumer's TV show and mind-expanding take on how to enjoy preparing food for and with friends, showcases some of his many talents. His recipe for guacamole heats up the action, making a "spicier, fresher-tasting variation of the traditional recipe." He suggests that adding a diced tomato is also good.*

SERVES 6 TO 8

2 ripe avocados (ripe ones indent easily with the firm press of a finger ... but don't let the produce person see you)

½ cup fresh cilantro, stems removed, finely chopped

1 dried hot red pepper, crushed

or 1 tsp chili peppers, crushed

1 garlic clove, minced

juice of 1 lemon

4 scallions, finely chopped

1 tsp fresh ground black pepper, or to taste

½ tsp salt, or to taste

⅛ tsp cayenne pepper (optional)

Slice avocados in half, discard skin, and reserve pit. In a bowl, add all ingredients. Blend with a fork or a double bladed chopper. (I prefer to leave my guacamole somewhat chunky.)

The guacamole is best the day it is made. Garnish it with a lemon twist if you wish, and serve with yellow or blue corn tortilla chips.

To keep the guacamole from going brown, either squeeze the juice of ½ of a lemon over top or place avocado pit in the mixture. Keep it chilled until use.

HUMMUS

This is a basic recipe that can be transformed in various ways, including some you might dream up yourself. Each added ingredient can be chosen for color, flavor, or texture.

SERVES 8 OR MORE

2 14-fl oz (398-ml) cans garbanzo
   beans (chickpeas)

juice of 1½ – 2 lemons
   (about 6 tbsp)

2 tbsp water

½ tsp salt, or to taste

Drain and rinse the garbanzo beans, then, in a food processor or blender, purée them, adding the lemon juice and water as soon as the beans are broken up. Process until smooth, and then adjust seasoning, adding the salt as necessary, since some canned garbanzo beans are already quite salty.

Many people like 3 tbsp tahini stirred into the basic recipe, and one or more cloves of garlic, chopped before processing.

Alternatively, process into the basic mixture:
3 tbsp oil-packed sun-dried tomatoes, diced or 2 – 3 tbsp parsley or basil, choppedor 3 tbsp spinach, cooked and chopped

JALAPEÑOS STUFFED
WITH CHÈVRE

These appetizer morsels are not for the faint of heart. You will need a jar of oil-packed or marinated jalapeño peppers, bright red and fiery tasting, available in some supermarkets, and specialty food stores.

MAKES 12

12 jalapeño peppers, packed in oil

¾ – 1 cup chèvre (soft goat cheese)

Drain the peppers and pat them dry with paper towel. Carefully fill each one with chèvre, arrange in a small container, and keep chilled until ready to use.

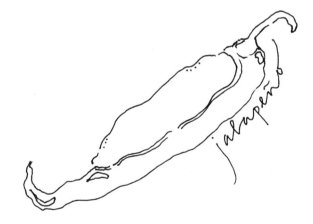

MARINATED MUSHROOMS

These tangy little darlings will keep well for a week. They are quite spicy and make an excellent hors d'oeuvre or side dish with cold meats or cheeses.

SERVES 6

1 lb (450 g) button mushrooms
(about 35 pieces)

¾ cup apple cider vinegar

⅓ cup water

1 tbsp whole peppercorns

1 tbsp whole cloves

1 tsp dried thyme leaves

1 tsp whole allspice (optional)

2 bay leaves (optional)

1 tsp salt

2 tsp honey

Wash or brush the mushrooms, dry them well, and cut off any brown ends of stems.

In a pot over medium heat, combine the rest of the ingredients and bring to a boil. Reduce heat to low and simmer for 5 minutes, then add the mushrooms, stirring them around gently as you bring the liquid back to the boil. The mushrooms shrink as they release their juice into the marinade, so you will not need to continue stirring after the first few minutes.

Reduce heat again and let them simmer, covered, for 5 minutes. Remove the pot from the heat and allow the mushrooms to cool completely. Spoon them into a jar with a lid, and cover them with as much of the marinade, spices, etc, as will fit in the jar. Refrigerate until ready to use.

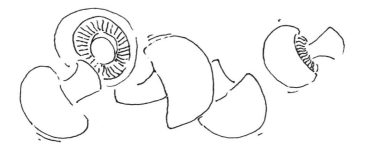

MARYLAND CRAB DIP

If you are lucky enough to have access to fresh crab meat, this is a heavenly way to serve it as an appetizer, hot or cool, with chunks of baguette or plain crackers. The recipe was given to us by Elisabeth's Maryland relative Cara Lynn F., who uses blue backfin crab, but the recipe would work well with the West Coast's Dungeness crab as well.

MAKES ABOUT 4 CUPS

½ lb (230 g) fresh lump crab meat

½ lb (230 g) softened cream cheese

½ cup sour cream

2 tbsp commercial salad dressing

1 tbsp lemon juice

1¼ tsp Worcestershire sauce

½ tsp dry mustard

pinch garlic salt

1 tbsp milk

¾ – 1 cup cheddar cheese, grated, divided into 2

½ – 1 tsp paprika

Preheat oven to 350°F (175°C).

Discard any cartilage from the crab meat and set the meat aside. In a bowl, mix the remaining ingredients, including half of the grated cheese, then gently fold in the crab meat.

Spoon the mixture into a greased 1-quart casserole, distribute the remaining cheese on top, and sprinkle with paprika. Bake in oven for 30 minutes, or until the mixture is bubbling and is lightly browned on top.

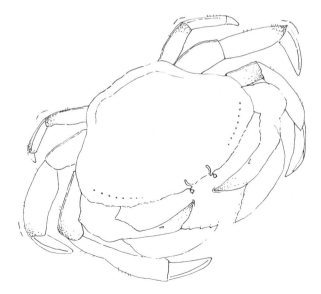

PEASE PORRAGE

Pease Porrage, a purée of split peas with flavorful spices and herbs, is the ancestor of the English "mushy peas" and it's surprisingly good, especially enriched with butter as this recipe is. (In Elizabethan times, ordinary folk would use fat pork rather than butter.) The use of garlic is uncommon in recipes of the time, because of its strong, vigorous powers, but it certainly contributes a tasty note to this one. Prepare the Pease Porrage just before picnic time or reheat it at the last minute, so that it can be eaten hot, with bread and extra butter.

SERVES 6 TO 8

2⅓ cups split yellow or green peas

5 cups water (you may need a little more)

1 small onion, finely chopped

1 tsp garlic, freshly pressed

1½ tsp coriander seeds, crushed

½ tsp ground pepper (or more to taste)

1 tsp salt (more as needed)

1 tbsp dried mint leaves, crushed

2 tbsp parsley, minced

¼ cup butter

In a pot over high heat, bring the peas to a boil in the water, with the onion, garlic, coriander seeds, pepper, salt, and mint. Reduce heat and continue to simmer. When the peas are completely soft (around 1¼ hours), add the butter and parsley and cook for a few more minutes. The mixture should be smooth and soft.

You can serve the porrage very thick, with small servings, or thin it to soup consistency towards the end of the cooking time by adding ½ cup water and ¼ tsp salt for every cup of porrage.

PECAN SALMON ROLL

Barbara-jo McIntosh, as she describes in Tin Fish Gourmet, *her cookbook that's a love letter to the sea, found the inspiration for this recipe in Lunenberg, Nova Scotia, and has used it extensively since, both for home use and in her career as a caterer. It's simple, scrumptious, and sustaining.*

Serves 6 to 8

9 oz (250 g) cream cheese

2 tbsp chèvre (soft goat cheese) (optional)

1 tbsp lemon juice

1 green onion, finely chopped

1 tbsp prepared horseradish

½ tsp cayenne pepper

1 15-oz (425-g) tin salmon, drained

½ cup pecans, finely chopped

2 tbsp parsley, finely chopped, plus a few sprigs for garnish

In a bowl, cream together cheeses, lemon juice, green onion, horseradish, and cayenne pepper. Add salmon and mix together. Refrigerate at least two hours.

Shape into a roll, about 8 x 3 inches (20 x 8 cm). Roll through the combined mixture of pecans and parsley to cover. Place on platter and garnish with parsley sprigs, Serve with sliced baguette or crackers.

For an Italian spin, substitute the onion, horseradish and cayenne with 2 tbsp of pesto sauce and 1 tbsp of sun-dried tomatoes, finely chopped, and replace the parsley with basil.

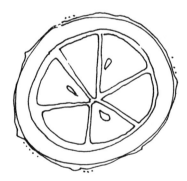

PICKLED MUSTLES

This Elizabethan method for marinating mussels (hence the recipe's spelling) is easy, and the results so more-ish you won't want to eat mussels any other way. They are ready to consume after a few hours in their pickling liquid, but can be made a day ahead, and will keep well for at least a couple of days, as long as they are kept refrigerated.

SERVES 6

3 lb (1.5 kg) fresh mussels

1 cup water

¾ cup apple cider vinegar

2 tsp black peppercorns

1 tsp whole cloves

½ tsp ground mace

1½ tsp salt

1 tsp honey

Scrub the mussels well, and snip off the beards. Discard any that are open.

In a large pot with a lid, bring the water to a boil over high heat. Place the cleaned mussels in the water, cover, and bring the water back to a vigorous boil. Shake the pot often to change the position of the mussels as they steam. Check them after 3 to 4 minutes, and take out the opened ones with a slotted spoon, setting them aside on a large plate. Leave the unopened ones to cook a little longer. All should be done in 5 to 7 minutes, and any unopened mussels at that point should be discarded. (Never try to force them open, because if they aren't open by this time, or at least part opened, they are spoiled.)

Remove the pot from the heat and let the liquid settle while you remove the mussels from their shells and put them in a jar or small casserole with a lid. Strain the water that the mussels were cooked in and measure ¾ cup into a small pot, discarding the rest.

Add the vinegar, spices, salt, and honey to the reserved liquid. Bring this mixture to a boil then pour it over the mussels. Cool, then refrigerate them.

To serve the mussels, remove them from the pickling liquid, and sprinkle them with a little more vinegar if desired.

POTTED SHRIMP INFUSED WITH SAVORY HERBS AND GARLIC

John Bishop, of Vancouver's famed Bishop's restaurant, has taken a British staple (well, just about!) food from its native shores, and made it his own. Simplicity itself to prepare and serve, this recipe makes fresh shrimp taste even more heavenly than usual.

SERVES 4

¼ cup butter

1 tsp garlic, chopped

1 tsp fresh thyme leaves, chopped

1 tsp fresh parsley, chopped

pinch of salt

pinch of grainy mustard

8 oz (250 g) fresh hand-peeled shrimp

toast fingers or sliced baguette

In a frying pan over medium heat, melt butter. Add the garlic and sauté until lightly colored, about 2 minutes. Stir in thyme, parsley, salt, and mustard. Remove from the heat.

Spoon shrimp into four 4-oz (125-ml) ramekins and pour butter mixture over top. Cover and chill thoroughly in the refrigerator before serving. (Will keep refrigerated for 4 to 5 days.)

To serve, place ramekins on plates, with toast fingers (or sliced baguette) on the side.

PRESSED YOGURT

By draining some of the liquid from skim yogurt, you can produce a thick creamy dairy product that is very low in fat and easy to combine with dressings or dips to add flavor and nutrition. It can replace cream cheese in many contexts. For example, pressed yogurt is delicious on a bagel or in a veggie sandwich, and blended with brown sugar it makes a low-fat cake topping or a dip for fresh strawberries. In some recipes that require sour cream, pressed yogurt can also be used, but it is not suitable for cooking, as it separates when hot.

MAKES 1 TO 3 CUPS, depending on how long you leave the yogurt to drain

1 quart (1 litre) yogurt

You need to start with a product that does not contain gelatin, pectin, or sweeteners, in other words, genuine live-culture yogurt. The straining is best done with a large (6-cup), clean, cone coffee filter holder, lined with a paper filter or several layers of cheesecloth, and placed over a thoroughly clean Pyrex coffee pot that fits the filter. It may also be done using a plastic or stainless steel colander or strainer, lined with cheesecloth and placed over a bowl.

Spoon the yogurt into the strainer, and refrigerate it for 3 to 8 hours. The liquid will continue to drain out of the yogurt until it is very stiff and much reduced in volume, so leave it to drip only until you are satisfied with its consistency. Start checking this after 3 hours.

When it is thick enough for the use you have planned for it, transfer the pressed yogurt to a storage container, and keep it refrigerated until ready for use. You may need to stir it before use to reintegrate any remaining liquid.

The liquid that has been strained out of it is quite nutritious, but I have not found a good way to use it, so I usually discard it. If you are using cheesecloth, wash it thoroughly before the next use.

RAITA

Vancouver chef, restaurateur (she and her husband own Rubina Tandoori, Vancouver's leading Indian restaurant), and food writer Krishna Jamal offers Raita as the perfect cool milky accompaniment for spicy food, and suggests serving it with the Beef Tikka in our Barbecue menu to quench the fires as needed.

MAKES 20 2-TBSP SERVINGS

2 cups thick yogurt

½ cucumber, seeded if necessary

1 carrot

1 tsp salt

1 tsp ground cumin

1 tsp sugar

fresh mint, chopped, to taste, or pinch
   dried ground mint

To prepare yogurt, start with a low- or nonfat unflavored yogurt with no gelatin or other thickeners. Pour yogurt into cheesecloth-lined sieve and cover with cloth. Place weight on top to press and put sieve in sink or large pan to catch liquid. Or, put yogurt into paper coffee filter in its plastic holder and use coffeepot to catch liquid. Yogurt will be reduced by half in 1 hour.

Grate carrots and cucumber. Place in sieve and press to squeeze out as much moisture as possible.

In a large bowl, stir together all ingredients. Seal bowl with plastic wrap and place in fridge to chill. Serve cold or at room temperature. If it weeps, simply stir before serving.

RATATOUILLE

This intensely flavored vegetable dish is equally good eaten hot, warm, or cold. With the addition of garbanzo beans (chickpeas), it can be used as an entrée. Although I find the flavor of garlic in this dish overpowers the subtler qualities of the other vegetables, many people prefer the garlicky version.

SERVES 6 TO 8 AS A SIDE DISH

1 tbsp olive oil

3 cup shallots, finely chopped

1–2 cloves garlic, crushed (optional)

2 cups fresh tomatoes with juice drained off, finely chopped

2 cups small zucchinis, chopped small

2 cups Japanese eggplant, chopped small

1 14-oz (398-ml) can garbanzo beans (chickpeas), rinsed and drained (optional, see note above)

1 tsp salt

½ 5½-oz (156-ml) can tomato paste

salt and pepper to taste

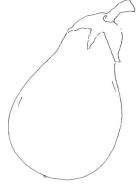

All the vegetables should be chopped to approximately the same size; i.e., small cubes or pieces.

In a large heavy pot over medium heat, heat the oil then sauté the shallots and garlic until they are soft and becoming translucent. Add the tomatoes and cook for a few minutes until the tomatoes become pulpy. Add the zucchinis, eggplant, garbanzo beans, and salt, and simmer, covered, for 20 minutes or until all the vegetables are completely cooked and soft.

Remove the vegetables with a slotted spoon and set them aside. Over medium-high heat, boil the remaining liquid in the pot until it is reduced in volume by about half. (May take 10 to 12 minutes but watch for burning and stir frequently.)

Turn off the heat, return the vegetables to the pot, and stir in as much tomato paste as is needed to make a thick smooth mixture. Taste and add pepper and salt as desired.

ROASTED PEAR AND GOAT CHEESE PHYLLO PASTRIES

Pear and chèvre are perfect complements for each other, and by roasting the pear before it joins the goat cheese, John Bishop achieves a wonderful intensity of flavor in these tasty morsels.

SERVES 4

2 Bartlett or Anjou pears

2 tbsp butter, melted

salt and black pepper to taste

4 oz (125 g) chèvre (soft goat cheese)

8 sheets frozen phyllo pastry, thawed

Preheat oven to 400°F (200°C). Line two baking sheets with parchment paper.

Peel and core pears, then cut them in half. Place pear halves, cut side down, on one of the prepared baking sheets. Brush with half of the melted butter, then season with salt and pepper.

Roast until golden brown and tender, about 30 minutes. Remove from oven and allow to cool. Leave the oven on.

Fold each sheet of phyllo pastry lengthwise twice (so that they are a quarter of their original width). Brush with the remaining melted butter.

Cut pear halves in half, then slice thinly from the stem end, leaving the bottoms attached.

Place a pear piece on each phyllo sheet and top with 1 tbsp goat cheese. Fold pastry over pear and cheese to form triangles. Place on the second prepared baking sheet and bake until pastry is golden and slightly puffed, about 12 minutes.

To serve as an appetizer, place pastry triangles in pairs on warmed plates. To serve as an *hors d'oeuvre*, arrange pastry triangles on a warmed plate.

SARDINE SPREAD ON CROSTINI

The good old reliable sardine is surprisingly upscaled in this easy recipe.

SERVES 6 TO 8

2 4-oz (120-g) cans of sardines, drained and mashed (about 1 cup well-packed)

3 tbsp mayonnaise-style dressing

2 tsp lemon juice

1 tbsp sweet onion, finely minced

¼ tsp cayenne pepper, or a dash of hot sauce

24 crostini squares (see note below)

1 hard-boiled egg, cooled and finely chopped (optional)

capers (optional)

12 sweet pickled gherkins (optional)

Drain the sardines. In a bowl, mash them until smooth with the mayonnaise, lemon juice, onion, and pepper. Spread a small quantity of the mixture on each crostini and top with a sprinkle of chopped egg, and a caper or two or a sliver of sweet pickled gherkin.

To prepare your own crostini:
Cut 6 large slices of thick bread into quarters, place them on a baking sheet and bake them until they are crisp in a 300°F (150°C) oven.

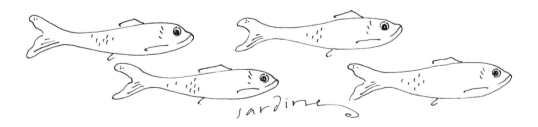

SESAME POTATOES

Eaten while still warm, these potatoes are particularly delicious, but they are also fine chilled, and can be made ahead of time.

SERVES 6

½ cup sesame seeds

2¼ lb (1 kg) small new potatoes (about 24 two-bite potatoes)

2 tbsp hoisin sauce

1 tbsp spicy blackbean sauce (or chili garlic soybean sauce)

1 tbsp sesame oil

In a dry pan over medium heat, toast sesame seeds just until they begin to change color. Set aside.

Scrub potatoes thoroughly or scrape. In a pot of salted water over high heat, bring potatoes to a boil, reduce heat, and simmer for 8 to 10 minutes or until tender. Drain and allow them to dry in a colander for a few minutes. Transfer to a bowl.

Combine the two sauces and oil and pour over the potatoes, moving them gently to cover them well with the sauce mixture. Sprinkle some of the sesame seeds on a plate, place some of the potatoes on them, and sprinkle with additional seeds. Lift them carefully into a serving container. Repeat the process until all the potatoes are coated with seeds. Do not seal the container en route to your picnic if the potatoes are still hot.

SHRIMP IN ROSY AGAR AGAR ASPIC WITH WASABI CREAM

The gentle aspic that holds these shrimp-laden mouthfuls together and gives them a rosy glow is not trying to compete with them, but to enhance them. If you add touches of garnish before you place the shrimp in their moulds, all the better. Possibilities might be a tiny edible flower or a colorful petal or two in the bottom of your little moulds, or a few snippets of chive. Serve each shrimp mould, topped with a dab of Wasabi Cream, on the wide end of a Belgian endive leaf, or in the bowl of a Chinese spoon.

MAKES 12 SMALL PIECES

6 oz (180 g) cooked salad shrimp
  (hand-peeled if possible)

½ cup clear fish or vegetable stock (use
  a cube if the color of the bouillon is
  light), cooled

½ cup rosé wine (dry)

1 squeeze lemon juice

1 tbsp agar agar flakes

Wasabi Cream

MAKES ABOUT 3 TBSP

4 tbsp wasabi powder

1 tbsp water

5 tsp commercially prepared
  mayonnaise

Using a mini-muffin pan with 12 cups or an ice-cube tray with rounded cups, place a garnish detail in each cup as suggested above, or simply divide the shrimp among the 12 cups. Put the tray of shrimps in the fridge to keep cool.

In a small bowl, combine the stock, wine, and lemon juice, and stir in the agar agar. Stir well and leave to soak for at least 15 minutes, stirring occasionally. Then transfer to a small pot, and, over low heat, bring to a boil, stirring constantly. Let simmer briefly, whisking thoroughly to help the agar agar to dissolve completely. Remove from heat. Taste and adjust seasoning if necessary.

As soon as the liquid is cool, spoon it over the shrimp in the small moulds, to almost but not quite cover the shrimp. You want only the minimum amount of jelly to keep them together. Refrigerate until serving time.

Wasabi Cream

In a tiny bowl or cup, mix the wasabi powder with the water to make a stiff paste. Turn the bowl upside down for 1 minute to let the flavor intensify. Mix the mayonnaise into the wasabi paste, and adjust for flavor, adding a little more mayonnaise, or wasabi powder, as needed.

To serve, slip the shrimp aspics out of their pan and serve as suggested above, or on a serving platter on a bed of lettuce.

STUFFED CELERY STICKS

Celery stays crisp when all sorts of tasty stuffings are spread along the washed and dried stalks. Two similarly sized stalks can be put face to face and tied with a chive to create a very portable and nutritious snack. The default stuffing is, of course, peanut butter, but there are other possibilities out there.

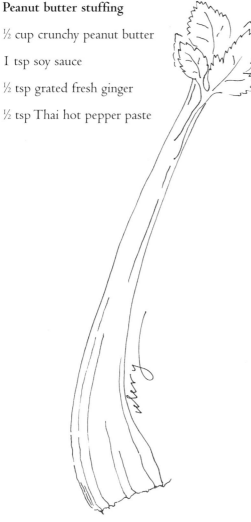

Peanut butter stuffing

½ cup crunchy peanut butter

1 tsp soy sauce

½ tsp grated fresh ginger

½ tsp Thai hot pepper paste

Cream cheese stuffing

½ cup cream cheese (light or regular)

1 tbsp sun-dried tomato, finely chopped

or

½ cup cream cheese (light or regular)

1 tbsp chives, finely diced

½ tsp pressed garlic

or

½ cup cream cheese (light or regular)

2 tsp anchovy paste

or

½ cup cream cheese (light or regular)

1 tbsp marmalade

SUMMER FRUIT RELISH

Cheeses are fabulous with something fruity and sweet and tart. Of course, you can buy a jar of chutney and it will taste good with your cheese plate, but why not make your own concoction, lightly cooked, with all the flavor and color of fresh summer fruit. You can use the fruit suggested here, or make your own blend of personal favorites, retaining the balance of fruit, sugar, spices, and lemon juice. The recipe needs around 5 cups of finely diced fresh fruit and will keep well in the fridge for a few days.

MAKES 3 CUPS

3 tbsp lemon juice

2 ripe peaches, peeled

2 ripe nectarines

2 or 3 ripe apricots (or more if they are small)

several ripe dark red plums

1 cup small seedless grapes, cut in half

3 – 4 tbsp sugar

1 tbsp (or more) fresh ginger, grated

½ tsp cinnamon

½ tsp mace

¼ tsp salt

Place the lemon juice in a saucepan.

Chop all the fruit except the grapes into very small pieces, adding them to the lemon juice as soon as they are cut. (Only the peaches need peeling. The other fruit skins add wonderful color.) Add the rest of the ingredients to the saucepan and bring to a boil over medium heat, stirring constantly until some juice flows, then frequently until it reaches boiling point.

Reduce heat to low and simmer for 10 minutes, then use a strainer to remove the fruit pieces from the juice.

Set the fruit aside and return the juice to boil for another 8 to 10 minutes, stirring constantly to avoid burning. The juice will reduce and become thick.

Remove from heat and stir in the reserved fruit. Taste to correct seasoning, then cool and refrigerate. It will keep well for several days in a covered jar in the fridge.

SUSHI ROLLS

With all the splendid Japanese sushi available in almost every urban area, you may prefer to buy it ready-made, whether it be Nigiri or California rolls, exotic fish or humble cucumber! But while it's not possible to expect to emulate the highly trained and professional sushi chefs, you can make delicious sushi rolls at home, with no arcane equipment or ingredients. You will need sushi rice, which is very sticky when cooked, although Arborio rice will suffice if necessary. If you can find seasoned rice vinegar, you will achieve good tasting rice more easily; if not, use regular rice vinegar and add a small amount of salt and sugar to it before you start stirring it into the rice, so that you can correct the seasoning to where you like it. A sushi mat for rolling your rolls will make the task easier, but if you don't have one, roll them on a piece of wax paper. If you don't have a sharp knife, though, stop here. You can't cut sushi rolls with a blunt one! The following quantities will serve 2 people generously, with either tuna or vegetarian sushi rolls.

Serves 2

1 cup sushi or Arborio rice

water, according to package directions for cooking the rice

1 – 2 tbsp seasoned rice vinegar (see note above)

4 sheets nori (a paper-like Japanese seaweed for sushi, readily available in supermarkets)

Cook the rice according to package directions or until tender, making sure the rice is steamed or drained as dry as possible when done. Place it in a large bowl and lift and turn it with a wooden spoon to let the steam out quickly. As you stir it in this way, sprinkle half of the seasoned vinegar over it and when that is well incorporated, add the rest. Taste for flavor and as long as the rice is not getting too wet, you can add a little more vinegar if required. A little extra salt or sugar may also be added at this point if needed. Keep gently turning the rice as it cools until it becomes cohesive and shiny.

To assemble the tuna sushi:
When the rice is cool, spread a sheet of nori on a mat, or a piece of wax paper, with the lines on the nori running vertically. Spread one quarter of the rice over the nori, leaving a 1-inch (2-cm) strip empty along the top and bottom edges. Work with

Filling (tuna)

4 oz (120 g) sashimi-grade tuna, cut in very thin long strips

2 tbsp wasabi powder

enough water to make a thick paste with the wasabi

Filling (vegetarian)

4 oz (120 g) smoked tofu, or prepared as for Tofu Sandwich Salad (p. 211)

1 small ripe avocado, peeled and pitted

several green onions, trimmed

1 tbsp sesame seeds

¼ cup carrot and/or daikon, finely shredded

2 tbsp wasabi powder

enough water to make a thick paste with the wasabi

For serving

Japanese soy sauce or tamari soy sauce for dipping sushi rolls

¼ cup Japanese pickled ginger (gari)

your fingers and a knife. It is much easier if you keep wetting your fingers and/or knife with water. Keep a bowl of warm water close to your work surface for this purpose, but don't let drips fall on the nori.) Lay one quarter of the tuna strips end to end about a third of the way up the rice. Spread a thin line of the wasabi paste along the rice right next to the tuna. (Keep the rest of the paste in a small container, as it will be used, on the side, when the sushi are served.) Start rolling the roll from the bottom edge, keeping it tight and straight with the mat, or the wax paper. Moisten the top edge of the nori, just before you finish the roll, so that it will seal the roll closed. Using the lines on the nori as a guide, cut the roll with a very sharp knife into small sushi pieces, usually eight per sheet of nori. Place them in a container with a lid. When all the rolls are completed, refrigerate them until ready to use. Serve them with soy sauce and the rest of the wasabi paste, as well as a clump of gari. These tuna rolls should be eaten as soon as possible after they are made.

To assemble the vegetarian sushi:
Please follow the instructions for the tuna sushi, but instead of tuna, your filling will be thin strips of tofu and avocado, green onions split in half down their length, a very thin layer of shredded carrot and daikon, and a sprinkle of sesame seeds, plus, of course, the wasabi paste. As long as you roll the sushi nice and tightly you can use a variety of vegetable strips (cooked shiitake mushrooms, green beans, squash, etc) and produce sushi rolls that are prettily colored in the center and very good tasting. Just make sure that your tofu, if not smoked, is well seasoned (soy sauce, a little honey, some hot pepper or ginger). Veggie sushi rolls will keep for a day, but the avocado will discolor.

THINGS ON TOOTHPICKS

All sorts of edibles can be cut into small pieces and served as finger food for picnics. Skewering them on a toothpick (wood, non-dyed) enables you to create tasty combinations, easy to prepare, transport, and eat. The prepared toothpicks can be arranged on a large tray, or stuck into unpeeled orange or grapefruit halves lying cut side down on a flat surface.

Melon and prosciutto:
Cut a fully ripe cantaloupe in two, remove the seeds, and use a melon baller to cut small balls of the flesh. Alternatively, cut slices of melon, cut off the skin and any green areas near it, then cut the slices into small cubes. Wrap each ball or cube in a small slice of prosciutto or ham, and fasten with a wooden toothpick.

Cheese and pineapple:
Most cheese goes well with pineapple or apple. For toothpick snacks, choose a cheese which can be cut into small cubes, and which has an assertive flavor, although if children are likely to be joining the party, they will probably prefer a mild cheddar to an aged one. Peel, core, and cut a fresh ripe pineapple into small cubes. Skewer each piece of pineapple with a toothpick, then add a cube of cheese.

Cherry tomatoes, basil and bocconcini:
Buy larger pieces of bocconcini cheese, cut them into small pieces and marinate them for several hours in a mixture of olive oil, chopped basil, and pepper for several hours. Drain them before use. Place a cube of marinated bocconcini on each toothpick, add a leaf of basil, and then a small ripe cherry tomato.

Gherkins with spicy sausage:
Cook spicy sausage links until cooked through, or purchase smoked sausage. Cut the cooked sausage into small cubes and skewer on toothpicks with half a small sweet pickled gherkin.

Other possibilities for toothpick things are, in various combinations:
Marinated rosebud beets; cooked tiny new potatoes; grapes; roasted red pepper pieces; smoked fish or meat pieces; marinated squid or octopus; cucumber; fresh or marinated mushroom caps.

TOMATO HERB TARTS

These small savory pastries are delicious warm or cold, and you can experiment with them by adding hot sauce, or adjusting the balance of herbs, or using a tangy cheese such as grated parmesan for topping.

MAKES ABOUT 24

½ recipe Rich Pastry (p. 268)

1½ cups canned crushed tomatoes

I large green onion, finely chopped

¼ cup parsley, minced

¼ cup finely chopped celery, including some tender young leaves

I tbsp fresh rosemary or basil leaves (not both!), chopped

salt and pepper to taste

3 – 4 small Roma tomatoes, thinly sliced into circles

½ – ¾ cup old cheddar cheese, finely shredded

Preheat oven to 360°F (180°C).

Roll the pastry using plenty of flour and cut with a cookie cutter into 3-inch (7.5-cm) circles. Place these circles in muffin pans, making sure each one is centered, so that the edge is slightly raised all round. In a bowl, combine the crushed tomatoes, onion, parsley, celery and rosemary or basil. Taste and add salt and pepper as needed.

Spoon the tomato mixture into the pastry circles, making sure that the quantity is sufficient to cover the base, but not to ooze over the pastry edge when it gets bubbly in the oven.

Place a tomato slice on each piece, and sprinkle lightly with cheese.

Bake in the oven for 20 minutes, or until the edges are nicely browned.

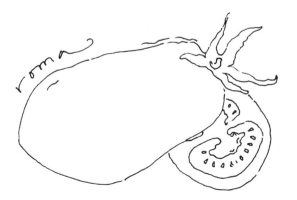

TOMATOES STUFFED WITH RICOTTA, PEAS, AND SUN-DRIED TOMATOES

Fresh herbs, cheese, and tomatoes ... mmm good!

MAKES 12

12 medium fully ripe tomatoes

2 – 3 cups ricotta or cottage cheese

1 cup fresh green peas, lightly cooked

4 – 6 pieces oil-packed sun-dried
   tomatoes, finely chopped

2 green onions, finely chopped

2 tsp parsley, finely minced

2 tsp mint, finely minced (optional)

salt and black or cayenne pepper
   to taste

paprika to garnish

Cut a slice off the stem end of each tomato, so that you can scoop out the interior, leaving the outside intact. Set aside the top slices, and the juice, seeds and flesh that you remove; they are good to use later in a tomato-based soup or stew. Turn the cut tomatoes open side down to drain while you prepare the filling.

In a bowl, place the ricotta or cottage cheese, assessing the quantity needed according to the size of the tomatoes. Add the drained peas, sun-dried tomatoes, green onion, and herbs. Mix well, then add salt and pepper to taste.

Scoop filling into the tomato shells, dash tops with paprika, and place in a wide shallow container, so that they remain upright. Chill until serving.

VEGGIE BUTTER

You can play around with the balance of flavors in this butter by adjusting the quantity of sun-dried tomatoes and lemon juice, adding olives and lashings of pepper if you like a bite to it. It should be served at room temperature, with fresh baguette slices or bagels, crackers, or hearty whole-wheat chunks. The vegetables can either be finely chopped by hand, or prepared in a blender or food processor.

MAKES ABOUT **2** CUPS

½ lb (1 cup) slightly softened butter

2 tbsp tomato paste

3 large oil-packed sun-dried tomatoes, finely chopped

3 tbsp green onions, minced

3 tbsp parsley, minced

1 tbsp red pepper, finely chopped

2 tbsp black olives, finely chopped (optional)

1 clove garlic, pressed (optional)

1 tbsp fresh lemon juice

salt, as required (depending on saltiness of butter used)

pepper to taste

In a bowl, mix all the ingredients until they are completely integrated, and then taste to adjust for salt and pepper. Spoon into a wide-mouthed container with a lid and refrigerate until half an hour to an hour before use, then allow to return to room temperature.

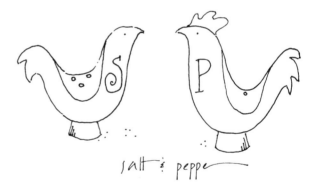

salt & pepper

VEGGIE PÂTÉ

This recipe has been around for some years now, too many for its origin to be clear, and has undoubtedly been tweaked here and there as it is passed on from friend to friend. Whatever its source, it is so delicious that you may never bother with chicken livers again! And it freezes well, so make plenty.

SERVES 10

1½ cups roast sunflower kernels, finely processed

⅓ cup engevita yeast

¾ cup whole-wheat flour

½ cup vegetable oil

1½ cups warm water

1 tsp each of dried thyme, sage, basil, salt, pepper

½ tsp ground cloves

1 tbsp lemon juice

1 clove garlic

1 carrot, grated or finely processed

1 onion grated or finely processed

1 medium potato, grated or finely processed

Preheat oven to 350°F (175°C).

In a bowl, mix all the ingredients thoroughly. Pour into a 10" x 10" casserole dish and bake in oven for 1 hour. While the pâté is still hot, stir it well with a fork, incorporating the browned surfaces, then allow it to cool completely before serving.

SOUPS

BULGARIAN BEAN SOUP

The recipe for this hearty cold-weather soup, full of the goodness of beans and the smoky tang of paprika, was given me by a friend who emigrated from Bulgaria long ago. It keeps beautifully, even better the second or third day! Note that other kinds of beans should not be soaked and cooked in salted water, because the salt prevents their tough skins from allowing the water to properly penetrate them. However, lima beans benefit from salt during their preparation because they have light, fragile skins and the salt helps to keep them intact.

SERVES 6 TO 8

½ lb (230 g) large white lima beans

8 cups water

1 medium onion

½ red bell pepper

1 large carrot, diced

3 stalks celery, halved

1 tbsp olive oil

2 tbsp dried mint leaves

1½ tsp salt, or to taste

3 tbsp olive oil

½ onion, finely chopped

3 tbsp flour

2 tbsp Hungarian paprika

1 14-oz (398-ml) can tomatoes, chopped

1 cup fresh parsley, mint, and celery leaves (combined), finely chopped

Soak the beans overnight in a generous quantity of lightly salted water, then drain them, and discard the water. In a large pot over high heat, combine the beans, water, whole onion, bell pepper, carrot, celery 1 tbsp olive oil, mint, and salt, and bring to a boil. Reduce heat and simmer, covered, for 1 hour or more, until the beans are cooked tender. Remove the onion, celery stalks, and bell pepper, and discard them.

In a small saucepan over medium heat, heat 3 tbsp oil, and sauté the chopped onion until transparent. Stir in the flour, and cook on low heat for a few minutes before adding the paprika and blending it into the roux.

Slowly whisk 1 cup of hot soup liquid into the roux, making sure the mixture is free of lumps. Whisk in another cup of liquid, then pour the contents of the small saucepan into the large pot, return to high heat, and stir gently until the soup boils.

Add the tomatoes, reduce heat again, and simmer for 10 minutes. Just before removing the soup from the heat, add the finely chopped herbs, tasting to adjust seasoning. This recipe freezes well.

CHILLED BORSCHT

For decades, my friend Joyce's mother-in-law has been making this borscht as a quick and easy summer soup. Although she uses canned beets and their juice in hers, and it's fabulous, and fabulously easy, I love to work with beets from the ground up as it were, and scrub and roast or simmer them myself before making the soup. If you use canned beets, reduce the salt in the recipe. (Begin by adding ½ tsp and taste before adding more.)

Serves 6 to 8

3 cups cooked beets, finely diced, or
   2 14-oz (398-ml) cans, including
   the juice

3 cups buttermilk

3 cups canned tomato juice

juice of ½ lemon

I tsp salt

pepper to taste

sour cream, about I tbsp per person
   (garnish)

chives, chopped, I tsp per serving
   (garnish)

cucumber, finely diced, I tbsp
   per serving (garnish)

In a large bowl, combine the first 6 ingredients, refrigerate for a couple of hours, then stir the soup well. Serve it with a dollop of sour cream, a sprinkle of chives, and a spoonful of finely diced cucumber in each serving. The soup can be made a day ahead and refrigerated.

COOL CUCUMBER AVOCADO SOUP

The unusual combination of avocado, cilantro, and apple juice really works, and the soup is a beautiful pale green, soothing on a hot day.

SERVES 8

4 ripe avocados, peeled and pitted

juice of 2 lemons, ⅓ – ½ cup

1 English cucumber, roughly chopped

6 green onions, roughly chopped

2 green bell peppers, seeded, roughly chopped

6 tender young celery stalks, including pale green leaves, roughly chopped

bunch of cilantro (about 1 cup, chopped small)

4 cups apple juice

½ tsp lemon zest

salt and pepper to taste

½ tsp cayenne pepper (optional)

fresh chives, chopped (garnish)

In a food processor or blender, combine the avocados and lemon juice. Purée until smooth.

Pour the avocado purée into a jug or bowl, then process the chopped vegetables and cilantro in batches, adding some of the avocado purée and just enough apple juice to each batch to enable the processor to work efficiently without spilling over.

Mix the processed ingredients with the remaining apple juice, lemon zest, and the seasonings, and adjust to taste. Chill the soup overnight if possible or for at least a few hours before use to let the flavors blend. Serve the soup as cold as possible. It may be garnished with chopped chives.

GAZPACHO

The tomatoes in this delicious chilled soup may be skinned to produce a smoother texture, but leaving the skins on gives the soup more color. To skin tomatoes, place them in simmering water for 25 seconds, then remove them from the pot, cool them briefly in a basin of water, and pull off the skins with a paring knife.

SERVES 6

1 medium cucumber, peeled, roughly chopped

1½ lb (700 g) tomatoes, roughly chopped

1 – 2 cloves garlic

1 small green bell pepper, seeded, roughly chopped

1 sweet onion or 4 large green onions, roughly chopped

1 tsp salt

2 tbsp olive oil

2 tbsp lemon juice

¼ cup cold water

fresh parsley, chives, and cucumber, finely chopped, 1 tbsp per serving (garnish)

Cut the cucumber lengthwise and remove any hard seeds if using a field cucumber. In a food processor or blender, process the chopped vegetables in small batches.

Place the processed mixture in a container and stir in the salt, oil, and lemon juice, and enough of the cold water to make a nicely flowing soup. Taste to adjust seasoning. Chill the soup well.

Stir just before serving. Garnish each cup or bowl with chopped green herbs.

LENTIL AND APPLE SOUP

Traditional lentil soup does not have the fruity flavor that apple juice lends to this version. It is a nutritious and satisfying soup for a cool-weather picnic.

SERVES 8

2 cups green lentils

7 cups vegetable stock (bouillon cubes work well)

1 cup frozen apple juice concentrate

1 onion, chopped small

4 or 5 medium carrots, thinly sliced

4 large stalks celery, chopped small

⅓ cup celery greens, chopped

½ tsp garam masala

¼ tsp cayenne pepper

1 tsp dried thyme leaves

1 tbsp olive oil

In a large pot over high heat, combine all the ingredients and bring to a boil.

Reduce heat to low and simmer the soup for 1¼ to 1½ hours, or until the lentils are puréed. Taste and adjust seasonings as needed.

PEA SOUP WITH HAM

A classic soup, with a little sting of ginger in its tail, this is a suitable choice for a cool-weather picnic. Ideally it would be made with smoked bacon, but a ham bone with plenty of meat on it, or strips of side bacon, not too fat, are a good substitute.

SERVES 6

1½ cups dried split peas

8 cups water

1 tsp ground ginger (or raw grated ginger to taste)

1 cup lean bacon, diced

1 large onion, diced

salt and pepper to taste

Pick over the peas and rinse them. In a large pot over high heat, combine the peas, water, and ginger, and bring to a boil. Reduce heat to low, and simmer gently for 30 minutes.

Add the bacon and onion and continue cooking for a further hour, or until the peas and onion are completely soft. Check the seasoning, and add salt and pepper as desired.

SALMON CHOWDER

Dill and lemon perfectly complement the flavor of salmon in this hearty hot soup.

SERVES 6 TO 8

¼ cup butter

1 medium onion, diced

2 tbsp flour

4 cups vegetable or fish stock, or water

4 medium potatoes (not the baking kind), diced

1½ lb (700 g) salmon, fillet or steak with any bones and skin removed

3 cups milk or half-and-half

1 tbsp fresh dill

good squeeze lemon juice

salt and pepper to taste

In a pot over medium heat, sauté the onion in butter just until it is clear, but not beginning to brown. Stir in the flour, making sure to stir out all the lumps. Cook the flour and butter over low heat for 4 to 6 minutes, without browning it.

Remove from heat and slowly add 1 cup stock, stirring until the roux is smooth, then return to low heat and add the rest of the stock slowly, stirring all the time. Add the potatoes, cover, and simmer until they are partially cooked, about 10 minutes.

Cut the salmon into bite-sized pieces, and add it to the soup. Simmer for 7 to 10 more minutes, or until the fish is cooked. Stir in the milk, dill, lemon juice, salt, and pepper, adjusting the seasonings as required.

Bring the soup back to just below boiling point but do not let it actually boil.

VICHYSSOISE

Cool, creamy, and subtle, this is a great soup to open a picnic meal, but keep it well chilled.

SERVES 6 TO 8

6 leeks, roughly chopped

3 tbsp butter

6 cups chicken or pale vegetable stock

2 medium potatoes, diced

1 tbsp parsley, chopped

3 tbsp chives, chopped, divided into 2

1 cup light cream

salt and pepper to taste

lemon juice to taste

Wash the leeks, removing the tough top and outer layers. In a pot over medium heat, sauté the chopped leeks in butter for 10 minutes, but do not allow them to brown.

Add the stock, potatoes, parsley, and half the chives. Reduce heat to low, and simmer for about 20 minutes, or until the leeks are completely tender. Traditionally the soup would be rubbed through a fine strainer, but it is quicker to food process the vegetables and recombine them with the liquid.

When the soup is completely cool, incorporate the cream gradually. Taste to adjust seasoning, adding salt, pepper, and a squeeze of lemon juice as desired. Serve chilled, topped with the remainder of the chopped chives.

SALADS

AHI TUNA SASHIMI AND GREEN PAPAYA SALAD WITH CHILI-LIME DRESSING

Rob Feenie, one of Vancouver's most highly recognized chefs, takes bar food to a new level with his book, Lumière Light. *The trick for this salad, he notes, is to get a center cut of grade-A ahi tuna. The subtle green papaya and the spicy, salty dressing balance flavor and texture perfectly.*

SERVES 4

Dressing

¼ cup fish sauce

¼ cup fresh lime juice

1 tbsp palm sugar (available at Asian food stores)

1-inch (2½-cm) piece lemongrass, roughly chopped

¼ – ½ Thai chili, roughly chopped

pinch of garlic, minced

½ cup water

In a blender or food processor, combine all dressing ingredients and process until smooth. Immediately strain through a fine-mesh sieve. Cover and refrigerate overnight to allow flavors to infuse.

In a saucepan over medium heat, combine dried shrimp and water, and bring to a boil. Remove from heat and immediately strain through a fine-mesh sieve; discard liquid. Place drained shrimp on a paper towel to dry. Mince shrimp, place in a covered container, and refrigerate until needed.

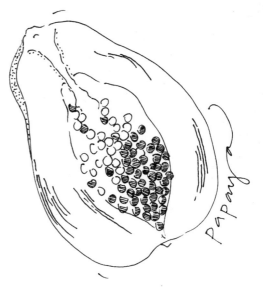

Salad

2 tsp dried shrimp

¼ cup water

½ cup green papaya, julienned

1 tbsp mint leaves, julienned

1 tbsp cilantro leaves, julienned

1 tbsp Thai basil leaves, julienned

4 tbsp toasted pine nuts

4 tbsp tomato concassé (blanch tomatoes and skin, remove inside flesh, and dice)

6 green beans, blanched and finely diced

8 slices grade-A ahi tuna loin (each 2 oz [50 g], ¼ inch [½ cm] thick)

¼ cup cilantro oil for garnish (grapeseed oil infused with an equal amount fresh cilantro and one half part fresh Italian parsley)

In a bowl, mix together the shrimp, green papaya, mint, cilantro, Thai basil, pine nuts, tomato concassé, and green beans. Add ¼ cup of dressing and toss gently.

Place 2 slices of ahi tuna in the center of each of 4 large chilled plates. Drizzle cilantro oil around the outside of the tuna. Spoon 2 tbsp of dressing over each serving. Divide salad and arrange on top of fish.

ASIAN NOODLE SALAD

This salad can be made with different kinds of pasta as available. It's zesty in flavor and full of crunch.

SERVES 8

3 cups thin Asian noodles, cooked *al dente*

1 tbsp vegetable oil

½ red bell pepper, julienned

½ green bell pepper, julienned

½ English cucumber, coarsely grated or shredded

1 large carrot, coarsely grated or shredded

¾ cup cilantro, chopped

1 cup bean sprouts

¾ cup water chestnut slices, diced

¾ cup roasted peanuts, chopped

1 recipe Peanut Dressing (p. 197)

1 tsp Thai red chili paste or dried chili flakes (2 or 3 for spicy heat)

Cook the noodles according to the package directions. Drain well, then toss gently with vegetable oil and spread them out on a flat tray or large plate to cool.

In a large bowl, combine the cooled noodles, peppers, cucumber, carrot, cilantro, bean sprouts, water chestnuts, and peanuts.

In a separate bowl, mix the Peanut Dressing with the chili paste. Toss the salad with the dressing, and taste to adjust seasoning. Chill and serve.

BEET, NOODLE, AND JICAMA SALAD

A gentle, mild-tasting salad, with particularly pleasing textural contrasts, Beet, Noodle, and Jicama Salad is remarkable for its color: brilliant deep pink. The pasta and jicama (a crisp sweet root vegetable shaped like a turnip), as well as the dressing, are dyed with the rich color of the beet juice, which becomes even more intense if the beets are roasted in the oven wrapped in foil, instead of boiled.

SERVES 10

2 large beets

8 oz (230 g) pasta (shells, elbows, etc)

2 tbsp olive oil

1 small jicama, peeled and grated, or enough for 3 packed cups

2 tbsp lemon juice

4 green onions, finely chopped

⅔ cup Boiled Dressing (p. 193) or commercially prepared mayonnaise

⅔ cup plain skim or low-fat natural yogurt

2 tbsp frozen apple juice concentrate

1 tsp salt

generous quantity of pepper

⅓ cup sunflower seed kernels

Scrub the unpeeled beets and, in a pot with water to cover, boil them, covered, for 45 minutes or until they are just tender. Drain, cool the beets a little, then slip off their skins, cut into small chunks, and set aside. (The preparation of the beets to this point may be done a day ahead if the cooked beets are refrigerated until use.)

Meanwhile, in a large pot of boiling water, cook the pasta according to the package directions, just until *al dente*. Drain well, and toss with the olive oil. Spread out on a large plate to cool.

In a large bowl, combine the jicama and lemon juice, tossing it well. Add the prepared beets and cooled pasta to the jicama, along with the green onions.

In another bowl, mix the dressing with the yogurt, frozen apple juice concentrate, and salt, then add pepper to taste.

In a dry hot frying pan, toast the sunflower seed kernels briefly. As soon as they are cool, sprinkle them over the salad.

CARROT, RAISIN, AND SESAME SALAD

The addition of sesame seeds to this traditional salad ensures a wider range of nutritional elements, as well as great flavor, but also adds calories from the extra oil. The sesame seeds and sesame oil may be omitted and you will still have a good salad.

SERVES 4

½ cup raisins

½ cup boiling water

3 tbsp sesame seeds

3 cups carrots, grated, packed tightly

¼ cup Rice Vinegar Dressing (p. 198), combined with 1 tbsp sesame oil, or use the dressing recipe below

In a bowl, soak the raisins for 10 minutes in the boiling water then drain well, discarding the liquid.

In a dry pan over medium heat, toast the sesame seeds until light brown, watching them carefully and tossing them frequently to avoid burning. They will be done in a very few minutes.

In a bowl, combine the carrots, soaked raisins, and toasted sesame seeds, then toss them with the dressing and sesame oil. Leave to marinate for up to several hours before using.

Dressing for Carrot, Raisin, and Sesame Salad

2 tbsp seasoned rice vinegar

¼ tsp salt

¼ tsp dry mustard

pepper to taste

2 tbsp sesame oil

In a bowl, mix these ingredients well, and adjust seasoning as necessary.

CELERIAC SALAD WITH LIME-COCONUT DRESSING

Celeriac is such an ugly-looking vegetable that its delicate flavor and deliciously chewy texture are often overlooked. Choose a larger one, avoiding any that are going green. To prepare it, you need to cut off the outer layer of brown fissured skin, as well as the knobbly base and top. As soon as the inside surfaces are exposed they start to brown, so the celeriac should be rubbed with a little lemon juice as soon as it is peeled. This salad is good as part of a salad buffet, or as one of several side salads eaten with a main course.

SERVES 6 TO 8

1 large celeriac

1 tbsp lemon juice

⅓ cup Lime-Coconut Dressing (p. 191)

Peel the celeriac, cut it into several pieces, and rub surfaces with lemon juice. Grate each piece into a bowl containing the dressing, and toss thoroughly.

Note: If you want to serve celeriac with a mayonnaise dressing, you need to grate it and toss it with a little lemon juice and salt, then drain after 10 to 15 minutes, to get rid of the watery juice which would otherwise thin out your mayonnaise. With this Lime-Coconut Dressing, though, there's no need for draining. And be advised, the effort of preparing celeriac is worthwhile!

COLESLAW

There are as many variations of this salad as there are good cooks! For a pleasantly sweet-sour slaw, use the Coleslaw Dressing. However, if you prefer the tangier taste of more vinegar and less sweetening, use the Old-Fashioned Boiled Dressing instead, or Traditional Vinaigrette. The slaw should be dressed at least a couple of hours before the picnic, and if any is left it will be great the next day, less crisp but still delicious. This quantity of vegetables needs a cup of dressing, and serves ten to twelve people as part of a salad buffet.

SERVES 10 TO 12

1 small or ½ medium head of cabbage, finely shredded

1 large carrot, grated

2 – 3 large celery stalks, very thinly sliced

1 large red bell pepper, julienned

4 – 6 green onions, finely chopped (include some of the darker green tops)

3 tbsp parsley, finely chopped

1 recipe Coleslaw Dressing (p. 188)

In a large bowl, mix the prepared vegetables and toss them thoroughly with the dressing.

For an unusual variation on traditional coleslaw, prepare the vegetables as above, but instead of using the Coleslaw Dressing, combine one cup of commercial mayonnaise or salad dressing with:

2 tbsp fresh ginger, grated

3 – 4 tbsp soy sauce

To make the salad, prepare the vegetables as above, then, in a large bowl, combine the mayonnaise, ginger, and soy sauce, taste to adjust seasoning, and pour dressing over the vegetables. Toss well.

COLESLAW WITH
CURRIED PEANUT DRESSING

Bill Jones, Canadian food writer, French-trained chef, author of 12 cookbooks, and salad guru, has created a new "fusion" version of good old coleslaw. The deliciously tangy peanut dressing on this salad makes it irresistible, as well as nutritious.

SERVES 4

2 tbsp mayonnaise

2 tbsp peanut butter

I tbsp curry paste

I tbsp white wine vinegar

I tbsp hot water

I tsp sugar

I tbsp fresh ginger, minced

2 tbsp cilantro, chopped

salt and black pepper to taste

I head of cabbage, shredded

2 medium carrots, shredded

I red onion, thinly sliced

½ cup dry-roasted peanuts, chopped (garnish)

In a large bowl, combine the mayonnaise, peanut butter, curry paste, vinegar, hot water, sugar, ginger and cilantro. Whisk until smooth, season with salt and pepper, and refrigerate until needed.

Add the cabbage, carrots, and onion to the dressing and toss well to mix. Chill until needed. Toss the coleslaw again and garnish with chopped peanuts just before serving.

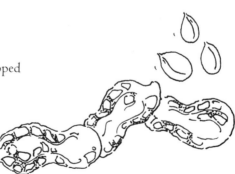

COUSCOUS VEGETABLE SALAD WITH ORANGE-MISO DRESSING

You can use whole-wheat or regular couscous for this salad. Combined with the garbanzo beans (chickpeas) and vegetables it makes a delicious and interestingly textured salad that can be prepared ahead of time and chilled until needed. If you like the tang of ginger, add an extra teaspoon of fresh grated ginger to the dressing before tossing the salad. Prepare the couscous according to package directions, and cool it before combining it with the other ingredients.

SERVES 8

2 cups prepared couscous

2 cups canned garbanzo beans
  (chickpeas), rinsed and drained

½ cup green onion, finely chopped

1 carrot, grated

½ yellow bell pepper, finely chopped

½ red bell pepper, finely chopped

⅔ cup cilantro, chopped

1 recipe Orange-Miso Dressing
  (p. 196)

In a bowl, combine all the ingredients and toss well, then chill before serving.

CURRIED CAULIFLOWER SALAD

Make this tangy dish as hot as you can stand, and serve it as a side with barbecued meat. Make sure you use fresh garam masala. (Making your own is a breeze if you have a spice grinder or a mortar and pestle! By buying whole spices and grinding them yourself, you guarantee freshness, and you can personalize the mix of spices to suit your own taste too.)

SERVES 4

½ large cauliflower

2 green onions, chopped

2 tbsp fresh ginger, minced

2 tbsp garlic, minced

1 tbsp vegetable oil

½ tsp or more chili flakes or 1 hot chili
  pepper, minced

1 tsp turmeric

2 tsp garam masala

2 tbsp peanut butter

1 tsp honey

½ cup plain yogurt

salt (optional)

¼ cup cilantro, chopped (optional)

In a pot over medium high heat, steam cauliflower (no salt added) until just tender, about 8 minutes. Cool and cut into bite-sized pieces, about 4 cups.

In a pan over medium high heat, sauté the green onions, ginger, and garlic in the oil for 3 to 5 minutes. Remove from heat and add the next 5 ingredients. Blend well and set aside to cool.

Add yogurt, and salt and cilantro if desired. Gently mix the dressing into the cauliflower pieces and let the salad sit for an hour or two in a cool place for the flavors to blend.

EDAMAME BEAN SALAD WITH GREEN PEAS

Edamame beans, green soy beans used in Japanese cuisine, can be purchased frozen, shelled, and ready to cook. They contribute nutritional value as well as flavor and texture to this tasty salad.

SERVES 4

1 heart of romaine or other sturdy lettuce, shredded

2 cups frozen edamame beans

2 cups frozen peas

1 sweet white onion, thinly sliced

¼ – ⅓ cup Rice Vinegar Dressing (p. 198)

Cook the edamame beans and the frozen peas (microwave or stovetop) until they are just tender. The beans will take a little longer than the peas, and if you cook them in the microwave oven, will require a few tbsp of water in the cooking dish. Drain and cool the vegetables thoroughly.

In a large bowl, place the shredded lettuce. In another bowl, combine the onions and cooled vegetables, then toss them with the dressing and pour them over the lettuce.

FIVE BEAN SALAD

Although you can start from scratch to make a bean salad, soaking the dried beans overnight and then cooking them is time-consuming. It is easier to use canned beans and the salad will still be nutritious. Because they are already cooked, they need only to be rinsed and drained well before use in the salad. There are many varieties available, of all sizes and colors, so the recipe below is only a starting point. Choose contrasting colors, and make sure to include garbanzo beans, which are highly nutritious and a good contrast to the other varieties in texture and shape. Green and wax beans, however, are more appealing in color and texture, and more nutritious, when cooked fresh.

SERVES 8 TO 10

1 14-oz (398-ml) can kidney beans, rinsed and drained

1 14-oz (398-ml) can garbanzo beans (chickpeas), rinsed and drained

1 14-oz (398-ml) can lima beans, rinsed and drained

2 cups green beans, chopped, lightly cooked and cooled

2 cups wax beans, chopped, lightly cooked and cooled

1 medium sweet onion, chopped small

½ cup celery, chopped small

½ cup red bell pepper, chopped small

¼ cup parsley or Italian flat parsley, finely minced

½ cup (or more to taste) Vinaigrette (p. 200)

1 tsp honey

2 tbsp balsamic vinegar

In a bowl, combine all the vegetables. In another bowl, blend the honey and balsamic vinegar into the vinaigrette and toss the vegetables with the dressing. Taste to adjust seasoning as necessary, since some canned beans are much less salty than others and may taste a little bland to some palates.

GOLDEN YAM SALAD

The color of this little side salad is intense. The sweetness of the yam marries with the salty miso and the tangy citrus to create a complex and delicious blend of flavors.

SERVES 4

1 large yam

1 large orange, peeled

¼ – ½ cup Orange-Miso Dressing
   (p. 196)

Wash and trim the yam, then either peel, cube, and steam it in unsalted water until it is just tender, or bake it whole in the oven along with other food you are cooking, until it is just tender.

If the yam is baked, you will need to peel it while it is still hot, and cut it into small cubes. Allow the yam to cool. Cut the orange into small pieces then toss both orange and yam pieces with the dressing.

GRAND MIXED SALLET

The presentation of this showy salad is described in Robert May's book, The Accomplisht Cook *(1660). Some of the ingredients in the original might seem unusual to us in a salad, and a couple (samphire and broom buds) are not available at all, but I believe our version is close enough to be credible as an Elizabethan salad. May makes it clear that the cook may choose from among the side garnishes. Individual cooks may also decide on the quantities of those that they serve. The basic chicken salad itself, as presented here, will serve 5 or 6.*

SERVES 5 OR 6

1 large roast chicken (use the Tarragon Chicken recipe [p. 236] for extra flavor), diced

1 tbsp fresh tarragon leaves, chopped small

1 tbsp parsley, minced

1 medium sweet onion, chopped small

1 small head romaine lettuce, trimmed and shredded

⅓ – ½ cup Vinaigrette (p. 200)

In a bowl, combine the diced chicken meat, tarragon, parsley, onion, and lettuce and toss with the vinaigrette, tasting to adjust seasonings. Add more vinaigrette if desired. Heap the salad in the middle of a large platter or tray and arrange a selection of the side garnishes in neat rows radiating out from the salad.

SIDE GARNISHES

capers
black olives
green olives
arugula, torn into small pieces
Marinated Mushrooms (see p. 111)
canned smoked oysters, drained
lemon wedges
orange wedges
raisins
lightly toasted almonds
fresh figs cut in half
cooked potato, cubed
lightly steamed snap peas

GREEK SALAD

Greek Salad is sometimes served over romaine lettuce but is ideal for a picnic as is. It can be made and dressed well ahead of picnic time, and kept cool.

SERVES 6 TO 8

½ lb (230 g) feta cheese, cubed

2 lb (900 g) ripe tomatoes, cut in wedges or cubed

1 large sweet onion, thinly sliced or chopped into small chunks

1 English cucumber, cubed

1½ cups black olives (calamata are particularly good here)

¾ – 1 cup Vinaigrette (p. 200)

In a large bowl, combine all the ingredients and mix well.

GRILLED ASPARAGUS SALAD WITH PROSCIUTTO, PARMIGIANO-REGGIANO, AND BALSAMIC VINAIGRETTE

A salad for spring and summer when asparagus is at its peak. Restaurateur Rob Feenie, of Vancouver's Lumière and Feenie's restaurants, sings the praises of smoky grilled asparagus, salty prosciutto and cheese, the tart sweetness of balsamic vinegar, the smoothness of olive oil. And well he should!

SERVES 4

Vinaigrette

1 shallot, finely chopped

1 tsp honey

2 tbsp balsamic vinegar

6 tbsp extra-virgin olive oil

salt and white pepper to taste

Salad

2 lbs (900 g) asparagus

4 tbsp extra-virgin olive oil

salt and white pepper to taste

8 thin slices prosciutto

4 cups mesclun or other salad greens

Parmigiano-Reggiano (parmesan cheese) for garnish

In a stainless steel bowl, combine shallot, honey, and balsamic vinegar. Whisking continuously, slowly add olive oil until emulsified. Season to taste with salt and freshly ground white pepper. Cover and refrigerate until ready to use.

Preheat the grill to medium high heat. Snap or cut off fibrous ends from asparagus. Bring a large saucepan of salted water to a boil. Blanch asparagus in boiling water for 1 minute, then immediately plunge into ice water to stop the cooking and to preserve color. Place asparagus on a paper towel to dry.

In a stainless steel bowl, toss blanched asparagus with olive oil to coat (to prevent asparagus from sticking to the grill). Season to taste with salt and freshly ground white pepper. Grill asparagus for 2 to 3 minutes, turning on all sides. (The cooking time is short as the asparagus is already partially cooked.)

Divide asparagus among four warmed plates. Spoon vinaigrette over and around asparagus. Place 2 slices of prosciutto on top of each serving. Top with mesclun (or other salad greens) and drizzle with a little more vinaigrette. Use a vegetable peeler or a sharp knife to thinly slice Parmigiano-Reggiano into curls and place a few on top of each serving.

HALIBUT AND POTATO SALAD

A fish salad needs to be kept carefully chilled before being eaten, but it is a flavorsome addition to any picnic, as part of a buffet or as the main dish.

SERVES 4

1 halibut steak, about 1 lb (450 g), or other firm white fish

1 tsp vegetable oil

1 lb (450 g) cooked new potatoes, cubed

3 or 4 green onions, chopped

½ cup celery stalks, finely chopped

½ cup Boiled Dressing (p. 193), Creamy Tofu Dressing (p. 189) or commercially prepared mayonnaise-style dressing (or more as desired)

1 tbsp old-fashioned (grainy) mustard

1 tsp honey (optional)

In a covered pan over medium high heat, fry the halibut steak in oil, for about 5 to 6 minutes, or until the fish is cooked through. Remove the skin and central bones from the fish and allow it to cool thoroughly.

Flake or chop the fish into small sections. In a large bowl, combine the fish, potatoes, onions, and celery, and mix well.

In another bowl, combine the remaining ingredients and taste to adjust for seasoning. Add this dressing to the fish and vegetable mixture and gently toss until everything is well coated. Allow the salad to chill well before use. Can be served on lettuce leaves.

JAPANESE SPINACH SALAD

The nutty-sweet taste of the dressing, combined with the cooked spinach and sesame seeds, provides a real zap of flavor, so the serving sizes for this salad, goma-ae, are very small. If keeping the dressing separate from the salad until serving time is a problem, mix the spinach and dressing as soon as the spinach is cool, and sprinkle the sesame seeds on top. The salad will taste just as good although it doesn't look as attractive.

SERVES 4 TO 6 AS PART
OF SALAD BUFFET

2 large bunches spinach

2 tbsp tahini or sesame butter

1 tsp sesame oil

3 tsp mirin (rice wine vinegar)

2 pinches salt, more to taste

2 tbsp water, more if needed

4 tsp lightly toasted sesame seeds
(garnish)

Wash the spinach thoroughly, then place it, still wet, in a pot with a lid. Over high heat, sauté for 2 or 3 minutes. Place it in a colander and drain well, pressing out excess moisture.

In a small bowl, mix the remaining ingredients, adding only enough water to create a smooth thick dressing. Press the spinach into a container to form a round or rectangle about 1 inch (2.5 cm) deep.

To serve, cut the spinach in wedges or squares and spoon some dressing over each serving, then sprinkle with sesame seeds.

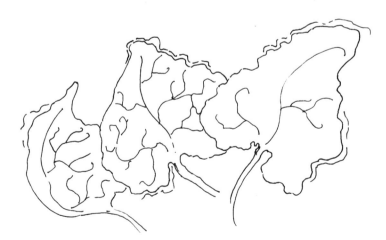

KIDNEY BEAN SALAD WITH WHITE WINE, CORN, AND PEPPERS

Salads with legumes such as the kidney beans in this recipe are ideal for large buffet-style picnics where, nowadays, there are likely to be some people who don't care to eat meat or fish. The legumes are a good source of vegetable protein, and for that reason are attractive not only to vegetarians but to people limiting the amount of cholesterol they consume.

SERVES 6 TO 8

2 cups dried kidney beans, soaked overnight in 6 cups water, or canned (see directions)

5 cups water

1 cup white wine

1 large onion, chopped small

1 cup cooked corn

⅓ cup each of red, yellow, and green bell peppers, diced

½ cup parsley, finely chopped

¼ cup green onions, chopped

1 (or more) cloves garlic, pressed or minced

½ – ¾ cup Miso Dressing (p. 192)

salt and pepper to taste

Drain the soaking water from the beans and place them in a pot with the water, wine, and onions. Simmer the beans for 1½ to 2 hours until they are soft. Do not boil hard. Drain the beans and onions, place them in a bowl and mix in the corn, peppers, parsley, green onions, and garlic.

Toss the salad with the dressing and adjust for seasoning. You may need to add more salt, because the beans are not cooked with salt. This salad is good warm.

If you prefer to use canned beans, you will need about 5 cups, and you will need to sauté the onions till soft before adding to the salad. To add that special tang the wine gives the beans, you might add 2 tbsp white wine to the dressing. The flavor of the salad will improve, too, if you marinate the beans and onions in the dressing for a few hours before adding the rest of the ingredients.

LENTIL, APPLE, AND ALMOND SALAD

Apart from the hazard of mushy lentils, this salad is very easy to prepare, and can be made a day ahead of the picnic. It is too delicious for you to care that it's also very nutritious.

SERVES 6

1 cup dried French lentils (very small, dark green)

4 cups water

¾ cup dried apples, chopped (measure after chopping)

¾ cup toasted almonds, slivered or chopped

¾ cup celery, including some of the young leaves, finely chopped

½ cup Vinaigrette (p. 200) made with olive oil and lemon juice, or use Creamy Tofu Dressing (p. 189) or Miso Dressing (p. 192)

pepper to taste

Rinse the lentils and, in a pot over medium heat, bring them to a simmer. Reduce heat to low, and continue to simmer them, covered, in the water until just tender. Do not let them boil or the lentils will get pulpy. Drain them well and place in a bowl with the dried apple, almonds, and celery. In a small bowl, mix the lemon juice, olive oil and salt together, adding pepper if desired. Mix the dressing into the lentil mixture, then chill the salad thoroughly.

LINGUINE SALAD WITH CHERRY TOMATOES AND AVOCADO DRESSING

Rich and sensuous, full of vibrant flavor and texture, this salad invites romance. The touch of cumin is to ensure the fidelity of your lover, and pepper will, reputedly, promote his or her good disposition. Ginger's power as an aphrodisiac, and that of lemons, garlic, and onions, may not be scientifically proven but why not give it the benefit of the doubt. Besides, they taste so delicious!

SERVES 2

1½ cups cooked (*al dente*) linguine noodles

1 tsp olive oil

⅓ cup sweet onion, very thinly sliced

⅓ – ½ cup Avocado Dressing (do not add the optional water in the recipe, p. 187)

½ tsp lightly toasted cumin seeds

½ tsp fresh ginger, grated

¼ tsp fresh squeezed garlic juice (optional)

pepper to taste

¾ cup cherry tomatoes (the smaller the better)

When the linguine is cooked and well drained, toss it gently with the olive oil and spread it out on a plate to cool. Then place it in a bowl with the onions and set aside. In a small bowl, combine the Avocado Dressing with the cumin, ginger, garlic, optional garlic juice, and pepper, taste for seasoning, and pour over the pasta and onions. Toss gently. Scatter cherry tomatoes around the edge of the bowl.

MARINATED ROASTED VEGETABLES

When I serve winter vegetables this way, I bring them to the table hot from the oven, but they are so delicious cold that leftovers are not just tolerated but craved! The fennel bulb adds a delicate flavor that marries extraordinarily well with balsamic vinegar, so even if you need to substitute other vegetables, try to include the fennel.

SERVES 8 TO 10

1 large potato

1 sweet potato

1 yam

2 large carrots

1 large mild onion

1 fennel bulb

2 parsnips

2 small turnips

3 tbsp olive oil

1 small bunch fresh thyme or rosemary

½ – 1 tsp salt, or to taste

½ tsp black pepper, or to taste

1 tbsp lemon juice

2 tbsp good quality balsamic vinegar

Preheat oven to 415°F (212°C).

Wash, peel, and cut all the vegetables into bite-sized cubes. Place them on a wide flat baking tray, toss them with the olive oil, and sprinkle them liberally with small sprigs of thyme or rosemary. Roast them in the oven, turning them after 30 minutes, until they are tender and beginning to brown (about 45 minutes, depending on the size and quantity of the vegetables).

When they are cooked, sprinkle them with salt and pepper then transfer to a bowl and sprinkle the lemon juice and balsamic vinegar over them, tossing them gently. Taste and adjust seasonings if desired, and allow to cool to room temperature.

MESCLUN GREENS WITH TOASTED PECANS, NECTARINE SLICES, AND SHERRY VINAIGRETTE

Mesclun greens, those tasty little leaves of all sorts of lettuces, are available fresh in most places in the summer, and are nicely complemented here with nuts, fruit, and sherry.

SERVES 4

4 cups fresh mesclun greens

¼ – ½ cup caramelized pecan halves (see directions)

½ tsp butter

1 tbsp sugar

2 tsp fresh lemon juice

1 large ripe nectarine, washed but not peeled

3 tbsp dry sherry

½ tsp salt

¼ tsp white pepper

2 tsp honey

3 tbsp light-tasting oil (canola, grape seed or sunflower seed)

Pack the greens in a food-safe plastic bag and keep them cool.

To prepare the pecans, toast them in a dry pan over medium heat, tossing them continually, until they smell aromatic, and begin to turn brown. Add the butter to the pan, toss the pecans to coat them, and turn them out on to a plate. Wipe the surface of the pan dry, then heat the sugar in it, over medium heat, watching it carefully so that it melts, but does not turn dark brown. Do NOT stir the sugar as it heats and melts. As soon as it is liquid, and has turned light brown, take the pan off the heat, add the hot pecans, toss them quickly in the caramel, and quickly turn them out on to the plate again. Let them cool then separate them and place them in a small container. Do not refrigerate them.

Just before the picnic, place the lemon juice in a small container, and slice the nectarine into it, cutting thin slices from the top of the fruit to the bottom and freeing them from the pit as you go. Toss the fruit gently in the lemon juice. In a small bowl, mix the sherry, salt, pepper, and honey, then whisk in the oil. Taste and adjust for seasoning. Pour the dressing over the nectarine slices in lemon juice, and gently combine the liquids around the fruit slices. Cover the container, and keep cool until ready to use.

To serve the salad, place the greens on individual plates, spoon nectarine slices, along with the dressing, over each portion, sprinkle with caramelized pecans, and eat immediately.

MUSHROOM MEDLEY

Although you can substitute other fresh mushrooms for the ones suggested below, the flavors and textures of oyster and shiitake are so perfect together in this tangy salad that it would be a pity to do so. You may wish to add half of the fresh thyme, then taste the salad before adding the rest; the thyme should not overpower the other ingredients.

SERVES 4 TO 6

¼ cup olive oil

I tsp garlic, crushed

4 cups oyster mushrooms, sliced

2 cups button mushrooms, sliced

2 cups shiitake mushrooms (stems removed), sliced

3 tbsp balsamic vinegar

⅓ cup sun-dried tomatoes (packed in oil), drained and rinsed, finely chopped

½ tsp fresh thyme, finely chopped

salt and pepper to taste

In a large pan over medium high heat, heat the oil and sauté the garlic and mushrooms until tender, 6 to 10 minutes. Add the balsamic vinegar, sun-dried tomatoes, thyme, and salt and pepper to taste, and cook gently for a few minutes. Serve warm or cold.

NAPA CABBAGE SLAW

*Although this light slaw-type salad does not require any oil, it can be made, if preferred, with
¼ to ½ cup of Peanut Dressing (p. 197) or Miso Dressing (p. 192) instead of the fish sauce
and lime juice.*

SERVES 6 TO 8

1 Napa cabbage, 2 – 3 lb
  (900 g – 1.3 kg)

1 tbsp salt

1 clove fresh garlic, minced

2 – 3 medium shallots, very thinly
  sliced

1 – 2 small Thai or jalapeño chilis,
  seeded and minced

2 tsp fresh lemongrass, minced

2 tbsp fish sauce (available in
  Asian markets)

2 tbsp fresh lime juice

Wash the cabbage and drain it, then shred it finely,
rub the salt well into it, and leave it to drain in a
colander for an hour. Rinse thoroughly under the tap
and squeeze any remaining water out of it. Place in a
large bowl, and add the remaining ingredients. Toss
well, taste, and adjust seasonings as desired. Chill the
salad before serving.

PENNE, ARUGULA, PROSCIUTTO, AND OLIVES WITH LEMON VINAIGRETTE

Another fertile combination from the king of salads, Bill Jones. The lemon, mustard, and garlic dressing is a perfect match for the penne and the zippy flavors of the vegetables and prosciutto.

SERVES 4 TO 6

Dressing

1 lemon (juice and zest)

1 tbsp Dijon mustard

1 tsp garlic, minced

1 tsp water

4 tbsp olive oil

salt and black pepper to taste

Pasta

6 cups water

1 tsp salt

2 cups penne

1 tsp olive oil

additional olive oil for drizzling

2 cups arugula leaves

2 oz (60 g) prosciutto, shredded

½ cup whole olives

additional prosciutto and olives
(garnish)

In a large bowl, combine the lemon juice, zest, mustard, garlic, and water. Drizzle in the oil, whisking constantly, until smooth and thick. Season with salt and pepper and set aside until needed.

In a large pot over high heat, bring the water and salt to a rolling boil and stir in the penne and oil. Bring back to a boil and cook until *al dente*, about 7 or 8 minutes. Drain, drizzle with a little oil and toss well. Transfer to a baking sheet and spread out evenly. Cool to room temperature and toss lightly to separate.

Add the cooled penne, arugula, prosciutto, and olives to the dressing and toss well to mix. Garnish with a sprinkling of extra shredded prosciutto and olives. Serve at room temperature.

PINEAPPLE CELERY SALAD

Nuts add great flavor, crunch, and healthy protein to this easy salad. Decorate it with a few of the tiny pale green leafy stalks from the inside of the celery heart.

SERVES 6 TO 8

3 cups fresh pineapple, cut in small cubes

3 cups young celery stalks, finely sliced

1 cup almond slivers

½ cup pine nuts

¼ cup Old-Fashioned Boiled Dressing (p. 193) or prepared mayonnaise

¼ cup Pressed Yogurt (p. 117), or sour cream

a little pineapple juice, if needed

Drain the pineapple cubes completely, then mix them in a bowl with the celery. Set aside a little of the juice to add to the dressing if needed.

In a pan over medium heat, toast the almonds and pine nuts until they begin to change color, tossing them well during this process. Cool them and add to the pineapple and celery.

In another bowl, stir the Boiled Dressing or mayonnaise into the pressed yogurt, add a little pineapple juice if it is too thick, and taste to adjust seasoning. Stir the dressing mixture into the salad, and chill it well before serving.

POTATO AND BACON SALAD

Nowadays, bacon is usually too lean to produce enough fat to dress this salad without the addition of vegetable oil, but if you should find bacon that is not, omit the extra oil. If your bacon yields very little fat (less than 2 or3 tbsp), add more oil. Either way, this is a tasty version of potato salad, mustardy enough to complement the bacon beautifully.

SERVES 6 TO 8

12 medium potatoes (red or new potatoes are best)

6 strips fat bacon

1 tbsp vegetable oil

1 large onion, finely chopped

¾ cup celery, thinly sliced

2 tbsp prepared mustard

1 tbsp honey

⅓ cup vinegar

black pepper to taste

2 tbsp mustard seeds (garnish)

In a pot of salted water, bring the potatoes to a boil, then reduce heat to low and simmer until just tender (10 to 14 minutes, depending on size). As soon as they are cool enough to handle, rub or pull off the skins, and dice them into a bowl. Set aside.

Chop the bacon into small pieces and fry it in a pan over medium high heat until crisp. Remove the bacon and combine it with the potatoes.

Leave the bacon fat in the pan and add vegetable oil. Sauté the onion and celery in the bacon fat and oil until they are soft. Add to the potatoes and bacon, making sure to include any fat remaining in the pan. Mix well.

In a small bowl, mix the mustard, honey, and vinegar together, and add black pepper to taste. Combine this dressing with the salad and taste to correct for seasoning.

In a small saucepan over medium heat, toast the mustard seeds until they start to pop. Sprinkle them on top of the prepared salad. Serve warm or at room temperature.

POTATO AND RED BEET SALAD

The red of the beets permeates this salad, but its rosy hue is only a small part of its appeal. The flavor combination is a delightful variation on the well-known but far from hackneyed theme of potato salad.

SERVES 4 TO 6

6 – 8 medium potatoes

1 cup marinated beets, drained and diced (measure after dicing)

2 tbsp onion, finely chopped

½ tsp white pepper

⅓ – ½ cup Vinaigrette (p. 200)

2 tbsp chives, chopped

2 tbsp parsley, chopped

In a pot of salted water over high heat, bring potatoes to a boil, reduce heat, and simmer until just tender (10 to 14 minutes, depending on size). As soon as they are cool enough to handle, rub or peel off the skins, and slice them into a bowl. Add the beets and onions. In another bowl, combine the pepper with the vinaigrette. Pour the dressing over the salad and toss well. Chill the salad for a couple of hours, turning it once during that time. Toss it again just before serving and sprinkle with the chopped chives and parsley.

QUINOA CORN SALAD
WITH CILANTRO, CHIVES, AND
LEMON-LIME DRESSING

Rebar salads, masterminded by Audrey Alsterberg and Wanda Urbanowicz, are famous in Victoria, B.C., and this grain and vegetable salad is a perfect example of why. They explain in their book (named after the restaurant, of course) that quinoa has been around for quite a while — it was used by the Incas. It has more protein than all other grains, and is a great source of calcium and other useful nutrients. Quinoa needs to be well rinsed before it is cooked; otherwise, it tastes a little bitter.

SERVES 6

1 cup quinoa

1½ cups water

½ tsp salt

2½ cups corn, fresh or frozen

1 small red onion, minced

2 jalapeño peppers, seeded and minced

½ red pepper, finely diced

3 tbsp lemon juice

3 tbsp lime juice

¼ cup cilantro, chopped

3 scallions, minced

2 tbsp chives, finely minced

1 tsp salt

½ tsp Tabasco sauce, or to taste

Place quinoa in a fine mesh sieve and rinse thoroughly with cold, running water. In a small pot, bring water to boil, add the quinoa and salt, and bring to a boil again. Cover and reduce heat to low for 15 minutes. Turn off the heat and keep the pot covered for an additional 5 minutes. Strain off any excess liquid and spread the quinoa out to cool on a tray while preparing the remaining ingredients.

Steam or lightly sauté corn until just tender and cool to room temperature. In a large bowl, combine all of the ingredients and gently toss. Season with additional salt, pepper or hot sauce to taste. Serve with fresh lime wedges.

RED CABBAGE SALAD WITH PISTACHIOS

James Peterson is a prominent U.S. chef, food writer, and teacher, and former owner of one of New York's leading French restaurants. This deconstructed coleslaw replaces traditional mayonnaise with vinegar and oil, and pays particular attention to the texture of the cabbage, which the salt rub brings to a soft yet sturdy condition. The nuts give the contrasting crunch, and the flavorings — top-quality nut or olive oil, and sherry or balsamic vinegar — give all the zing required. Call it Salade de Chou Rouge aux Pistaches and amaze friends and family!

SERVES 6

1 small red cabbage (1½ lbs [675 g])

1 tbsp coarse salt

1 cup pistachios (husked), whole pecans, or walnut halves

⅓ cup sherry vinegar or other flavorful wine vinegar, such as balsamic

½ cup walnut, hazelnut, or pistachio oil made from roasted nuts, or extra-virgin olive oil

freshly ground pepper to taste

Discard loose or wilted leaves from cabbage and cut in four pieces through the bottom core. Slice the wedge of white core out of each quarter. Shred each quarter as finely as you can. This is easiest if you have a plastic vegetable slicer or a mandoline, but if you don't have one, place each quarter on a cutting board and slice it as fine as you can with a very sharp chef's knife.

Lay nuts of choice out on a baking sheet. Toast in a 350°F (175°C) oven for 10 to 15 minutes, then allow to cool. If using walnuts, chop halves into smaller pieces.

In a large bowl, combine the cabbage with the salt, and rub it between your fingers for about 2 minutes until the salt dissolves and you can't feel any more salt. Transfer the cabbage to a colander, set the colander over the large bowl, and let drain for about 30 minutes. Squeeze the cabbage in your hands, in little balls, to extract as much liquid and salt as you can — you'll be amazed how much liquid comes out — and put the squeezed cabbage in a clean mixing or salad bowl (if you're serving or passing it at table). Use a fork to toss the cabbage with the vinegar and oil. Stir in the nuts just before serving so they don't get soggy. Season to taste with pepper.

SALADE NIÇOISE

There are lots of variations of this salad, but to be in any way "authentic" it should be dressed with vinaigrette rather than a mayonnaise dressing. If authenticity is important, it should also be noted that Salade Niçoise is traditionally made with high-quality oil-packed canned tuna rather than the glorious slices of rare ahi tuna that grace some contemporary dishes of this name in fine restaurants. (I never was a stickler for authenticity!)

SERVES 6

24 small new potatoes, lightly cooked and cooled, halved

1 lb (450 g) green beans, cut in 1-inch (2.5-cm) pieces and lightly cooked

6 medium tomatoes, chopped, or 18 cherry tomatoes

1 sweet onion, thinly sliced

12 anchovy fillets, or 2 7-oz (213-g) cans good quality chunk tuna, drained and separated with a fork

½ cup Vinaigrette (p. 200)

2 tbsp tarragon, chopped

6 hard-boiled eggs

24 or more pitted black olives

In a large bowl, combine the potatoes, beans, tomatoes, onions, and halved anchovy fillets or tuna.

In another bowl, combine the tarragon with the vinaigrette, pour it over the salad and toss gently. Slice the eggs or cut lengthwise into four sections, and arrange the eggs and olives decoratively on top. The salad can be chilled at this point for up to several hours.

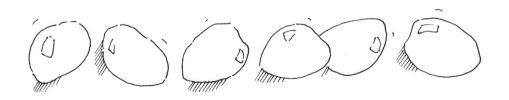

SUNFLOWER TOFU SALAD

Tofu is great in a salad because it can assume whatever flavor you wish it to, as well as adding texture, and some good high quality protein. The sweetness of jicama and the tartness of apple are compatible bedfellows in this scrumptious salad.

SERVES 6

1 cup sunflower seeds

2 cups prepared firm tofu (see directions) or smoked tofu, finely diced or shredded

3 tbsp tamari sauce

1 cup tart apple, diced

2 tbsp lemon juice

1 cup celery, finely sliced

½ cup red onion, chopped

1 cup jicama, diced or grated

½ – ¾ cup Miso Dressing (p. 192) or Creamy Tofu Dressing (p. 189)

Toast the sunflower seeds by placing them in a dry pan over medium high heat. Keep them moving in the pan until they begin to brown. Allow to cool.

To prepare tofu, slice the block into slices about ¼ inch (½ cm) thick, then into small rectangles. Toss them gently in the tamari sauce. Place them on an oiled cookie sheet and bake them for 25 minutes in a 375°F (190°C) oven, turning once. They should be brown and beginning to crisp. Cool before using.

In a serving bowl or container, add the diced apple to the lemon juice. When the apple pieces are well coated, add the rest of the ingredients and toss well.

SWEDISH PICKLED CUCUMBER

This recipe may have originated in Sweden but it has been around the rest of the civilized world for at least as long as any of my oldest recipe books and files, with many minor variations in the proportions but very similar basic ingredients. Its simplicity is as attractive as its gentle flavors.

SERVES 4 TO 6

1 large English cucumber, peeled and thinly sliced

3 tbsp white vinegar

2 tbsp water

2 tbsp sugar

¼ tsp salt

pinch of white pepper

1 tbsp parsley and/or chives, chopped

In a large dish, place the cucumber slices. In a bowl, combine the remaining ingredients, mix well, and pour over the cucumber. Allow the salad to chill for several hours, then pour off and discard most of the liquid from it just before serving.

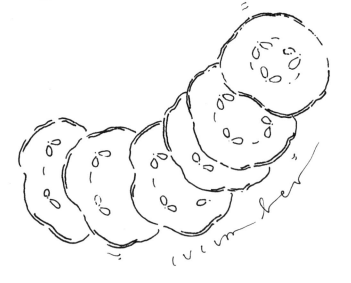

TABOULEH SALAD

Fresh-tasting, interestingly textured, and nutritious, Tabouleh Salad is a great addition to a picnic buffet. It keeps well, and is all the better for being made a few hours or even a day before your picnic.

SERVES 6

1 cup bulgur wheat

4 cups water (for soaking bulgur wheat)

¾ cup parsley, finely chopped

½ cup green and/or sweet onion, finely chopped

¼ cup mint, finely chopped

¼ cup cilantro, finely chopped (optional)

1½ cups English cucumber, unpeeled, finely diced

2 large tomatoes, finely chopped and drained

¼ – ½ cup lemon juice

2 tbsp olive oil

salt and pepper to taste

Soak the bulgur in the water for 20 minutes, then drain it thoroughly, pressing out any remaining water. Shake the grains into a bowl, and add the prepared vegetables.

Mix well, then add ¼ cup of the lemon juice, 1 tbsp of the olive oil, and a sprinkle of salt and pepper. Mix well, taste, and add the rest of the lemon juice and olive oil to taste.

THAI-STYLE BEEF AND CUCUMBER SALAD

This is a fiery salad, but you can adjust the level of heat by reducing the number of Thai hot peppers or omitting them altogether.

SERVES 4

3 cups rare roast beef, julienned

2 cups peeled cucumber, julienned

1 cup canned water chestnuts, diced small

¾ cup cilantro, chopped

¾ cup green onions, chopped

3 tbsp seasoned rice vinegar

1 tbsp fresh lime juice

2 small Thai hot peppers, minced

1 tsp hot chili flakes

1 tbsp fresh ginger, minced

2 inches (5 cm) lemongrass, minced

¼ tsp salt (more if desired)

In a large bowl, combine the first 5 ingredients. In another bowl, mix the remaining ingredients to make a dressing, then add to the salad and toss well. Chill before serving. This salad could be served in hollowed-out half cucumbers.

TOMATO AND CUCUMBER SALAD

The simplicity of this salad is perfect for a hot summer's day.

SERVES 6

6 large ripe tomatoes, sliced

1 English cucumber, peeled, or 2 field
cucumbers, peeled and seeded, sliced

1 sweet onion, sliced

¼ cup Vinaigrette (p. 200)

2 tbsp chopped chives

You can peel the tomatoes by immersing them in boiling water for 25 seconds. The skins should slide right off when you cut round the top core of the tomatoes. However, you may prefer to leave the skins on.

In a large bowl, arrange the tomatoes, cucumber, and onion in layers. Pour the Vinaigrette slowly over the surface. Sprinkle with the chives. The salad is best if left to marinate for an hour or more, and may be served at room temperature or chilled.

TOMATO AND POTATO SALAD

I first ate this salad in France decades ago, sitting with my friends Jacqui and Chantal (who had made the salad) on a picnic blanket, gazing out over the rolling slopes of the Jura foothills. I was able to duplicate the salad, if not the ambiance, when I returned home, and have made it every summer since then.

SERVES 6

8 medium cooked new potatoes, thinly sliced

8 medium fully ripe tomatoes, thinly sliced

1 large sweet onion, thinly sliced

4 tbsp chives, chopped

3 tbsp mint, chopped (optional)

½ cup Vinaigrette (p. 200) or preferred dressing

In a large pot of salted water over high heat, bring the potatoes to a boil, reduce heat to low, and simmer until just tender (10 to 14 minutes). In a large bowl, layer the hot potatoes, tomatoes, and onions, sprinkling chives (and mint) over each layer, and reserving some for the top.

Pour the vinaigrette slowly over the top layer, then sprinkle with the reserved herbs. Allow the salad to cool and marinate for an hour or two before serving time. It can be eaten warm or at ambient temperature.

TOMATO BOCCONCINI SALAD WITH BASIL

Fresh tasting and pretty, as simple as a salad can get, this is always a crowd pleaser.

SERVES 4

2 cups fresh tomatoes, diced

2 cups diced bocconcini, or "baby" bocconcini cut in half

½ cup basil leaves, coarsely chopped

¼ cup Vinaigrette (made with balsamic vinegar and olive oil, p. 200)

In a large bowl, toss all ingredients together and allow to marinate for at least 30 minutes before serving.

TRADITIONAL POTATO SALAD

Using the Boiled Salad Dressing, you will achieve a potato salad "like Grandma used to make," tangy and quite tart. If you prefer a milder taste, cut the salad dressing with cream or buttermilk, and add a little sugar or honey to taste, or use a commercially prepared mayonnaise.

SERVES 6

12 medium potatoes (red or new potatoes are best)

½ – ⅔ cup Boiled Salad Dressing (p. 193) or prepared mayonnaise

2 tbsp parsley, chopped

2 tbsp chives, chopped

1 tbsp onion or green onion, finely chopped

The following are optional additions to choose from:

3 hard-boiled eggs, chopped

½ cup green olives

2 large dill pickles, finely chopped

1 cup celery, including some young green leaves, finely chopped

3 tbsp capers

2 tbsp fresh dill, chopped

3 tbsp pimentos, chopped

In a large pot of salted water over high heat, bring the potatoes to a boil, reduce heat to low, and simmer until just tender (10 to 14 minutes depending on size). As soon as they are cool enough to handle, rub or pull off the skins, and dice them into a bowl.

While the potato cubes are still warm, add the salad dressing, parsley, chives, and onion, and any of the additions you favor. Do not add hard-boiled eggs, though, until the salad is cool.

TUNA AND RICE SALAD
OR INSALATA DI TONNO E RISO

Award-winning U.S. author Joyce Goldstein, former owner of the illustrious Square One restaurant in San Francisco, includes in her book, Enoteca, recipes from chefs working in traditional neighborhood wine bars throughout Italy. She uses basmati rice rather than the more traditional Arborio for salads, and suggests using spelt as a substitute for rice in this delicious recipe. Although she gives a choice of canned or cooked fresh tuna, she says that in Italy, the canned tuna is more popular because it is such an excellent product. (Look for tuna labeled "ventresca di tonno," packed in good olive oil.) The salad may be garnished with anchovy fillets or marinated roasted peppers. Tomato wedges, too, when tomatoes are in season.

SERVES 4

Rice

1 cup long-grain white rice,
   preferably basmati

1½ cups water

1 tsp salt

Vinaigrette

⅔ cup extra-virgin olive oil

2 tbsp mild red wine vinegar

¼ cup fresh lemon juice

salt and black pepper to taste

In a saucepan over high heat, combine the rice, water, and salt. Bring to a boil, cover, reduce the heat to low, and cook until the rice is tender and all the water is absorbed, 15 to 18 minutes.

In a small bowl, whisk together the olive oil, vinegar, and lemon juice. Season with salt and pepper.

½ cup red onion, finely chopped

¼ cup fresh flat-leaf parsley, chopped

10 – 12 oz (300 – 350 g) olive oil–packed Italian tuna or cooked fresh tuna

8 olive oil–packed anchovy fillets, drained and cut into narrow strips or chopped (optional)

1 red bell pepper, roasted, peeled, seeded, and cut into long narrow strips or coarsely diced (optional)

tomato wedges (optional)

Transfer the warm rice to a bowl. Drizzle with some of the vinaigrette, toss well with a fork, and let cool. Fold the onion and parsley into the cooled rice, then toss again with a fork to fluff. In another bowl, break the tuna into large chunks with your fingers and toss with some of the remaining vinaigrette.

To serve, spoon a mound of rice on to each of 4 individual serving plates. Top with the dressed tuna; anchovies, if you like them; and the roasted pepper, if using. Drizzle with the last of the vinaigrette. (Alternatively, arrange on a single large platter, family style.) Garnish with tomato wedges, if desired.

WALDORF SALAD

This salad's success depends on a wise choice of apples, and really fresh walnuts. Granny Smith apples have a pleasing tartness and a pretty color, but tart red-skinned ones are also attractive. Many varieties of apples turn brown as soon as they are cut, so as soon as each apple is diced, toss the pieces in some lemon juice.

SERVES 6 TO 8

3 cups apples, diced

2 tbsp fresh lemon juice or juice of half a lemon

2 cups celery, diced

1½ cups fresh walnut or pecan pieces

1½ cups seedless green grapes

¾ cup Boiled Salad Dressing (p. 193), combined with ¼ cup cream

or 1 cup prepared mayonnaise or salad dressing

In a bowl, prepare the apples and toss the pieces in the lemon juice, then set aside. In another bowl, combine the rest of the ingredients.

Drain the apple pieces thoroughly and add them to the salad, making sure they are separated and that all are covered with the dressing. Taste and adjust seasoning as desired.

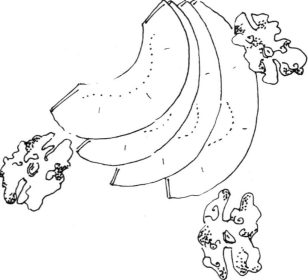

SALAD DRESSINGS

AVOCADO DRESSING

The luscious smoothness of avocado and its oil content make for a sensuous dressing that is good with greens, vegetables, or grains.

MAKES I CUP

1 small ripe avocado

¼ cup lemon juice (juice of 1 lemon)

½ tsp salt

1 small clove garlic, pressed

⅓ cup buttermilk or plain yogurt

1 – 2 tbsp water (optional)

salt and pepper to taste

In a bowl, mash the avocado with the lemon juice until it is smooth. Add the other ingredients and blend well, adding the water only if you need a thinner dressing. Taste and adjust the seasonings as desired, adding pepper and salt if required. The dressing will not keep well, so use it the same day it is made.

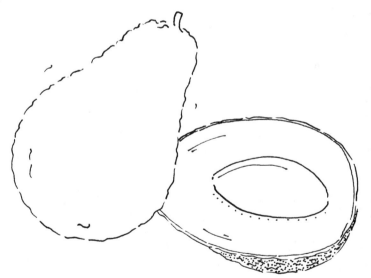

COLESLAW DRESSING

Simple to make, it keeps for days in the fridge, and is perfect for to the hearty crunch of coleslaw.

MAKES I CUP

½ cup sweetened condensed milk

½ cup apple cider vinegar

2 tsp prepared mustard

I tsp salt

½ tsp cayenne pepper or hot sauce

In a bowl, combine all the ingredients and mix well. Cover and keep refrigerated until use.

CREAMY TOFU DRESSING

Mustardy, lemony, sweet-sour, this dressing can be used on tossed green salads, with steamed vegetables, in sandwiches, or anywhere you might use salad dressing or mayonnaise, although it is a little thinner than either.

MAKES ¾ CUP

½ pkg firm silken tofu, about 5 oz (150 g)

¼ cup seasoned rice vinegar

1 tbsp lemon juice

1 tsp honey

¼ tsp dry mustard

½ tsp salt

pepper to taste

1 tbsp milk or water (optional)

In a food processor or blender, process all except the milk or water until completely smooth. Add the milk or water only if needed to correct the consistency of the dressing. Cover and keep chilled before use.

GREEN DRESSING

Here's a tangy dressing that will appeal to garlic fans. It can be used on a tossed salad or in any vegetable salad that needs a flavor boost.

MAKES 1½ CUPS

3 large dark-green romaine leaves, coarsely chopped

2 or 3 stems of parsley

1 green onion, coarsely chopped

1 clove garlic, chopped

¼ tsp salt

pepper to taste

2 tbsp fresh lemon juice

½ tsp honey, or more as desired

½ cup buttermilk

In a food processor or blender, process the romaine leaves, parsley, green onion, and garlic with the seasonings, lemon juice, and honey until smooth. Pour in a bowl, then gradually add the buttermilk and mix well. Cover and let the dressing chill for a few hours before use to blend the flavors. Taste and adjust seasoning if necessary.

LIME–COCONUT DRESSING

The fresh flavors of lime juice and coconut can be used as a background for a fiery hot Thai-style dressing, or they can star on their own in a salad that is delicately fruity.

MAKES ABOUT ¾ CUP

juice of 1 lime

6 tbsp coconut milk, ½ 5.6-fl oz (165-ml) can

½ tsp salt

½ tsp honey

good pinch of cayenne pepper

1 or more tsp Thai hot chili paste (optional)

In a bowl, combine all the ingredients and mix well. Taste and adjust for seasoning. Cover and keep chilled before use.

MISO DRESSING

Miso, a Japanese condiment made from soy beans, is so tasty that if you haven't used it until now, you'll wonder what took you so long. It can be dark and intensely flavored, or lighter in color and flavor. This recipe works well with Aka miso, a medium one, so if you use another sort, experiment with quantity and adjust as necessary. If you do not have seasoned rice vinegar, add a small amount of sugar and salt to rice vinegar, just enough to be tasty.

MAKES ABOUT 1¼ CUPS

¼ cup miso paste

¼ cup seasoned rice vinegar

2 tsp honey

¼ – ½ cup fresh lemon juice (start with ¼ and add more to taste)

4 tbsp tamari soy sauce

2 tbsp sesame oil

1 tbsp canola or other mild-tasting oil

1 tbsp *dashi* (available in Asian markets) (optional)

In a bowl, mix the vinegar into the miso paste a little at a time until it is smooth. Add the other ingredients, mix well, and taste to adjust for seasoning. You may add *dashi* (dried flaked tuna) to this dressing, and substitute *mirin* (rice wine vinegar) for the seasoned rice vinegar, to make a more assertive dressing. Cover and keep chilled until use.

OLD-FASHIONED BOILED SALAD DRESSING

During the hard times of the Great Depression, eggs were very scarce where my family lived, and boiled salad dressing made sense as a cheap and easy replacement for mayonnaise in an era and location where all salad dressings were made at home. Today it's a luxury because of the time it takes to prepare, but it so exactly recreates the flavor of old-fashioned picnic potato salad that it's worth the time for that alone. Since its flavor is intense, it may be thinned with a little cream or buttermilk before use. As a substitute for mayonnaise, it avoids the problem of using raw eggs, and it keeps for a couple of weeks covered in the fridge. Like mayonnaise, it can assume many guises.

MAKES ¾ CUP

⅔ cup vinegar

2 tbsp water

1 large egg

1 tsp cornstarch

½ tsp dry mustard

2 tsp sugar

½ tsp salt

1 tbsp butter

pinch cayenne pepper

In a small bowl, combine all the ingredients and mix well. Place the bowl over a pot of simmering water, or use a double boiler to cook the mixture until it has thickened, stirring constantly. Cover and keep refrigerated until use.

Note: These are some of the things you can add to change your dressing's character and give each salad a distinctive flavor. To a half cup of dressing, add:

Tartare Sauce

1 tsp Dijon mustard

1 tbsp sweet gherkins, chopped

1 tbsp green olives, chopped

1 tbsp capers, chopped

1 green onion, chopped

Thousand Island Dressing

1 hard-boiled egg, chopped

1 tbsp green olives, finely chopped

1 tbsp green onion, finely chopped

1 tbsp green bell pepper, finely chopped

1 tbsp red bell pepper, finely chopped

1 tbsp parsley, finely chopped

1 tbsp tomato paste

½ tsp cayenne pepper or Tabasco sauce

Tangy Russian Dressing

1 tbsp prepared horseradish

1 tsp Worcestershire sauce

1 tbsp tomato paste

1 green onion, chopped

½ tsp cayenne pepper

OLD-FASHIONED SALAD CREAM

Rich and creamy, this dressing looks like golden whipped cream and has a delicate subtle flavor. It makes an exotic alternative to mayonnaise, and can be used as a dressing for any mixed vegetable or fruit salad, or served on the side at a salad buffet picnic.

MAKES ¾ CUP

2 freshly hard-boiled eggs

½ tsp salt

2 tsp sugar

½ tsp dry mustard

½ cup whipping cream

5 tsp apple cider vinegar, or more
  as desired

Cut the warm eggs in half and scoop out the yolks. Set the whites aside.

In a bowl, mash up the hard-boiled yolks with the salt and sugar until smooth and creamy. Add the mustard, then fold in a couple of tbsp of the cream and mix until smooth. Mix in the rest of the cream and whisk for a minute or two, only until the dressing is slightly fluffy and just beginning to thicken. (It will thicken more when you add the vinegar.)

Fold the vinegar in gently, then finely chop the egg whites and add. Add more vinegar, a teaspoonful at a time, and mix well, until the flavors are pleasantly balanced. Cover and keep refrigerated until use.

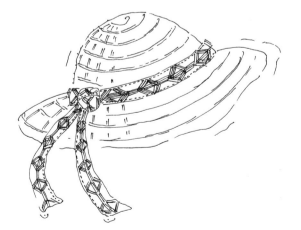

ORANGE-MISO DRESSING

The pronounced orange flavor of this tasty dressing suggests a marriage with almonds (or pecans) and fruit. Try it in our Golden Yam Salad (p. 155), or with salad greens, toasted almond slivers, and sliced oranges or grape halves. The flavor of the dressing will alter according to the kind of miso you use. Some are light colored and salty sweet, others are darker and more intense in flavor.

MAKES ¾ CUP

4 tbsp frozen orange juice concentrate

2 tsp maple syrup

4 tsp miso paste

1 tsp salt

1 tsp fresh ginger, grated (optional)

4 tbsp olive oil

In a bowl, combine the first 4 ingredients (plus the ginger if desired), whisking and stirring until the miso paste is completely blended. Add the olive oil and whisk it in until the dressing is smooth, then taste and adjust seasoning as desired. Cover and keep chilled until use.

PEANUT DRESSING

The texture of this dressing varies according to whether you use crunchy or smooth peanut butter, but it is always richly nutty in flavor, and complements salads with fruits and grains particularly well. The heat can be enhanced with your favorite hot sauce, chili paste, or fresh hot peppers.

MAKES A GENEROUS CUP

½ cup seasoned rice vinegar

2 tbsp soy sauce

½ tsp ground or crushed Szechuan peppercorns or black peppercorns

3 tbsp natural peanut butter (see note)

2 tsp fresh ginger, grated

1 tsp salt

¼ cup peanut oil

In a bowl or jar, whisk or shake the first 5 ingredients, then add the oil and whisk or shake until smooth. Cover until use.

Note: if you prefer to use salted peanut butter, omit the salt from this dressing and taste for flavor before serving.

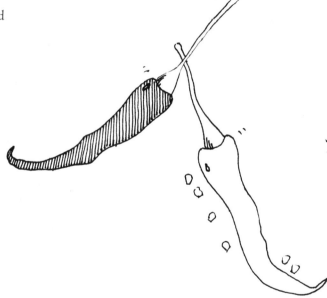

RICE VINEGAR DRESSING

I use this dressing on my tossed green salads, and never tire of its delicate sweetness and the tang of the mustard, just right for the bitter green salad mixes I often serve.

MAKES I CUP

½ cup seasoned rice vinegar

½ tsp dry mustard

½ tsp Mrs Dash seasoning (or other salt-free vegetable-based dry seasoning)

½ cup olive oil

salt and pepper to taste

In a bowl or jar, whisk or shake the first 3 ingredients together well, then add the oil and whisk or shake until smooth. Pour into a bottle. The dressing keeps well for several weeks without refrigeration.

SIMPLE SOUR CREAM DRESSING

The mustardy flavor and creamy texture of this dressing make it a delicious choice for coleslaw, potato salad, or other dishes where you might use mayonnaise.

MAKES 1 CUP

1 cup sour cream (light will work)

1 – 2 green onions, finely diced

2 tbsp sweet pickle juice

1 tsp grainy or Dijon mustard (more to taste)

½ tsp salt

pepper or hot sauce to taste

In a bowl, combine all the ingredients and mix well together until smooth. Cover and keep well chilled until use.

VINAIGRETTE

The classic French vinaigrette has approximately three or four parts oil to one part vinegar, but since most North Americans prefer a lighter version, my recipe is less authentic than delicious! To further "lighten" the flavor, you can substitute 1 tbsp of water for the same quantity of vinegar. Many people prefer a sweeter salad dressing than this vinaigrette, so 1 tsp or more of honey or sugar may be added if desired. It is important, above all, to buy high quality oil and vinegar and ensure that you enjoy the flavor of each of these two key ingredients on its own. A well-dressed salad is a lightly dressed salad; just enough dressing to coat the vegetables.

MAKES ABOUT 1 CUP

⅓ – ½ cup white, malt, or wine vinegar, or lemon juice

½ tsp salt or to taste

½ tsp pepper or to taste

1 or more tsp sugar or honey (optional)

½ cup high quality olive oil, preferably cold-pressed

In a bowl, combine all the ingredients except the oil, and whisk together, adding the oil gradually, until smooth. Alternatively, combine all the ingredients in a bottle and shake.

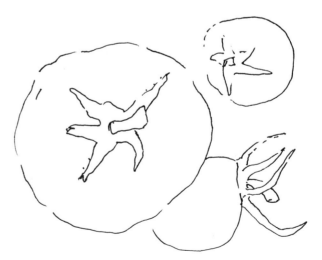

**To the basic vinaigrette,
add any of the following:**

1 – 2 tsp prepared honey mustard

½ – 1 tsp dry mustard

2 tbsp blue cheese, crumbled

handful green herbs, minced

1 – 2 tsp fresh garlic, pressed or minced

1 ripe avocado mashed with 2 tsp lemon juice

1 tsp or more wasabi powder

1 tbsp capers, chopped

2 tbsp sweet gherkins, chopped or dill pickles
   and 1 tbsp pickle juice

1 tbsp tomato paste and 1 tbsp green onions,
   chopped

1 tsp curry paste, 1 tsp sugar, and some
   pressed or minced garlic

For the suggested vinegar, substitute:

cider vinegar

balsamic vinegar

tarragon vinegar

rice vinegar

raspberry vinegar

or any other good quality flavored vinegar

For the olive oil, substitute:

grapeseed

peanut

safflower

canola

or another oil of your choice, depending on
   your budget and taste or health preferences

Note: Some of the more strongly flavored or
expensive oils (walnut, for example) can be
used half-and-half with a more neutral oil
such as canola.

For the salt, substitute:

1 or more tbsp tamari or soy sauce, or

anchovy paste, or

2 tsp or more of miso paste

SANDWICHES

CROQUE-MONSIEUR

Although these grilled sandwiches would be eaten hot in order to be authentically French, they are also delicious cold, with dill pickles on the side or chili sauce. An alternative version using smoked salmon instead of ham, and Gruyère cheese instead of Emmenthal, would benefit from a smear of dill mayonnaise rather than the mustard.

SERVES 4

8 slices bread (slightly stale is good)

2 tbsp soft butter

2 eggs

1 cup milk

4 oz (115 g) Emmenthal cheese, sliced

4 thin slices cooked ham

Dijon mustard

Butter the bread slices, and place four of them, butter side down, on a working surface. Spread each with mustard. Place cheese and a slice of ham, then a bread slice on each, butter side up.

In a small bowl, beat the eggs with the milk, and transfer to a wide shallow container, to fit the sandwiches. One at a time, and holding them together carefully, place each sandwich in the milk mixture, and turn it over to coat the other side. In a large non-stick pan, or a griddle over medium high heat, cook the sandwiches for about 5 minutes on each side or until they are brown and the cheese is melted. Press them firmly before they cool to make sure they stay together when cold.

LAYERED SANDWICHES

Layered sandwiches, like rolled sandwiches, are small dainty morsels, good as a picnic *hors d'oeuvre* or for a grand afternoon tea in the English style. Of great importance is very thinly sliced bread; standard sliced bread will be too thick, but the flat breads recommended for rolled sandwiches are a little too dense for these layered ones. If you can find a square loaf that you can slice yourself, or a sliced loaf for dieters, you're well on the way to success. Thin bread slices can be hard to butter, but if you slice them yourself with a bread knife and butter the loaf very lightly just before you cut each slice, you can achieve very thin buttered slices quite easily.

However, not all your slices will need buttering. Although for some fillings, butter will help keep the layers together, you can use, as a butter substitute, a thin layer of mustard or mayonnaise or yogurt flavored with mustard or capers or tomato-flavored cream cheese, etc; whatever is appropriate for the ingredients of your sandwiches.

To make a tasty layered sandwich, you need to combine fillings that will be compatible. Having decided on, say, three fillings (although two fillings and three slices of bread is also a good choice, and somewhat easier to handle), place a slice of bread on the working surface, spread it with filling number one, and place another bread slice face down on the filling. Then spread filling number two on its upper side, and put on another slice of bread, butter side down. Then spread filling number three on top of it and finally, the top slice of bread. When this sandwich is assembled, place your hand on it quite firmly and trim the crusts from the four edges with a sharp knife, then put the sandwich aside while you prepare the next one. When you have assembled all the sandwiches, wrap them two or three in a pile in plastic food wrap and chill them. Close to serving time, cut each sandwich into four small rectangles, or triangles, or even into three long rectangles, for slightly larger sandwiches. As you arrange the sandwiches on the serving plate or in the carrying container, make sure, by the way you place them, that it is clear that they are layered sandwiches.

Filling combinations for layered sandwiches:

ham, tomato, and cheese

cold cuts, cucumber, and tomato

pâté, sandwich pickles, and shredded lettuce

scrambled egg, bacon, and salsa

cream cheese with tomato paste, cucumber,
and carrot, finely shredded

bacon, apple, and onion

blue cheese, cream cheese, and alfalfa sprouts

smoked salmon, cream cheese with dill,
and onion

egg salad, smoked salmon, and
shredded lettuce

thinly sliced roast beef with horseradish
cream, cucumber, and tomato

thinly sliced roast lamb, cream cheese, mint,
and cucumber

More suggested fillings to mix and match:

traditional tuna, salmon, or egg salad

cheese of all kinds, thinly sliced

cooked asparagus, mashed with a squeeze of
lemon juice and some pepper

carrot, finely grated, with a teaspoon of fresh
grated ginger, and a little sour cream

hummus with parsley, cilantro,
or mint, chopped

devilled ham

salad shrimp, lightly mashed with a little
mayonnaise or salad cream

pressed yogurt with green herbs

marinated beets, finely chopped, with
pressed yogurt

sun-dried tomatoes, chopped,
with mayonnaise

steamed white fish with mayonnaise

smoked fish, with parsley and mayonnaise

anchovy fillets, mashed with lemon juice

salami slices, cut paper-thin

cress

tahini

olives, chopped

celery, chopped

arugula, shredded

ROLLED SANDWICHES

An array of little rolled sandwiches is eye-appealing, and perfect for the kind of "grazing" people like to do when lying back on a picnic blanket in idyllic summer weather. Although we've suggested rolled sandwiches for our afternoon tea picnic, to conform at least a little to the traditions of afternoon tea *à l'anglaise*, they make excellent pre-meal nibbles, too, tasty little mouthfuls to whet the appetite and get picnickers in the mood for the feast to follow.

Thin breads such as lavash, chapati, or soft tortillas make good rolled sandwiches, but the rectangular shape of lavash bread, and its softness, make it particularly good for this purpose. It is available from Greek and Middle Eastern bakeries and delis.

Using whatever flatbread you have, make rectangles about 9 inches long and as wide as you can make them. Take enough of any one of your prepared fillings to cover the rectangle with a thin layer. Roll the bread into a long neat roll, then cut it into rounds about an inch thick, as you would cut a sushi roll. Each piece should be bite-sized.

To enhance both eye appeal and flavor, place something along the edge of the filling before you start to roll it up: sweet pickled gherkins; slender asparagus spears; alfalfa sprouts; cucumber cut into thin lengths; spicy chutney if it is good and thick; the white part of green onions, left whole but well trimmed of looser outer layers; strips cut from slices of marinated beets; very finely grated carrot; pimientos or sun-dried tomato strips, well drained of oil.

Whatever you place on the edge before you start rolling will end up in the center of each sandwich, so it needs to be held in place both by the tightness of the roll and by the consistency of the spread you use to cover the bread.

Filling suggestions:

Using 1 cup of cream cheese or pressed yogurt as the base, add salt and pepper as required and any of the following, making sure the mixture remains easily spreadable:

2 tbsp blue cheese, crumbled and 2 tbsp parsley or celery, minced

2 tbsp tomato paste and ½ cup ham, finely shredded, or crisp bacon, crumbled

½ cup smoked salmon or gravlax, finely chopped and 1 tbsp chopped capers

1 – 2 tbsp canned anchovies, minced or 2 tbsp anchovy paste

3 large canned sardines, finely mashed and 1 tbsp sweet onion, finely minced

½ cup parmesan cheese, grated and 2 tbsp mayonnaise-style dressing

¼ cup marinated beets, finely chopped

¼ cup sun-dried tomatoes, chopped

¼ cup pitted black olives, finely chopped

½ cup fresh chervil, finely chopped

¼ cup hot fruit chutney

¼ cup toasted sunflower seeds, finely chopped and 2 tbsp orange marmalade

¼ cup crushed pineapple and 1 tsp fresh mint, finely chopped

Here are some other fillings that do not need cream cheese to provide the appropriate consistency:

egg, tuna, salmon, shrimp, lobster, or tofu sandwich salad, as long as the texture of all the ingredients is finer than usual

cooked asparagus, mashed with a squeeze of lemon juice and some pepper

hummus with parsley, cilantro, or mint, chopped

devilled ham with 2 tbsp chili sauce or ketchup, or crushed pineapple

tahini or sesame butter sprinkled with toasted sesame seeds

peanut butter topped with sweet onion, finely diced, or alfalfa sprouts

Marmite mixed with twice its volume of soft butter, sprinkled with chopped walnuts

SALAD SANDWICHES

These traditional picnic salads can be served on lettuce or used as sandwich fillings. They are good inside a hollowed-out baguette cut into serving-sized chunks. All these salads have the same basic ingredients, and should contain at least twice as much of the main ingredient (tuna, salmon, shrimp, lobster, crab, chicken, turkey, ham, egg, or tofu) as the other ingredients.

The combinations I have suggested can be varied according to your own taste, and any of these salad sandwich fillings could be further enhanced with fresh chopped herbs, such as chives, parsley, cilantro, basil, mint, chervil (especially good with egg) and others. The stronger-flavored herbs need to be used very moderately.

The dressing that gives the salads their cohesion is usually a mayonnaise of some kind, but for picnics it is wise to use a commercially prepared one or a cooked salad dressing, rather than a home-made mayonnaise prepared with uncooked eggs. To every three to four cups of salad ingredients, use ¾ to 1 cup of dressing, depending on the proportion you like. The tangy Boiled Salad Dressing recipe, p. 193, can be cut with plain yogurt, buttermilk, or whipped cream, and its flavor can be tweaked with any of the suggested additions listed under the basic recipe, as long as they do not overwhelm the flavor of the principal ingredients.

TUNA OR SALMON SALAD

MAKES ABOUT 3 CUPS

2 cups cooked tuna or salmon, flaked,
  or canned tuna or salmon, drained
  and flaked

½ cup celery, diced

1 tbsp chives or green onions,
  finely chopped

½ cup dressing

In a small bowl, combine all ingredients well. Cover and refrigerate until ready to use.

LOBSTER, SHRIMP, OR CRAB SALAD

MAKES ABOUT 3 CUPS

2 cups steamed lobster, shrimp
  or crab meat (or equivalent canned
  and drained)

½ cup cucumber, finely diced

1 tbsp parsley, chopped

½ cup dressing (dressing made with
  lemon juice instead of vinegar is
  particularly good with fish salads)

In a small bowl, combine all ingredients well. Cover and refrigerate until ready to use.

CHICKEN OR TURKEY SALAD

MAKES ABOUT 3 CUPS

2 cups cooked chicken or turkey,
  minced or diced

⅓ cup celery, diced

½ cup seedless grapes, halved
  (with chicken)

or ½ cup cooked or dried cranberries
  (with turkey)

or ½ cup toasted almond slivers

½ cup dressing

In a small bowl, combine all ingredients well. Cover and refrigerate until ready to use.

HAM SALAD

MAKES ABOUT 3 CUPS

2 cups cooked ham, minced

⅓ cup celery, diced

⅓ cup sun-dried tomatoes, finely chopped

or ⅓ cup marinated beets, finely chopped

½ cup dressing

In a small bowl, combine all ingredients well. Cover and refrigerate until ready to use.

EGG SALAD

MAKES ABOUT 3 CUPS

8 hard-boiled eggs, cooled

¼ cup parsley, chervil, or chives, finely chopped

¼ cup (or more) celery, finely chopped

2 or 3 green onions, finely chopped

½ cup dressing

salt and pepper to taste

In a small bowl, combine all ingredients well. Cover and refrigerate until ready to use.

TOFU SALAD

MAKES ABOUT 3 CUPS

1½ cups firm or extra-firm tofu, julienned

1 tbsp vegetable oil

2 tbsp soy sauce

1 tsp honey

¼ cup diced celery

½ cup halved seedless grapes

½ cup toasted almond slivers

⅓ cup dressing

In a pan over medium heat, sauté the tofu in the oil until it is pale golden. Remove from the heat and add the honey and soy sauce. Toss the tofu to coat, and allow it to cool completely.

In a small bowl, combine the tofu with the celery, grapes, almonds, and dressing, and toss well. Cover and refrigerate until ready to use.

MAINS

APPLE–MARINATED CHICKEN DRUMSTICKS

Gentle in flavor, easy to prepare, and appealing to kids, these drumsticks need to be completely cooled and chilled before you pack them to take on a picnic. (They are good eaten hot, but when chilled, the apple flavor really emerges. Yummy!)

MAKES **10** PIECES

10 chicken drumsticks

½ cup lemon juice

½ cup vegetable oil

1 cup apple juice

1 clove garlic, crushed

1 stock cube, crushed (quantity for 2 cups liquid)

¼ cup brown sugar or maple syrup

Place the chicken drumsticks in a food-safe plastic bag.

In a bowl, combine the remaining ingredients and mix well until the sugar and stock cube are dissolved, then pour over the chicken. Seal the bag and sit it in a dish or casserole in the refrigerator. Allow to marinate for 4 hours, turning the bag over several times.

When the meat is ready to be cooked, preheat oven to 425°F (220°C). Discard the marinade and place the drumsticks on a greased rack in a roasting pan.

Cook them in the oven for about 30 minutes, until they are brown and the meat is tender, turning them only if necessary to prevent excessive browning.

BACON AND EGG PIE

Rich and satisfying, this pie makes a good hearty centerpiece for an energetic group of picnickers. A layer of sliced ripe tomatoes in the middle of the filling would provide an extra flavor boost, but with or without them, a slice of this pie is great with a dollop of ketchup.

SERVES 6

Rich Pastry (p. 268), or your choice of pastry dough, for a two-crust pie

bacon slices, lean or back, enough to cover your pan area twice

7 large eggs

1 cup green onions, chopped

½ tsp salt

pepper or hot sauce to taste

Make or buy your favorite pastry dough, or try the Rich Pastry recipe. Roll it out to a shape that will cover your pan (a 9" x 9" pan will accommodate this recipe).

Preheat oven to 375°F (190°C).

Place bacon slices in a single layer over the pastry, then crack eggs over the bacon. Pierce the yolks with a fork. Sprinkle green onions and salt over the eggs, and a generous quantity of pepper or hot sauce. Add another layer of bacon, then the top crust.

Bake in the oven for 25 minutes, then reduce heat to 350°F (175°C) for another 15 to 20 minutes. Pastry should be golden brown, and eggs completely set when you insert a cake tester into the center of the pie.

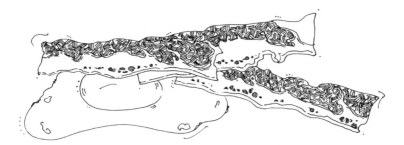

BREADED TOFU PICNIC SLICES

A tasty alternative to cold cuts or other cold meat, this tofu recipe can be prepared the day before and kept refrigerated until picnic time. Children and most adults will enjoy the flavor just as it is, but some heat, such as cayenne, hot sauce, or freshly grated ginger, could be added either to the marinade or to the coating if desired. If you are not a regular user of tofu, buy it in a sealed pack (labelled Extra Firm), rather than loose, to guarantee freshness and quality.

SERVES 6 TO 8

⅓ cup soy sauce (tamari if possible)

¼ cup tomato ketchup

2 tbsp sesame oil

1½ lbs (700 g) extra firm tofu, cut in slices about ¼ inch (0.7cm) thick

1¼ cups (about) fine dry breadcrumbs

¼ cup sesame seeds

Preheat oven to 375°F (190°C).

Combine the soy sauce, ketchup, and sesame oil in a food-safe plastic bag large enough to hold all the tofu slices in its bottom third.

Place the tofu slices in the bag and seal the top, then very gently turn and move the slices until they are all well coated with the marinade. Set aside.

In a bowl, combine the breadcrumbs and sesame seeds and set aside.

Oil a 9" x 13" baking tray. Remove the slices of tofu, one at a time, from the bag and dip them in the breadcrumb/sesame seed mixture. As each slice is coated, place it on the baking tray.

Bake in the oven for 15 minutes, then turn the slices over carefully and bake for 10 minutes more, then remove the slices to a cooling rack. When completely cooled, they can be placed in layers on wax paper in a lidded container and refrigerated.

BREAST OF DUCK RAPIDO

Good quality meat, simply prepared, and you have a recipe for success. Vancouver restaurateur and author Umberto Menghi's mustardy breading is just right for the rich juicy duck breasts.

SERVES 4

4 medium duck breasts

4 cloves garlic, cut in half

salt and black pepper to taste

2 tbsp olive oil

4 tbsp Dijon mustard

2 eggs, beaten

I cup breadcrumbs

Preheat oven to 375°F (190°C).

Make a couple of small incisions on the skin side of each breast and insert the garlic into the meat. Salt and pepper the breasts to taste.

In a sauté pan over medium heat, heat the oil and place the duck breasts in, skin side down. Fry them for 4 to 5 minutes per side, or until they're browned all over. Remove the breasts from the pan and dry them thoroughly with paper towels.

Brush the breasts on all sides with mustard. Place beaten eggs and breadcrumbs in separate flat bowls. Dip each breast first in egg, then in the breadcrumbs.

In a baking dish, place the breasts skin side up and roast in the oven for about 20 minutes. The duck is done when the meat offers some resistance when pressed but still has some give to it.

BROILED CHICKEN

Another very simple way of preparing nutritious finger food for a picnic, this recipe works well if you have an efficient broiling element in your oven. This chicken could be served with a tasty chutney, or a mayonnaise-style sauce enhanced with green herbs, sun-dried tomatoes, and green onion.

SERVES 6

6 whole chicken legs

garlic, crushed (optional)

2 tbsp melted butter or oil

salt and pepper to taste

Set oven to broil.

Rub a little garlic into the pieces of chicken if desired, then brush the pieces of meat with the butter or oil and sprinkle them with salt and pepper. Rub or spray a large shallow broiling pan with a little oil, and place the meat skin side down in it.

Place pan under broiler and broil until the pieces are brown on both sides, turning only once, and keeping the meat about 6 to 8 inches (15 to 20 cm) from the heat source. This process will take about 15 minutes, depending on the heat of the broiler.

Then move the pan to the middle rack, change heat of oven to 325°F (160°C), and bake the chicken until it is tender and completely cooked through (15 to 20 minutes).

BRUNCH BURRITOS

These burritos don't need to be reserved for brunch; they're good any time, and don't require cutlery or plates to be enjoyed alfresco.

SERVES 4

4 large flat breads, soft tortillas or similar

1 large baked potato, diced small

¾ cup hot tomato salsa

4 – 6 large eggs, scrambled in a little butter

1 cup sharp cheese, grated

½ cup cilantro, chopped

black pepper to taste

salt to taste (optional)

Place ¼ of the potato at one end of each tortilla. Drizzle a quarter of the salsa over the potato, and then a quarter of the scrambled egg, ¼ cup of the grated cheese, a quarter of the cilantro, and finally a sprinkle of black pepper. Add salt if desired. (Cheese and salsa are both quite salty, but the egg and potato need some salt for flavor.)

Roll each tortilla firmly, folding the ends in when the roll is half completed. Secure each burrito with a toothpick or wrap firmly in plastic food wrap. Keep cool until ready to eat.

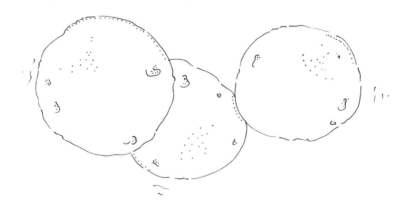

CHEESE AND ONION TART

Another traditional dish, this simple tart is great for picnics. Its flavor can be tweaked by the use of either very old, or quite mild cheese, and by the addition of more cayenne or hot sauce. This tart recipe can also be made into small tarts, using muffin pans, and adjusting the cooking time accordingly.

SERVES 6 TO 8

6 oz (170 g) pastry dough, unsweetened

2 medium parboiled onions, chopped

1 tbsp flour

¼ tsp salt

¼ tsp cayenne pepper or hot sauce

3 – 4 oz (85 – 100 g) medium or old cheddar, grated

2 tbsp milk

Preheat oven to 425°F (220°C).

Roll half of the pastry dough to fit a 10" pie plate. In a bowl, combine the onions, flour, salt, and pepper. Pour mixture on the rolled pastry in the pie plate, and sprinkle the cheese over it, then drizzle the milk evenly over all.

Roll the remaining pastry, cut it into strips, and place them over the pie in a neat lattice pattern.

Bake in the oven for 35 to 40 minutes, making sure it does not get too brown. Serve cold or warm.

FRITTATA WITH MIXED VEGETABLES

The flavor of your frittata can be varied by the use of different cheeses and vegetables. Make sure you include vegetables that will contribute color as well as flavor and texture.

SERVES 4 TO 8

1 large onion, finely chopped

4 cups mixed vegetables, chopped (any combination of green beans, zucchini, carrots, broccoli, cauliflower, snap or snow peas, red, yellow or orange bell peppers)

2 tbsp olive oil

6 eggs, beaten

¼ – ½ cup cheese, grated (freshly grated parmesan is good, or old cheddar)

¼ cup cream or milk

¼ tsp pepper (or more, as desired)

¼ tsp salt

Preheat oven to 350°F (175°C).

The frittata will be served from the pan, which needs to be usable both on the stove top and in the oven.

Divide the chopped vegetables into those that cook quickly and those that need more time. In a large pan over medium heat, sauté the onion in the oil for about 4 minutes.

Add those vegetables that need longer cooking, sauté for 4 more minutes, then add the remaining vegetables and sauté briefly, until all the vegetables are tender.

In a bowl, combine the beaten eggs, cheese, cream, pepper, and salt. Add the mixture to the vegetables, and cook over medium-high heat until the bottom is set.

Place the pan in the oven and bake for 5 to 7 minutes or until the mixture is set all the way through. Allow it to cool to room temperature, but it is best if not refrigerated. Serve it from the pan. This frittata is a main dish for 4 people, but will serve 6 to 8 if it is part of a buffet picnic meal.

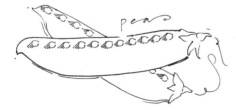

peas

JELLIED SALMON

While Elizabethan cooks needed to boil animal bones and cartilage to produce jellied meats and fish, we can reach for a packet of gelatin, which makes this dish a lot easier to prepare. Note that this recipe calls for enough gelatin to make a very firm aspic, able to be sliced, rather than a somewhat softer dessert-style jelly. Keep it chilled until serving time, when you can turn it out on to a platter and garnish it with lemon wedges, hard-boiled egg wedges, cucumber slices, and some salad greens.

SERVES 6 TO 8

6 thick salmon steaks (between 3 and 4 lbs [1.5 – 2 kg] of fish)

2 cups dry white wine

2 cups water or chicken stock

salt as needed (if you're using water rather than stock, start with 1 tsp)

1 medium onion, cut in pieces

1 lemon, sliced thinly

4 or 5 stems of parsley

4 or 5 stems of thyme (or 1 tsp dried leaves)

1 tbsp peppercorns

½ tsp ground mace

2 envelopes gelatin (or package recommendation for 4 cups liquid)

Chill a deep 5" x 9" loaf pan in the fridge.

Wash the salmon steaks and set them aside. In a large wide pan (big enough to accommodate the fish later), place all other ingredients except gelatin. Over high heat, bring this poaching liquid to the boil, then reduce heat to low and let it simmer for 10 minutes, covered.

Add the salmon steaks, making sure all are in the liquid. Over medium heat, bring the pan liquid back to a slow simmer, reduce heat again to low, and let the fish gently poach, without a lid, until it is cooked through (15 minutes). Turn the steaks after 7 minutes of poaching.

Remove the fish to a plate and strain the liquid, discarding the seasonings. Measure 3 cups of liquid into a small saucepan and discard any remaining. Taste and adjust for flavor, adding salt and lemon juice as desired.

While the fish is cooling, bring the liquid to a boil, then remove from the heat and sprinkle the gelatin over the top of it. Stir it well, until all the gelatin is dissolved. Set the liquid aside to cool as quickly as possible by sitting it, in its saucepan, in a large bowl or sink of ice water. Stir it occasionally and do not let it set!

While it is cooling, skin the fish, debone it carefully, and cut or break it into small pieces. Place it in the fridge. As soon as the gelatin mixture is at room temperature, arrange the salmon pieces in the chilled pan, and pour the liquid over the fish. Refrigerate the jellied salmon overnight, and keep it well chilled until ready to eat.

JUMBO SHRIMP (PRAWNS) SAUTÉED IN LEMON BUTTER

Whether you call them jumbo shrimp or prawns depends on where you live rather than what creatures you're cooking. Either way they are an expensive treat, but so delicious that they deserve a star billing from time to time. Cooking them this way brings out their fabulous flavor without overpowering it, and the shrimp can be eaten very pleasantly straight from the container they are carried in, using only your fingers, or perhaps a toothpick.

SERVES 4

1 lb (450 g) jumbo shrimp tails, shelled

½ cup butter

¼ cup lemon juice

zest of 1 lemon

salt and pepper to taste

Wash and pat the shrimp dry. In a sauté pan over medium heat, melt the butter then cook the shrimp until just done, opaque and firm to the touch. Do not cook them for more than a few minutes.

Add the lemon juice and zest and stir into the pan juices, then remove the shrimp with a slotted spoon and set aside, while the pan juices bubble and reduce.

When the liquid is reduced to a syrupy thickness, add a sprinkle of salt and some pepper, remove from the heat, and toss the cooked shrimp in it, making sure each piece gets well covered. Place the shrimp in a container and allow them to cool, then chill until ready to eat.

KID KEBABS

To use toothpicks or skewers safely while eating, children need to be well-supervised. That said, they really enjoy the idea of being able to help themselves to whatever tidbits they fancy, and create their own ready-to-eat shish kebabs. To serve Kid Kebabs, arrange all the items you plan to provide in small containers on a tray or in a shallow box, provide a small container of sturdy toothpicks or small bamboo skewers, and let the children help themselves.

The following list is a guide only, because you need to suit your items to the children you are serving (who will appreciate the chance to make creative suggestions ahead of time too). All the items should be bite-sized at most, and soft enough to skewer easily. You may choose to serve a dipping sauce, which could be anything: yogurt, soy sauce seasoned with a little ginger or garlic, peanut butter with orange or pineapple juice, ketchup and sour cream — whatever your children might enjoy.

hot dog wieners, split lengthwise and cut in small chunks

tofu chunks, marinated for an hour or two in tamari soy sauce or half soy sauce and half ketchup or a thick mixture of peanut butter and orange juice

cheese cubes

veggie wiener chunks

omelette chunks, plain or cheese

cherry tomatoes

grapes

pineapple chunks

apple chunks

dried apricot or pitted prune halves

tiny new potatoes steamed and chilled, halved if necessary

cooked carrot chunks

button mushroom caps, cooked or raw

lupini or broad beans, cooked

cucumber chunks

small florets of raw or cooked broccoli or cauliflower

banana chunks

LETTUCE WRAPS

Large leaves of iceberg lettuce create a delectable finger food out of a Thai-style delicacy that you'd otherwise have to eat with a fork. A good-sized iceberg, carefully taken apart, yields about 10 leaves large enough to use in this way. The filling can be packed in a lidded container, the noodles left in their bag of purchase, and the wraps assembled at the picnic as people are ready to eat them.

MAKES ABOUT 10 WRAPS

1 medium onion, finely chopped

2 or more Thai or other hot peppers, trimmed and seeded, or 2 or more tsp chili flakes

3 tbsp oil, divided (only 1 tbsp of oil needed if you are using chicken)

1 8-oz (227-ml) can peeled water chestnuts, whole or sliced, finely chopped

1 14-fl oz (398-ml) can unsweetened pineapple chunks (reserve ¼ cup of the juice), coarsely chopped

2 tsp fresh ginger, grated

2 tsp cornstarch

¼ cup soy sauce

1 tbsp sugar

3 tbsp orange juice, or 1 tbsp frozen orange juice concentrate with 2 tbsp water

In a medium pot over medium heat, sauté the onions and hot peppers in 1 tbsp oil, until the onions start to caramelize.

Add the water chestnuts, pineapple chunks, and ginger.

In a small bowl, mix the cornstarch with the soy sauce, reserved pineapple juice, orange juice, and sugar until it is lump free, then stir it quickly into the vegetable mixture. Heat until thickened, stirring constantly. As soon as it has come to the boil, remove from the heat and prepare the tofu.

In a pan over medium-high heat, heat 2 tbsp oil and fry the tofu cubes until browned. Drain them on a paper towel before adding them to the hot mixture, along with the mint and cilantro. If using the chicken option, add the chicken pieces instead of the fried tofu.

iceberg lettuce

12 oz (350 g) extra firm tofu, diced small (about 3 cups)

or equal quantity of cooked chicken meat, finely chopped

¼ cup each of cilantro and mint, chopped small

leaves of 1 iceberg lettuce, washed and dried

3 cups fried steamed noodles

Dipping Sauce

¼ cup soy sauce

1 tbsp orange concentrate

1 tsp seasoned rice vinegar

½ tsp fresh ginger, grated

1 tbsp mint, chopped

1 tbsp cilantro, chopped

1 tbsp green onion, chopped

Taste the mixture and adjust seasoning if desired. When ready to eat, each diner takes a lettuce leaf, puts in some noodles and a spoonful of the tofu mixture, and wraps the lettuce leaf to make a neat parcel, which may be dipped in the sauce below, or any other tangy Asian-style sauce.

LOIN OF PORK WITH PRUNES (SWEDISH STYLE)

Prunes marry extraordinarily well with pork, their sweet intensity a foil for the rich meat flavor, and the loins slice nicely when the meat is allowed to cool completely.

SERVES 6 TO 8

2 filets of pork, about 1½ lbs (675 g) each

16 large pitted prunes, chopped

1 tsp salt

½ tsp pepper

1 tbsp vegetable oil

1 cup vegetable or chicken stock

Cut the filets down their length to butterfly them. Make sure you do not cut them all the way through.

Arrange the prune pieces evenly inside each cut filet. Sprinkle with salt and pepper. Use thin string or strong thread to tie the filets closed.

In a large skillet or a Dutch oven over medium high heat, heat the oil and brown the filets on all sides (about 15 minutes in all). Pour ½ cup stock over, reduce heat to low, and simmer covered for about 1 hour, adding a little more stock as needed to keep liquid in the bottom of the pan. Let cool completely and cut into slices.

MILLET PIE

My first experience of Millet Pie was near sunset, at a music festival in midsummer. Someone had set up a little stall with all sorts of vegetarian delights for sale, and I decided to try one of the big wedges of savory pie. One mouthful and I was an addict, but it took me several attempts at home to make it myself, to get the flavor and texture just right. This is a hearty pie, good warm or cold.

SERVES 6

pastry dough for a two-crust pie, Rich
  Pastry (p. 268) or see the recipe for
  Vegetable Anise Pie pastry (p. 245)

1 cup millet

2½ cups water

½ tsp salt

3 medium leeks (white parts and tender
  green leaves), washed and finely
  chopped

2 tbsp butter

2 large mashing potatoes, peeled and
  chopped into 6 or 8 pieces

1 tsp salt

1 tsp dried thyme leaves

1 tsp lemon pepper

In a pot over high heat, combine the millet, water, and ½ tsp salt. Bring to a boil, then reduce heat to low and simmer covered for 15 to 20 minutes, or until the grains are soft but not mushy. Add a little more water if necessary during the cooking, and drain as soon as it is done.

While the millet is cooking, in a pan over medium-high heat, sauté the leeks in the butter until they are translucent and limp (partial cooking only). Set them aside.

While the leeks and millet are cooking, in a pot of water over high heat, bring the potatoes and salt to a boil, reduce heat to low, and simmer until they are soft enough to mash. They should be cooked in about 8 to 10 minutes. Drain them well.

Mash the potatoes, but not really smooth, or chop them with two knives. Add the thyme and lemon pepper, then the leeks with any juice from the pan, and the drained millet. Mix this filling well, and taste to adjust seasoning, adding salt and pepper as desired.

Preheat oven to 450°F (230°C).

When the filling is cool, prepare the pie crusts for a 10" pie dish. Spoon the filling into the bottom crust, place the top crust over, and seal the edges with a little water. Cut 2 or 3 steam vent holes in the top crust, and flute the edges. Bake in the oven for 12 to 15 minutes, then reduce heat to 350°F (175°C) for 30 minutes, or until the crust is golden brown. This pie is really good with tomato sauce, ketchup, hot sauce or a spicy chutney.

NORI NUT ROLLS

A friend gave me this recipe and suggested I soak the nuts for 8 hours then let them dry again for 8 hours, to get their juices flowing, as it were. Although I have to confess I seldom do that, it does alter slightly the texture of the nut rolls, and apparently adds much to their nutritional value. Either way, this is a nourishing and high protein dish, satisfying and portable for a picnic. Nori is a seaweed, used to make sushi rolls.

MAKES ABOUT **48** PIECES

I cup almonds, with skins

I cup hazelnuts

½ cup tahini

I red bell pepper, seeded and chopped

I clove garlic

½ cup parsley, chopped

I tsp dried basil

I tsp dried oregano

I stalk celery, chopped

I large carrot, chopped

tamari soy sauce to taste

6 – 8 nori sheets

I cup alfalfa sprouts

In a food processor or blender, process the almonds and hazelnuts to a fine mince. Add tahini, pepper, garlic, and herbs, and process to produce a thick paste.

Set aside in a bowl, then process the celery and carrot finely. Combine the two mixtures together, using a little tamari soy sauce to enhance the flavor and soften the mixture a little as needed.

Place as much of the nut mixture onto each sheet of nori as you wish, for thin or fat rolls, adding a tbsp or two of sprouts before rolling the nori into a neat roll, and sealing the edge with a little moistening of water. A sushi mat will help the rolling but it will work even without a mat.

Wrap the rolls in plastic wrap and refrigerate them for an hour or two before cutting them into bite-sized pieces. This recipe makes 3 to 4 cups of nut paste. An average-sized roll would need ½ to ¾ cup of paste, and cuts nicely into 8 pieces.

OLD-FASHIONED CORNISH PASTIES

A staple of brown bag lunches in the days when Mom baked at home while the rest of the family headed out to work or school for the day, pasties are the perfect meal to go. Cornish pasties traditionally include potato, turnip, and meat, but you can vary the proportions according to what you have and what you like.

SERVES 4

8 oz (230 g) flaky or Rich Pastry (p. 268) or any other unsweetened pastry dough

8 oz (230 g) lean round steak, cut fine but not ground

1 medium potato, peeled and cut into small cubes

1 medium white turnip, peeled and cut into small cubes

1 small onion, diced

1 tbsp flour

pepper to taste

2 tsp thyme leaves

2 tsp salt

1 tbsp water

1 small egg, beaten with 2 tbsp water (to seal and brush tops of pasties)

Preheat oven to 400°F (200°C).

Cut the pastry into four pieces and roll each into a circle about 5 to 6 inches (12 to 15 cm) in diameter. You can use a saucer or side plate to get the size and shape.

In a bowl, mix the meat, vegetables, flour, pepper, thyme, salt, and water together, and divide into four portions.

Place one portion of filling in the centre of each pastry round. Wet the edges of the circles of pastry with a smear of the egg/water mixture, then bring them together in two halves so that the join line is along the top of the pasty. Pinch closed with finger and thumb, making sure the join line is well sealed.

Prick the pasties on each side of the centre join with a fork. Brush the top surfaces lightly with the egg/water mixture.

Bake on a cookie sheet or shallow oven pan in the oven for about 30 minutes. Test carefully with a thin bladed knife or cake tester, to make sure inside is soft.

OXFORD KATES SAUSAGES

These sausages were served in Elizabethan times, typical of the sort of skinless sausages that would be made at home and eaten right away, rather than smoked and kept. The original of our recipe called for a great deal more butter than modern cooks would care to use, but the result is still delicious with the smaller amount specified here.

SERVES 6 TO 8

2 lb (1 kg) lean pork meat (or veal)

¼ lb (120 g) butter or suet

1 tsp black pepper, crushed or
   coarsely ground

¼ – ½ tsp ground cloves

1 tsp mace

2 tbsp finely shredded fresh sage
   (or dried sage leaves, crumbled)

2½ tsp sea salt, or to taste

3 egg whites

2 egg yolks

To chop the meat fine, use a food processor in brief pulses, so that the meat is not mashed, or use two sharp knives.

In a bowl, combine all the ingredients except the eggs, then mix in the lightly beaten eggs until the mixture is smooth and well-blended.

In a non-stick pan over medium high heat, fry about 1 tsp of the mixture, then taste to adjust the spices and salt as necessary. Shape the rest of the mixture into sausages about the length and thickness of your largest finger. Fry them over medium high heat until they are nice and brown. Serve them with honey mustard.

PEPPERS STUFFED WITH CORN, POTATO, EGG, AND VIOLET SALAD

James Barber, TV's "The Urban Peasant," makes simple food seem like gourmet extravagance. This dish has loads of eye appeal, and it's worth going out of your way to get fresh organic violets, just to see your guests react to the outrageous colors of these delectable stuffed peppers.

SERVES 4

1 each of red, green, yellow, and orange bell peppers

2 fresh cooked corn cobs

2 cups cooked new potatoes, diced

4 hard-boiled eggs, chopped

2 sticks celery, finely chopped

½ red bell pepper, finely diced

½ green bell pepper, finely diced

½ yellow bell pepper, finely diced

½ onion, finely chopped

1 tsp capers, finely chopped

½ cup mayonnaise

½ tsp curry powder

salt and pepper to taste

1 bunch fresh organic violets (garnish)

1 bunch watercress

Cut a slice off the top of each pepper and remove the seeds. Cut the sides to resemble flower petals and set aside. Cut the kernels off the cooked corn and, in a bowl, mix with the rest of the ingredients, reserving the violets and watercress. Stuff the peppers with the mixture, garnish with violets, and lay on a bed of watercress.

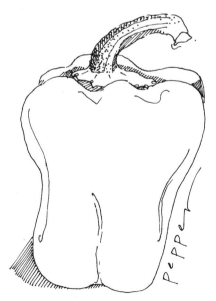

Pepper

POTATO PIZZA

James Barber's recipe for pizza dough saves mucking about with yeast and kneading and all that, but still produces a tender, delicious pizza crust. This garlicky potato pizza will go down well with the brunch crowd, but it's good any time of day or night.

SERVES 4

I cup flour

I tsp baking soda

I tsp cream of tartar

I tsp salt

¾ cup milk soured with I tbsp vinegar

olive oil

Topping

I lb (450 g) potatoes, washed and trimmed, sliced wafer-thin

4 cloves garlic, finely chopped

olive oil

salt and pepper to taste

I tbsp fresh rosemary

2 tbsp parmesan cheese

Preheat oven to 475°F (240°C).

For the crust: sift the flour, baking soda, cream of tartar, and salt into a bowl. Add the sour milk and stir to make a soft dough. On a floured board, knead lightly to make a ball. Halve the ball and roll into 2 circles. Place both on a dry, flour-dusted baking sheet. Ridge the edges and brush with olive oil.

For the topping: arrange the potato slices in overlapping circles over the dough (like a French apple tart). When the dough is completely covered, scatter the garlic over both pizzas, brush with olive oil and sprinkle with salt, pepper, rosemary, and parmesan. Bake in the oven for 20 minutes.

QUICHE LORRAINE

You will probably need to double the recipe and make two, because everyone will want second helpings!

SERVES 4

1 recipe Rich Pastry (p. 268) or
   short pastry dough, for a 9"
   single-crust pie

2 eggs

1 cup half-and-half (milk and cream)

1 cup cheese (any firm, tasty cheese you
   like), grated

4 slices back bacon, diced

pepper to taste

Preheat oven to 425°F (220°C).

Line a deep quiche dish (7" diameter) with
the pastry.

In a bowl, beat the eggs with the milk mixture, then
add cheese and bacon. Grind some pepper into the
mixture then pour it slowly and carefully into the
pastry-lined dish.

Bake in the oven for 15 minutes, then lower heat to
350°F (175°C) and bake for 25 to 30 minutes
more, until the quiche is golden brown and the
filling is well set.

ROAST CHICKEN WITH TARRAGON

What could be easier and more delicious than a whole roast chicken as the centerpiece of a casual picnic? Especially if you can purchase a grain-fed chicken, so flavorful and juicy. The distinctive flavor of tarragon here is delectable and the butter keeps the chicken moist during roasting.

Serves 4 to 6

3 – 3½ lb (1.5 – 2 kg) chicken

salt and pepper to taste

2 tbsp soft butter

2 tbsp fresh tarragon leaves, finely chopped

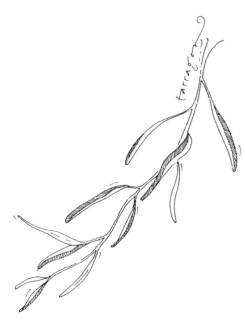

Preheat oven to 350°F (175°C).

Wash and pat the chicken dry and sprinkle the cavity with salt and pepper. Take a piece of foil large enough to wrap the chicken in, and rub a little butter on it where the chicken will sit. Place the chicken on the foil.

In a small pot over medium-high heat, melt the butter and add the tarragon, then brush half of it over the skin of the chicken, and distribute the rest in the cavity. Wrap the chicken and place it in a roasting pan.

Roast in the oven for 45 minutes then open the foil and continue cooking for another 15 minutes to allow the chicken to crisp up a little. Check for doneness, then continue cooking as necessary with the foil open until the chicken juices run clear and the legs move easily. Let cool, then wrap it and refrigerate it until picnic time. It can be prepared a day ahead.

ROMAN MEATLOAF

This tasty meatloaf can be served warm or cold, and it can also be used on top of bruschetta. Joyce Goldstein, prolific and award-winning U.S. food writer and former restaurateur, recommends a tomato sauce with the meatloaf if you serve it hot, but for picnic purposes it would be excellent cold, and does not need the sauce. She adds that at Bottega Bleve, where this recipe originates, it is often served with a plate of concia, sautéed zucchini with lemon juice, and chopped mint.

SERVES 6

1 lb (450 g) ground beef

¾ cup fresh breadcrumbs, soaked in beef stock or water then squeezed dry

½ cup flat-leaf parsley, chopped

2 or 3 cloves garlic, minced

½ cup onion, grated (optional)

1 or 2 eggs, lightly beaten

salt and black pepper to taste

nutmeg, grated (optional)

3 hard-boiled eggs

1½ cups roasted bell peppers, diced

2 cups tomato sauce (Goldstein provides a recipe in her book, *Enoteca*, or you may use a commercially prepared substitute if you decide to serve the meatloaf with sauce)

Preheat the oven to 350°F (175°C).

In a bowl, combine the beef, breadcrumbs, parsley, garlic, and onion. Mix in 1 egg; if the mixture is too dry, add the second egg. Season with the salt, pepper, and nutmeg. In a small lightly oiled pan over medium high heat, fry a nugget of the mixture in oil to test the seasoning.

Form half of the mixture into a rectangle and place in an oiled baking pan. Make an indentation lengthwise down the center and place the hard-boiled eggs in a row in the indentation. Distribute the diced peppers over the eggs. Cover the eggs with the remaining ground meat mixture, encasing them fully. If desired, brush the top with a bit of the sauce.

Bake in the oven for about 1¼ hours or until cooked through when tested with a knife. Remove from the oven and let rest for 10 minutes. Meanwhile, reheat the sauce. Cut the meat loaf into thick slices and serve with the warm sauce. You can also serve the meat loaf at room temperature with or without the sauce.

SALAD ROLLS

*These are my own take on Vietnamese Salad Rolls, which use grated tofu rather than meat or fish,
plus tahini or peanut butter and sesame seeds to enhance their nutritional value.*

MAKES 8 ROLLS

8 oz (225 g) vermicelli noodles

¼ cup sesame seeds

8 oz (225 g) cooked fish, chicken,
    shrimp, or tofu

1 cup carrot, finely shredded

½ cup tahini or unsalted peanut butter

½ cup tamari soy sauce

¼ cup water

1 tsp honey, or more if desired

2 tbsp sesame oil

8 circular sheets of rice noodle

8 green onions, trimmed

8 lettuce leaves

In a pot over high heat, bring 6 cups water to a boil,
then turn off heat and add the vermicelli noodles.
Allow them to soak for 5 to 7 minutes, then drain,
rinse in cool water, and drain again. Cut them a little
to make them easier to handle, and set aside.

In a dry pan over medium high heat, roast the
sesame seeds until they are pale brown.

In a large bowl, combine the noodles, sesame seeds,
fish or tofu (if using tofu, prepare it according to
the note on following page), and carrot.

In another bowl, mix the tahini, tamari, water, honey,
and sesame oil together until smooth. Set half aside
to use later as dipping sauce, and add the other half
to the noodle mixture.

To assemble the rolls, fill a large bowl with very hot
water. Holding one rice circle at one edge, immerse it
in the hot water, then turn it, until it is all wet. This
takes only 5 seconds. Set it on the work surface. It
will continue to soften as you shape the roll. As soon
as the rice circle is soft enough, fold over the first
third of it, and on this double thickness place a
lettuce leaf, and an eighth portion of the noodle

filling. Fold the ends of the rice circle in a little and place the green onion on top of the filling so that it will protrude from one end when the roll is made. Roll firmly and place with the edge down in a serving container. Repeat the process with the other 7 rolls.

Store the remainder of the sauce in a small lidded container, and use it for a dipping sauce when the rolls are served.

Note on preparation of tofu:

8 oz (225 g) firm tofu, grated

1 tbsp oil

2 tbsp tamari soy sauce

2 tsp honey or maple syrup

2 tsp sesame oil

In a pan over medium high heat, sauté the tofu with the oil for 5 to 7 minutes. Remove from heat and add the tamari, sweetener, and sesame oil. (This can be messy as the liquid hits the hot pan!) Return to the heat briefly and allow the tofu to absorb the sauce.

SALMON CAKES

This recipe is equally good with canned tuna.

SERVES 2 TO 4

7 oz (200 g) potatoes, cooked with salt

1 tbsp butter

2 tbsp milk

1 tsp onion, finely chopped

2 cups canned salmon, drained well

1 egg, separated

salt, pepper, and cayenne pepper
   to taste

2 tsp lemon juice, or to taste

breadcrumbs for coating

oil for frying

Mash the potatoes well with the butter, milk, and onion. Remove any skin from the fish and break it up with a fork. (The canned bones, well mashed, add nutrition and are soft enough not to be noticed in the mix.) Set the fish aside.

In a saucepan over medium heat, reheat the mashed potato mixture. When thoroughly heated, add the fish and the yolk of the egg and mix well. Continue cooking until the mixture is very hot and thick. Add salt, pepper, cayenne, and lemon juice to taste.

Spoon the mixture onto a buttered plate to cool, smoothing it round and flat. Let cool, then divide into 8 to 10 portions and shape into small flat circles. Brush the cakes with the beaten egg white, and coat them in dry breadcrumbs. In a pan over medium high heat, fry both sides in a little oil. Use an oil sprayer if you have one. Serves 2 to 4 people as a main course, more if smaller cakes are made and served as appetizers or part of a picnic buffet.

SLICED MEAT ROLLS

Cold cuts, including sliced ham, various sausages, and pressed and smoked meats, can all be served with each whole slice wrapped around a sliver of dill pickle, or a couple of sweet gherkins. The pickles need to be cut lengthwise into 4 or 6, and then, for easier eating, the rolls can be cut into bite-sized pieces, each secured if necessary with a toothpick.

Another way to make meat rolls is to spread a thin layer of cream cheese over meat slices and roll them firmly. A tablespoon or two of hot chutney or tomato paste, or of finely diced and drained pineapple or strawberries mixed in with the cream cheese works particularly well with cold cuts served in this way. Fresh green herbs are also delicious in meat rolls with cream cheese. Basil, mint, chives, or thyme all add distinctive flavor, making plain ol' cold cuts a more interesting picnic offering.

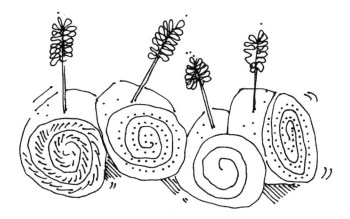

SOUCED FISH

Many fish recipes from Elizabethan recipe books call for vinegar or wine, salt, and spices, presumably to counter the effects of time and warmth on unrefrigerated fish. The fact that souced fish still appears in recipe books of quite recent vintage proves it also tastes good!

SERVES 6

2 lbs (900 g) skinned white, firm-fleshed fish (e.g., halibut, snapper, cod)

1 large sweet onion, thinly sliced

1 tsp whole peppercorns

8 – 10 whole cloves

3 – 4 sprigs fresh thyme

2 bay leaves

3 – 4 sprigs parsley

¼ tsp cayenne or 2 shakes of hot sauce

½ tsp salt

1¼ cups white vinegar

2 tbsp water

1 lemon, cut into thin wedges (garnish)

several sprigs parsley (garnish)

black pepper to taste

Preheat oven to 350°F (175°C).

Wash and dry the fish, and cut into pieces large enough for 1 per person.

Place fish in an oven-proof casserole with a close-fitting lid, large enough so that the fish is one layer deep. Place onion slices over the fish, then add the other ingredients, except for the vinegar, water, and garnishes, distributing them evenly.

In a bowl, mix the vinegar and water and pour it over the fish. Bake in the oven, tightly covered, for 20 to 25 minutes. Remove and let cool. The fish will continue to cook in the hot broth so make sure it is only very lightly cooked when you take it out of the oven.

Remove the fish from the liquid and seasonings, which should be discarded, and arrange it in a serving container with some fresh parsley sprigs, lemon wedges, and a sprinkle of black pepper. Keep the fish cool till serving.

TURNOVERS

Turnovers are the ultimate finger food; their tasty fillings can be as varied as your imagination can make them, and their tender crusts hold everything safe inside until you are ready to eat! Here is a dough that, although it requires yeast, is relatively easy to make, with help from your microwave oven. (It is also an excellent pizza crust.) For turnovers, it produces crusts that are not too hard but hold their shape for the duration of a picnic. Warning: no turnover crust can withstand a sloppy filling for very long, so select your filling with care!

MAKES 6

Crust

1 cup warm water

2 tsp fast-acting yeast

1 tbsp sugar

1½ tsp salt

2 tbsp vegetable oil

1¼ cups unbleached flour

up to 2 cups whole wheat flour, or enough to make a stiff dough

1 cup boiling water in a microwave-safe cup or small jug

In a large bowl, combine the warm water, yeast, sugar, salt, and oil. Beat in the unbleached flour to make a smooth mixture. Add the whole wheat flour ½ cup at a time, until a stiff dough is achieved.

Turn the dough out onto a floured counter top and knead for a few minutes until smooth. Transfer to a lightly oiled bowl and cover with a clean dry cloth.

Place the cup of boiling water in the microwave oven and put the covered bowl of dough in beside it. The boiling water adds necessary moisture as the dough is in the oven proving. Microwave the dough for 10 minutes at your oven's lowest heat. (I learned the hard way that the Defrost setting is much warmer than Low.)

After heating, keep the microwave oven door closed, and let the dough sit for another 10 minutes. When you remove it from the oven, it should have approximately doubled in size.

Suggested fillings:

I cup sweet corn kernels, canned or frozen

1½ – 2 cups mashed potatoes

¼ cup green herbs (chives, parsley, thyme, basil, green onions), chopped

½ cup sharp cheddar cheese, grated

hot sauce

1½ cups cooked potatoes, cut into small cubes (or mixed potatoes and carrots)

I cup onion, sautéed

I cup sharp cheddar cheese, grated

½ cup bacon bits or soy bits

I cup leek, sautéed

I cup mushrooms, sautéed

1½ cups ricotta cheese

salt and pepper to taste

3 cups mixed peppers, including some hot ones, sautéed

½ cup thick tomato sauce

2½ cups ricotta cheese

½ cup parmesan cheese, grated

½ cup pine nuts

¼ cup fresh basil, chopped

I tsp garlic, crushed

3 – 4 cups pre-prepared chili

3 – 4 cups any Indian-style curried meat or vegetables

2 cups cooked meat (chicken, beef, pork), diced

I cup seasoned mashed potatoes

½ cup onion, sautéed

¼ cup mixed green herbs

pepper to taste

Gently squeeze and press it thin for use as required. This quantity of dough makes 6 turnovers.

Preheat oven to 400°F (200°C).

To shape the turnovers, divide the proved dough into 6 pieces, and press each one out into a thin round crust. Place ¼ to ½ cup filling on one half of each circle, leaving I inch (2.5 cm) around the edge of the filled half. Moisten the edge of each circle with water, fold in half over the filling, and press the edges until they are well-sealed. Cut a couple of steam vents in the top of each turnover, and place on a flat baking pan that is lightly sprinkled with flour or cornmeal.

Bake in the oven for 20 to 25 minutes.

VEGETABLE ANISE PIE

Don't be put off by the seemingly mundane ingredients for this pie. It's amazingly good, with subtle flavors and pleasing textures, transforming humble cabbage into a gourmet feast.

SERVES 6

Pastry dough for a 2-crust pie, such as Rich Pastry (p. 268), or the one below

½ medium head of cabbage, finely shredded

2 large carrots, grated

1 medium fennel bulb, finely shredded

¼ cup butter

6 tbsp flour

4 tbsp milk or cream

1 tsp salt

Prepare the pastry for a 10" pie dish. Preheat oven to 425°F (220°C).

In a large pot or deep pan over medium-high heat, melt the butter and sauté the vegetables until they are soft but not completely cooked. Sprinkle the flour over them, stir in quickly, then add the milk or cream and blend the ingredients well. Add the salt, then taste and adjust seasonings if desired.

Let filling cool before spooning into bottom crust, then cover with remaining pastry. Bake in the oven for 12 to 15 minutes, then reduce heat to 350°F (175°C) and bake for about 30 minutes more, or until the pie is golden brown. This pie is delicious warm or cool.

Whole Wheat Pie Crust

1 cup whole wheat cake and pastry flour

1 cup white flour

⅔ cup of shortening or butter

½ tsp salt

ice water to blend

Sift the flours and salt, and cut in the shortening or butter until the mixture looks like coarse cornmeal. Sprinkle ice water over it, tablespoonful by tablespoonful, just enough to help the dough adhere together into a soft ball.

Knead a few times, then chill for about 30 minutes, well-wrapped.

BARBECUE

HOW TO GRILL THE PERFECT STEAK

The late David Veljacic, a Vancouver firefighter and internationally renowned captain of the grill, was the author of The Fire Chef. *The book really says everything there is worth saying on the subject; if you have any aspirations as a grill rider, go buy the book. Here are David's modest notes on how to achieve barbecue perfection.*

6-oz (170-g) filets mignons, 1 inch (2½ cm) thick

Bring the steaks to room temperature.

Season the steaks with sea salt and tellicherry pepper, a meat seasoning rub or a no-salt seasoning. Let the steaks sit while you preheat the barbecue to medium to high (350 to 400°F/150 to 200°C).

Place the steaks on the grill directly over the heat. Close the lid. After about 1 minute, flip the steaks. Close the lid. Continue to turn the steaks every minute for 6 minutes.

By this time the meat will be cooked between rare and medium. If you want a medium steak, grill for 2 minutes more on each side.

Don't use a knife to test for doneness because you will lose the juices. Learn to test by pressing the meat with your finger. When meat is raw, a finger indentation will come up slowly. The indentation will rise faster as the meat progresses through the stages of doneness. Eventually the meat will not hold an indentation, at which point it is overcooked.

BASIC BARBECUE SAUCE

Fire Chef David Veljacic's standard approach to a sauce used in the final minutes of barbecuing or as a dip for cooked meats.

3 cups ketchup

1 cup brown sugar

½ cup vinegar

2 tbsp chili powder

2 tbsp garlic powder

1 tbsp Worcestershire sauce

1 tbsp black pepper

1 tbsp salt

1 tbsp savory powder

½ tsp ginger powder

½ tsp cayenne powder

In a stainless steel pot over medium high heat, combine all the ingredients, bring to a boil, and stir well. Reduce heat to low and simmer for about 30 minutes, blending and stirring often.

BARBECUED BUTTERFLIED LAMB LEG

This delicious recipe is a celebration in itself. A large lamb leg is a luxury, but cooked this way, it's one you won't regret splurging on. It is not intrinsically difficult to butterfly a leg of lamb at home; however, a good butcher can generally do it more quickly and efficiently than the home cook. Once the meat is opened out in this manner, it is a great candidate for the barbecue grill.

SERVES 8 TO 10

4 – 4.5-lb (around 2-kg) lamb leg, bone removed, butterflied

3 tbsp soy sauce

3 tbsp sherry

2 cloves garlic, crushed

1 tbsp fresh ginger finely grated

2 tsp wasabi powder, or
½ tsp cayenne pepper

Pat the lamb dry with paper towel and lay it out flat. In a bowl, combine the remaining ingredients and spread the mixture over all the surfaces of the meat. Place the meat in a food-safe plastic bag and tie it closed. Refrigerate for 3 to 4 hours, turning the bag over several times during this time.

Barbecue the meat on a grill over medium heat for approximately 50 minutes, about 8 inches (20 cm) from the heat source, turning it every 8 to 10 minutes to avoid burning. To be at its best the lamb should still be pink in the middle, but if you want it well-done, it may take another 20 minutes or more.

BARBECUED LEMON CHICKEN

Anne Lindsay, Canada's diva of Heart-Smart cuisine, combines simplicity and wonderful flavor in this healthy barbecue choice. Grain-fed or free-range chicken will add to the good taste.

SERVES 4

4 boneless, skinless chicken breasts

juice of 1 lemon

2 tsp olive oil

2 cloves garlic, minced

1 tsp dried oregano

pinch cayenne pepper

In a shallow dish, arrange chicken in single layer.

In a bowl, combine the lemon juice, oil, garlic, oregano, and cayenne, and mix well. Pour mixture over chicken and turn to coat both sides. Let stand at room temperature for 20 minutes or cover and refrigerate for up to 6 hours.

On a greased grill, cook chicken over medium heat for 4 to 5 minutes on each side or until meat is no longer pink inside.

BARBECUED MUSHROOM CAPS WITH SUN-DRIED TOMATO AND HERB DRESSING

A tasty and quick-cooking appetizer that will whet the appetite with its aroma alone. Prepare the mushrooms and the stuffing ahead of time, and fill the caps just before you place them on the grill.

MAKES 12 PIECES

1 cup fresh breadcrumbs (see note)

3 tbsp oil-packed sun-dried tomatoes, drained and finely chopped

1 clove garlic, pressed or minced

3 tbsp minced parsley

1 tbsp fresh basil leaves, minced

½ tsp cayenne pepper (or more)

2 tbsp melted butter (optional)

12 large white mushrooms, brushed or washed and stems removed

1 egg

In a bowl, combine all the ingredients except the mushrooms and egg, and mix well.

Just before grilling time, break the egg into the stuffing mixture, and combine thoroughly. Fill the mushroom caps with the stuffing, then sit them, stuffing side up, on an oiled grill over medium high heat, until the mushrooms are soft and juicy and the stuffing heated through. Serve immediately.

Note: To prepare fresh breadcrumbs, leave several slices of whole-wheat bread to dry out a little for a few hours. In a food processor, process them to a fine crumb and measure required quantity. Any remaining crumbs can be frozen in an airtight bag and used at a later time.

BARBECUED PORK CHOPS

Great on the barbecue with a little oil and some lemon juice, pork chops should be cooked through before being served. Butterflied, they will cook more quickly, but many people believe that the flavor is better if they are cooked with the bone still on.

SERVES 4

4 lean pork chops

2 tbsp vegetable oil

¼ cup lemon juice

½ tsp dried sage leaves, crumbled

salt and pepper to taste

Pat the chops dry and place them on a greased grill over medium high heat. In a bowl, combine the remaining ingredients and baste the chops with the mixture, turning them every 5 to 7 minutes until they are cooked through.

BARBECUED STEAK WITH TARRAGON MARINADE

Use the following recipe to marinate steaks for several hours before cooking. Use additional marinade to baste the steaks as you grill them over the barbecue to the desired level of doneness. (See David Veljacic's How to Grill the Perfect Steak, p. 247.)

SERVES 4 TO 6

1 steak per person (sirloin, T-bone, porterhouse, club, or any of the tenderloin or filet steaks)

Marinade

2 tbsp fresh tarragon leaves, finely chopped

4 tbsp fresh lemon juice

¼ cup green onions, including some of the green tops, finely diced

2 cloves garlic, minced

1 cup olive oil

1 cup red wine

1 tbsp salt

1 – 2 tsp black pepper

In a bowl, combine all the marinade ingredients. Pour mixture over the steaks and refrigerate or keep over ice until close to cooking time.

BARBECUED TOFU KEBABS

Serve these vegetarian kebabs with a couple of sauces on the side, a spicy one (see recipe on next page) and a milder one, maybe a mango chutney.

SERVES 4

½ cup olive oil

6 tbsp lemon juice

2 tbsp soy sauce

½ tsp black peppercorns, crushed

zest of 1 lemon

2 tbsp parsley or cilantro, finely minced

1 lb (450 g) extra-firm tofu, cut into bite-size pieces

16 small mushrooms, brushed or washed and stems removed

16 cherry tomatoes

16 chunks of Japanese eggplant (3 or 4 eggplants)

In a bowl, mix the oil, lemon juice, soy sauce, pepper, lemon zest, and parsley or cilantro and add the tofu and prepared vegetables, making sure all the pieces are exposed to the marinade. Cover and refrigerate for 1 or 2 hours or until ready to use, turning occasionally.

Thread chunks of tofu, mushrooms, tomatoes, and eggplant pieces on metal or well-soaked bamboo skewers and grill over medium-high heat until the tomatoes are beginning to turn brown, and the eggplant and mushrooms are soft and tender, exact time depending on the heat of your barbecue. (For vegetarians, the kebabs will need to be cooked on a clean grill.) Serve with Peanut-Chili Sauce (see next page) on the side, and a fruit chutney if desired.

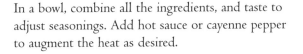

Peanut-Chili Sauce

½ cup chunky peanut butter

1 (or more) jalapeño peppers, seeded and finely chopped

1 small clove garlic, crushed

¼ cup orange juice

zest of 1 orange

1 tbsp brown sugar

salt to taste

2 tbsp lemon juice

2 tbsp soy sauce

hot sauce or cayenne pepper to taste (optional)

In a bowl, combine all the ingredients, and taste to adjust seasonings. Add hot sauce or cayenne pepper to augment the heat as desired.

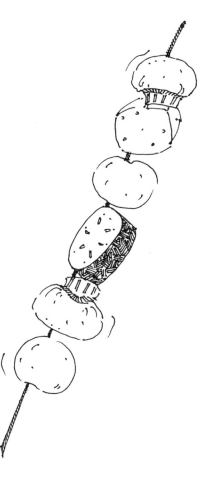

BEEF OR LAMB TIKKA

Krishna Jamal and her husband own and run Vancouver's highly regarded Rubina Tandoori restaurant. Her recipes always excite the tastebuds, and this Beef or Lamb Tikka is no exception. Serve these spicy tender morsels with her Raita (p. 118) to cool the fires. It's important, of course, to use fresh spices, and toasting before you blend them with the other ingredients brings out all the flavor.

MAKES 4

1½ lbs (750 g) sirloin tip beef or boneless spring lamb

2 tsp cumin seeds

½ tsp carom seeds or black pepper

1-inch (2.5-cm) piece ginger

6 – 8 cloves garlic

2 red chilis or 1 tsp *sambal oelek* or to taste

1 tbsp low-fat yogurt

1 tsp vegetable oil

Cut meat into 1-inch (2.5-cm) cubes and place in a bowl.

In a small, heavy, unoiled pan over low heat, toast cumin and carom seeds. Remove from heat when fragrant. (Not necessary for black pepper.)

In a blender or food processor, process seeds and remaining ingredients into paste. Pour mixture over meat, ensuring all pieces are coated, then cover and refrigerate for 6 to 8 hours.

Thread on metal or well-soaked bamboo skewers and barbecue over high heat, for 10 minutes, turning on all sides. Serve with raita, tamarind or mint chutney, and fresh vegetable relish.

GRILLED TANDOORI CHICKEN

With this heavenly-tasting recipe using skinless chicken breasts, Anne Lindsay, well-known Canadian chef and author, offers a low-fat alternative to the more usual barbecue-blackened chicken skin.

SERVES 4

1 tbsp Dijon mustard

1 tbsp canola oil

½ cup low-fat plain yogurt

2 tbsp fresh ginger, minced

1 tsp ground cumin

1 tsp ground coriander

½ tsp ground turmeric

¼ tsp cayenne

2 tbsp canned green chili, chopped or
   1 jalapeño, seeded and chopped

2 tbsp lemon juice

2 lbs (900 g) skinless chicken breasts

In a mixing bowl, add the mustard then whisk in oil, drop by drop, until well blended. Stir in yogurt and ginger. Set aside.

In a skillet over medium heat, cook the cumin, coriander, turmeric, and cayenne 1 to 2 minutes or until fragrant. Add to the yogurt mixture, then add green chili and lemon juice, and mix well.

Using a knife, make very small cuts in the chicken. Arrange in a shallow dish or place in a food-safe plastic bag; pour yogurt-spice mixture over chicken and be sure to coat all pieces. Cover and refrigerate for at least 8 hours or up to 24 hours.

On a greased grill over medium heat or under a broiler, grill chicken for 15 to 20 minutes on each side (15 minutes if top is down on barbecue) or until chicken is tender and juices run clear when chicken is pierced with fork. Watch carefully and turn to prevent burning.

INDONESIAN PORK

Crank up the heat by increasing the amount of chili paste you use, but cook these delectable morsels slowly, over low heat, so they don't burn before they are cooked through. The marinade can be prepared the night before the picnic and the pork placed in it first thing in the morning for a late afternoon grill. (If the sauce congeals in the fridge overnight, warm it to smoothness again before marinating the meat.)

SERVES 6

2 pork tenderloins (about 2½ lbs [1.1 kg] in total)

¾ cup salted roast peanuts

2 tbsp coriander seeds (or 2 tsp ground)

2 cloves garlic, minced

2 – 3 tsp Thai hot chili paste

1 cup green or sweet onion, finely chopped

⅓ cup lemon juice

⅓ cup tamari soy sauce

2 tbsp brown sugar

½ cup melted butter

½ cup chicken or vegetable stock

Cut the meat into 1-inch (2.5-cm) cubes, removing any fat or sinew, and place it in a bowl.

In a blender or food processor, blend the peanuts, coriander seeds, garlic, chili paste, onion, lemon juice, soy sauce, and sugar until it becomes a fine paste. Add the melted butter in a thin stream, and a little of the stock. Remove from the blender and add the rest of the stock.

Pour mixture over the pork and refrigerate for several hours.

Thread the pork onto metal or well-soaked wooden skewers. Grill them slowly over low heat until the meat is well cooked, turning on all sides and basting with the marinade.

LAMB KEBABS WITH GREEN HERBS AND GARLIC

Lamb and mint are made for each other, and this tasty marinade with its herbs and garlic ensures tenderness as well as flavor. Lean meat and the use of olive oil in the marinade make this a healthy choice too.

SERVES 6 TO 8

3½ lb (1½ kg) lean lamb (deboned leg)

½ cup apple cider vinegar

¾ cup olive oil

4 cloves garlic, crushed

2 tbsp fresh mint leaves, finely chopped

2 tbsp fresh oregano, finely chopped

2 tsp black pepper

1 tsp salt (or more)

Cut the meat into 1-inch (2.5-cm) cubes and set aside. In a bowl, combine the remaining ingredients, and add the meat. Cover and refrigerate for several hours.

Thread the lamb onto metal or well-soaked bamboo skewers. Grill them on the barbecue over medium high heat until they are brown and tender, turning on all sides and brushing with the marinade.

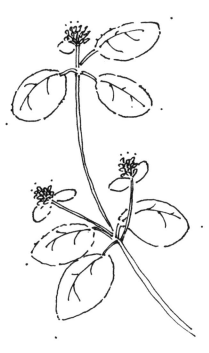

PRUNES IN BACON

Even people who profess to "hate prunes" enjoy these tasty mouthfuls; few eaters guess that the tidbit in the middle of the bacon is a prune, since it is transformed by the bacon fat, and the heat!

MAKES 24 SMALL PIECES

24 large pitted prunes

24 slices of bacon, about ½ a strip each (not too lean)

Place a prune on the end of a bacon slice and roll it up. Put a well-soaked bamboo skewer through the middle to hold the roll in place. Repeat with the rest of the prunes and bacon, placing 4 or 5 rolls on each skewer as one serving.

Grill over medium-high heat until the bacon sizzles and browns. Eat them while piping hot.

Note: To use this recipe without a barbecue, skewer each bacon-wrapped prune with a toothpick. Place the rolls on a broiling pan and broil under a hot broiler, turning the rolls several times. As soon as the bacon is cooked, they are ready to eat.

SALMON GRILLED BETWEEN ROMAINE LETTUCE LEAVES

This recipe from Bob Blumer — writer, artist, and more recently, the Surreal Gourmet — serves two, and we have left it that way, although you can easily make it as big as you need. He suggests that it can be prepped hours ahead of cooking time as long as it is kept refrigerated (or well-chilled).

SERVES 2

4 large romaine lettuce leaves

6 tsp olive oil

2 salmon steaks or salmon fillets,
  1-inch (2.5-cm) thick, about 6 oz
  (175 g) each

salt and pepper to taste

2 tbsp capers

4 sprigs fresh dill

2 lemons, 1 juiced, 1 sliced thinly

2 pieces of twine, or other
  nonflammable natural fibre,
  3 ft (1 m) long

Soak twine in hot water for 15 minutes.

Rinse romaine leaves in water; do not dry. Rub 1 tsp of the oil over the inside (concave) side of each lettuce leaf.

Pat salmon dry. For each serving, place salmon in center of one leaf (concave side up). Season with salt and pepper. Pour 1 tsp oil and the juice of ½ lemon over salmon, trapping the drippings with the leaf. Top with capers, dill, and one lemon slice.

Place second leaf over salmon, fold ends of bottom leaf up to keep juices trapped, and wrap the twine around the leaves to seal. Tie twine in a knot.

Grill fish over high heat for 5 minutes. Turn and grill for another 5 minutes. Cooking time will be slightly less for fillets and will vary according to the exact thickness of the steak. Do not overcook the salmon. To test, make an incision in the middle. Tastes vary, but most people like their salmon a light pink with just a faint hint of red in the very center.

Cut twine and remove top leaf. (You may want to leave string on for presentation value.) Serve on warmed plates, and garnish with a lemon twist.

BREADS
& MUFFINS

APPLESAUCE BRAN MUFFINS

This has to be the easiest muffin recipe to make, and the fruity taste and moist texture win top marks.

MAKES 24

3 cups raisin bran cereal

½ cup milk

2 cups applesauce

⅔ cup oil

2 eggs

2 cups whole wheat flour

1 cup white flour

3 tbsp baking powder

1 tsp soda

1 tsp salt

2 tsp cinnamon

⅔ cup brown sugar

Preheat oven to 350°F (175°C).

In a large bowl, combine cereal, milk, applesauce, oil, and eggs, and mix well. In another bowl, combine the remaining ingredients and mix well. Add the dry mixture to the wet one and mix well. Grease 24 muffin pans, spoon the mixture into them, and bake in the oven for 15 to 20 minutes.

BUTTERMILK SCALLION SCONES

These light and tender scones are delicately flavored with onion and parsley. They are wonderful still warm from the oven but will stay fresh all day. Although scones are traditionally served with butter, these are moist and tasty enough not to need it.

MAKES 16

⅔ cup butter, cubed

2 green onions, finely chopped

3 tbsp parsley, finely chopped

2 cups all-purpose flour

½ tsp baking soda

1 tbsp baking powder

½ tsp salt

¾ cup buttermilk

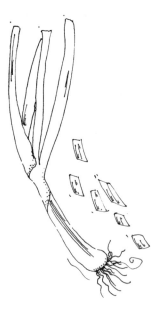

Preheat oven to 450°F (230°C).

In a small pan over medium heat, melt ½ to 1 tbsp butter. Add the onions and parsley, and sauté until just softened, about 3 minutes. Let cool.

In a large bowl, combine the flour, baking soda, baking powder, and salt.

With your fingers, rub the remaining butter in the flour mixture until it resembles coarse crumbs. Running your fingers under cold water then drying them will help keep the butter from melting.

Make a well in the center and pour in the buttermilk and onion-parsley mixture. Mix with a fork until the flour mixture is just moistened.

Turn dough out onto a floured surface and gather into a ball. Knead gently 10 times or until smooth. Pat out dough into a square ½-inch (1-cm) thick. Don't allow the dough to become overworked or too thick in places. Cut into 16 squares.

Place on an ungreased cookie sheet 2 inches (5 cm) apart to allow spreading. Bake for 12 to 15 minutes or until biscuits have risen and bottoms have browned.

FETA AND SUN-BLUSHED TOMATO SCONES WITH BLACK OLIVES

Nadine Abensur, of the U.K.'s elegant Cranks restaurants, uses sun-blushed tomatoes, which are a registered trademark for tomatoes dried and packed in oil scented with herbs and garlic. If you can, please use them; otherwise, substitute oil-packed, sun-dried tomatoes. Ms Abensur says the scones can be frozen and then heated in a very hot oven just before use, so make them ahead and spare yourself some work on picnic day.

MAKES 8

6 oz (170 g, or 1⅓ cups) flour, plus extra for dusting

2 oz (60 g, or ½ cup) whole-wheat flour

4 tsp baking powder

2 tbsp extra virgin olive oil

1 small red chili, finely chopped

½ tsp English mustard

2½ oz (75 g) feta cheese, cut in small cubes

2 oz (60 g) sun-blushed tomatoes, drained and roughly chopped

10 calamata olives, pitted and roughly chopped

several basil leaves, roughly torn

1 egg

2 – 3 tbsp milk, plus extra for brushing (depending on flour type and quality, you may need to add a little more milk to make a soft dough)

Preheat oven to 425°F (220°C).

Into a large bowl, sift the flours and baking powder, folding the leftover bran from the sieve back in. Add the oil, chili, and mustard, and mix with a fork until the mixture turns to small lumps. Stir in the feta, sun-blushed tomatoes, olives, and basil.

In a bowl, beat the egg, then add the milk and beat again. Gradually pour into the flour mixture, bringing it all lightly together with your fingers until you have a ball of soft, but not sticky, dough.

Roll out on a floured surface to a depth of 1 inch (2 cm) and cut out with a 2-inch (5-cm) round, fluted cutter.

Line a tray with baking parchment and place the scones in rows on it. Brush them lightly with milk and bake on the oven's highest shelf for 12 to 15 minutes, until golden brown. Transfer to a wire rack and eat them when still warm.

MOUSETRAPS

Even if you believe you don't like Marmite (a kind of yeast extract, available in most supermarkets), give these cheesy snacks a try. They are salty, tasty, and after their initial crunchiness has disappeared, if there are any left, they become delightfully chewy. (They keep well, and don't need refrigeration.)

MAKES 20 TO 24

¼ cup butter

3 tsp Marmite (or Vegemite if
 you must!)

½ loaf whole-wheat bread, thinly sliced

1 cup cheese, grated (mild or medium
 if you are making these for kids)

Preheat oven to 275°F (135°C).

In a bowl, mix the Marmite into the softened butter and spread this mixture thinly on one side of each slice of bread. Stack the slices and cut them in half with a serrated knife.

Place the half slices closely together on a greased large cookie sheet, Marmite side up, then sprinkle grated cheese evenly over them. Bake for up to 1 hour, but start checking for doneness after 35 minutes or so. The exact length of cooking time depends on the bread type and thickness. Really thin slices of white bread may take as little as 35 minutes to dehydrate and become crisp.

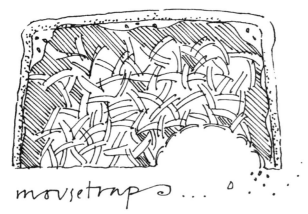

mousetraps ...

OAT BRAN MUFFINS

Good, and good for you, these muffins are straightforward to make, and keep well. They make a sturdy snack.

MAKES 18

2 cups whole wheat flour

2 tsp baking powder

1 tsp salt

2 cups oat bran cereal

½ cup butter

½ cup brown sugar

2 large eggs

1 cup molasses

1⅓ cups buttermilk

1 cup raisins

Preheat oven to 400°F (200°C).

In a bowl, combine the flour, baking powder, salt, and cereal. In another bowl, cream the butter then add the brown sugar, and beat well. Add the eggs and molasses, and mix well.

Add the dry ingredients to the butter mixture in three portions, alternating with the buttermilk, and mixing well after each addition. Stir in the raisins. Spoon the mixture into 18 well-buttered muffin pans, and bake in the oven for 15 to 18 minutes.

Raisin Bran Muffins:
Use wheat bran instead of the oat bran cereal, and add ¼ cup more flour; otherwise follow the recipe above. Makes a slightly less dense muffin.

RICH PASTRY

Many are the variations of this method for making pastry. The one we are presenting here has been in my family for many decades, used by my mother and grandmother for making mince pies, and by me for almost everything, except when I need to cook vegan!

MAKES 2 DOUBLE-CRUST PIES OR AROUND 4 DOZEN TARTLETS

1 cup unsalted butter or shortening

2¾ cups flour

1 egg, beaten lightly

1 tbsp vinegar

1½ tsp salt

cold water

Blend butter into flour using a pastry cutter, two knives, or chilled fingertips.

In a measuring cup, combine the egg, vinegar, and salt, and add cold water to make 1 cup liquid in total. Add the liquid to the flour and butter mixture, blending with a fork, then kneading gently until a moist pastry dough is obtained.

Separate into two portions, wrap in plastic food wrap, and chill before rolling out with plenty of flour. This dough may be frozen, but needs to be completely thawed out again before use.

RED RIVER PUMPERNICKEL BREAD

This recipe, and close variants of it, was very popular in the '70s, and deserves an encore. It's easy to make, is very flavorful, and keeps well. In fact, it's even better the next day.

3 cups Red River cereal

1 cup whole wheat flour

2 tsp baking soda

1 tsp salt

3 cups very hot water

½ cup molasses

In a bowl, mix the cereal, flour, baking soda, and salt. In another bowl, pour in the nearly boiling water, and stir in the molasses. Add this liquid to the dry ingredients, and mix well.

Let the mixture stand at room temperature for 2 hours, then spoon it into a greased 5" x 9" loaf pan. Preheat oven to 275°F (135°C). Cover the pan with foil, dull side facing out, and bake in the oven for 3 hours, or until a tester comes out clean from the center. Cool the loaf for 10 minutes before removing it from the pan.

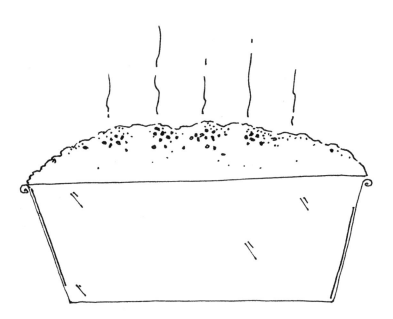

WELSH CAKES

Sweet, rich, and scented with nutmeg, my friend Ann K.'s Welsh Cakes are great for filling the empty corners. They can be made some hours ahead of picnic time, and need no adornment, unless you fancy a little jam.

MAKES 16

2 cups flour

¾ cup chilled butter

2 tsp nutmeg, freshly grated

¾ cup sugar

¼ cup dried currants

1 egg

milk (see directions)

Sift the flour and incorporate the butter, using a pastry cutter or two knives. The mixture should look like coarse cornmeal when the butter is sufficiently blended in. Add a pinch of salt if using unsalted butter.

Add the grated nutmeg, currants, and sugar and mix lightly. Break the egg into a measuring cup and add enough milk to make ¾ cup. Beat together, then add the liquid to the flour mixture and use a fork to combine them. (You may need a drop or two more milk, depending on your flour.)

Flatten the dough to ½-inch (1-cm) thickness on a well-floured surface, sprinkle the top with flour, and cut circles with a cookie cutter or a large tumbler.

On a medium-low (325°F [160°C]) griddle or large flat pan over medium low heat, cook the cakes for 15 minutes on each side. Adjust the heat as needed to make sure they brown, without burning before they cook through. Cool on a rack.

DESSERTS

APPLE CAKE WITH GINGER AND CARDAMOM

Serve this eggless cake straight from the pan, warm or cool. Use apples that will keep their shape when cooked — Fuji, Spartan, Braeburn, to name a few — rather than apples that pulp, such as McIntosh or Granny Smith.

2 cups unbleached flour

I tsp baking soda

I tsp baking powder

I tsp powdered ginger

½ tsp cardamom or grated nutmeg

3 medium apples, washed, peeled and cored

¾ cup soft butter

½ cup honey

I tbsp vinegar

½ cup hot water

Preheat oven to 350°F (175°C).

In a large bowl, combine the flour, baking soda, baking powder, ginger, and cardamom.

Chop the apples into very small pieces and mix them with the dry ingredients until they are well coated. In another bowl, combine the butter, honey, and vinegar with the hot water until they are well mixed. Pour this liquid over the apples and mix gently just to combine.

Spoon the batter into a well-greased 8" x 8" pan, and bake in the oven for about 45 minutes, until nicely brown and firm. This cake needs no frosting, but a topping of Pressed Yogurt (p. 117) and brown sugar spread on just before serving or on the side adds to perfection.

APPLE POLENTA FLAN

The ingredients for this dessert are simple and cheap, and the result, served warm or cool (with a dollop of whipped cream or sweetened pressed yogurt), is surprisingly elegant and delicious. A fine-ground cornmeal produces a more smoothly textured flan, but medium-ground, or polenta cut are also suitable for use here, although they may take a little longer to cook with the milk.

SERVES 6

2 large apples (not pulpy cookers), peeled and finely chopped

2 tbsp water

4 cups milk

1 cup brown sugar

3 tbsp butter

grated zest of 2 lemons

1¼ cups fine ground cornmeal

juice of 2 lemons

½ cup whipping cream

¼ cup pecans or walnuts, chopped (optional)

⅓ cup raisins (optional)

3 tbsp maple syrup

Preheat oven to 350°F (175°C).

Grease and flour a 9" or 10" spring-form pan. Steam or microwave the apples in water until just tender.

In a pot over medium heat, combine the milk, sugar, butter, and lemon zest, stirring to dissolve the sugar. When the liquid is near boiling point, whisk in the cornmeal, bring back to the boil, and add the lemon juice. Reduce heat to low and simmer for 6 minutes, stirring constantly.

Remove from heat, and add the drained cooked apple and cream. You may add a handful of chopped nuts and/or ½ cup raisins at this point, if desired.

Pour the mixture into the prepared pan, smooth the surface, and drizzle maple syrup over the top. Bake in the oven for 1 hour. Serve warm.

Note: For a fancier-looking dessert, you may like to top it with a ring of thinly sliced apples before you add the syrup.

BANANA BREAD

A tried and true family recipe, given to us by friend Mark B.

MAKES 1 5" X 9" LOAF

½ cup soft butter

¾ cup sugar

2 eggs

1 cup unbleached flour

1 tsp baking soda

½ tsp salt

1 cup whole wheat flour

1 tsp vanilla extract

3 large ripe bananas, mashed

½ cup walnuts, coarsely chopped

Preheat oven to 350°F (175°C).

Cream the softened butter and sugar until light and fluffy. Add the eggs one at a time and beat well after each addition. Sift the flour, baking soda, and salt, and combine them with the whole wheat flour. Add these dry ingredients to the creamed mixture. Fold in the bananas, vanilla, and walnuts.

Spoon into a greased 5" x 9" loaf pan. Bake in the oven for 50 to 60 minutes, or until cake tester comes out clean from the center of the loaf.

BANANA-STRAWBERRY LAYER CAKE

Strawberries and bananas are old friends, and they walk out in fine style in this picture perfect layer cake, with Regan Daley's helpful instructions to guide you through the process to the delectable end result.

SERVES 10

Cake Layers

¾ cup unsalted butter, at room temperature

1 cup granulated sugar

2 large eggs, at room temperature

1 tsp pure vanilla extract

1⅓ cups mashed overripe bananas (about 3 large), at room temperature

2 cups cake-and-pastry flour

¾ tsp baking soda

¼ tsp salt

⅓ cup full-fat sour cream

Preheat oven to 350° (175°C). Grease and lightly flour two 9" round cake pans and tap out the excess flour.

In the bowl of an electric or stand mixer fitted with the paddle attachment, or a large mixing bowl if mixing by hand, cream the butter and the sugar until light and fluffy, about 1½ to 2 minutes. Add the eggs, one at a time, beating well and scraping down the sides of the bowl after each addition. If your butter is too warm, or your eggs too cold, the batter may begin to separate; don't worry, it will come together when the last ingredients are added. Add the vanilla and the mashed bananas and blend well. Again, this addition may seem to completely curdle the batter if the ingredients were not the correct temperature. No need to panic — all will be well!

Sift together the flour, baking soda, and salt. Add ½ of this mixture to the banana mixture, blending just to moisten the flour. Scrape down the bowl and beat in the sour cream. Scrape again, then add the remaining flour mixture, stirring just until the batter is evenly mixed. Divide the batter between the 2 pans and smooth the tops with a rubber spatula.

Set the cakes on the center rack of the oven and bake for 25 to 30 minutes, or until the tops are light golden and spring back when touched and a wooden

Cream Cheese Icing

I lb (2 8-oz [225-g] packages)
   Philadelphia-brand cream cheese, at
   room temperature

½ cup unsalted butter, at room
   temperature

I package (500 g, about 4 to 4⅓ cups)
   icing sugar, sifted

½ tsp vanilla extract

I tsp fresh lemon juice

additional butter and all-purpose
   flour for greasing and dusting the
   cake pans

I quart (4 cups) fresh ripe strawberries,
   washed and dried, if necessary

skewer inserted into the centre of each cake comes out clean. Rotate the pans once during baking so the cakes bake evenly.

Cool the cakes in the pans on wire racks for 7 minutes, then invert onto the racks and cool completely before icing or wrapping and storing. (The cakes can be made up to this point up to one day ahead, then wrapped tightly in plastic wrap and stored at room temperature. They may also be frozen up to 3 months; thaw and bring to room temperature before proceeding.)

Prepare the Cream Cheese Icing: in the bowl of an electric or stand mixer fitted with the paddle attachment, beat the cream cheese and butter together until they are smooth, light and creamy, about I½ minutes. (The icing can also be made by hand – a strong one! – by beating with a wooden spoon.) Add the icing sugar, a cup at a time, re-sifting it over the cream cheese mixture. Beat well and scrape down the sides of the bowl. Continue adding the sugar one cup at a time, until almost all the sugar has been smoothly incorporated. Beat in the vanilla and lemon juice, then the remaining sugar.

Taste the icing: it should be rich, cheesy and sweet, but not achingly so. If necessary, add a few drops more lemon juice or vanilla to your taste.

Cover the icing and refrigerate it for 15 to 30 minutes before using to firm it up enough to support the layers. (The icing may be prepared up to 2 days ahead of time, and stored covered in the refrigerator. Allow the icing to return to room temperature or near it before spreading.)

Place one layer of the cake on a cardboard cake circle or platter. (If you are going to ice the cake directly on the platter, slip strips of waxed or parchment paper around the bottom of the cake. These will protect the platter from gobs of icing and can be pulled cleanly away when you're finished decorating.) Spread the top of the first layer with a generous amount of icing, not going over the edges. Place the cake in the refrigerator for 15 minutes, to firm up the icing again.

Meanwhile, reserve 10 to 12 pretty, small strawberries, and one large one. Hull the remaining berries and cut them in thirds from hull to point. Remove the iced layer from the refrigerator and cover the top with slices of strawberry. Feel free to overlap the slices slightly, but don't pile or stack them, or your next layer will topple over! Top the strawberries with the second cake layer, centring it over the bottom tier. Press down gently to make it adhere to the berries and icing. Spread the top and sides generously with the remaining icing, then immediately place the entire cake in the refrigerator, for at least 20 minutes, or up to 24 hours, before serving.

If the cake has been chilled for more than a few hours, remove it from the refrigerator 30 to 45 minutes before serving so it is not too cold. Just before serving, cut the large reserved strawberry several times from point to hull, not cutting through the stem. Push down lightly on the fat part of the berry, and it will fan out. Place this in the very centre of the cake. Cut the remaining berries once from point to stem, again not severing the halves from the hull, then twist slightly, "fanning" the little berries. Settle one berry at each of ten evenly spaced places around the outside of the cake, one for each piece.

Once the cake has been decorated, it should be served within 6 hours or so, as the strawberries tend to pull the moisture from the icing, creating runny pink patches in the cream cheese. If the cake is to be made ahead, keep the icing chilled until needed, the cake layers wrapped and stored separately and assemble just before serving.

BARBECUED DESSERTS

Adrienne O'Callaghan is normally to be found working wonders behind the range at Barbara-Jo's Books to Cooks in Vancouver. Who knew about this secret grill side to her? The following is her eye-opening account of the sweet side to barbecue. "A decent gas or charcoal grill is all you need to produce some pretty amazing sweet finales. Humble campfire favorites like s'mores and sophisticated stuffed crepes are equally at home on the grill, whose slightly smoky infusion makes a surprisingly delightful complement to fruit, chocolate, and pastry."

GRILLED FRUIT

Pineapple is most often cited as a good fruit to grill, but peaches, apricots, plums, pears, bananas, and even grapes are also amazing when their sugars are kissed by intense heat. Pineapple slices, quartered bananas, grapes on the stem, and halved and pitted stone fruits all benefit from a basting with the following mixture during cooking:

4 tbsp melted unsalted butter

½ vanilla bean, split and scraped out

zest of 1 lemon or orange, finely grated

1 tbsp pure maple syrup

FLAVORED SUGAR

Another favorite taste booster for grilled fruit is flavored sugar, made simply by pulsing spices or fresh herbs in the food processor with granulated sugar. Sprinkle fruit with the sugar at the end of grilling or just before serving. Serve grilled fruit as is or pair it with cookies, biscotti, crème fraîche, whipped cream, or ice cream. Vanilla is fabulous, as is chocolate with pears or bananas, ginger with apricots ... the combinations are limitless.

Some ideas:
cilantro sugar with pineapple

mint or lemon-balm sugar with almost any fruit

cinnamon sugar with pears and Italian plums

cardamom sugar with apricots or peaches

vanilla sugar with any fruit

rosemary and thyme sugars (although not very pretty because they darken) are good with sturdier fruits like pears, peaches, and nectarines, especially when sprinkled on with the basting butter.

POUND CAKE

Brush slices of pound cake with plain or flavored butter and grill (also good served with grilled fruit).

CREPES

Stuff crepes with sweetened mascarpone scented with lemon zest and vanilla, tuck in a few berries (raspberries and blueberries are spectacular), tie up in a beggar's purse with a thin strip of scraped vanilla pod, and grill over medium heat until warm. Serve with chocolate sauce if you dare.

PAIN PERDU

The fancy name for French toast betokens a barbecue natural. Soak slices of challah or brioche in a mixture of beaten eggs, a little sugar, the seeds from a vanilla bean, a pinch of salt, and a few tablespoons of milk. Grill over medium heat for about 4 minutes per side, until puffed, golden, and grill-marked, then serve with fresh berries, thinned crème fraîche, and your favorite syrup or caramel sauce (also a great brunch dish).

PHYLLO PASTRY

Fill individual pastries with any of these combinations: chopped bittersweet chocolate and raspberries; lightly sweetened ricotta or quark and rum-soaked raisins; an equal mix of mascarpone and Nutella or peanut butter; bananas and caramel sauce. Brush the outside of the pastries with melted butter and grill over medium heat for about 3 minutes per side, until crisp and golden.

BLUEBERRY CAKE

Serve this beauty in blueberry season straight from the pan, still warm if possible, and with a big dollop of whipped cream, sour cream, or pressed yogurt and brown sugar. This particular recipe originates in Vermont, but variations on the theme appear nowadays in restaurants and recipe books all over North America, wherever blueberries are loved.

SERVES 6 TO 8

Batter

¾ cup sugar

¼ cup soft butter

1 egg

2 cups unbleached flour

½ tsp salt

2 tsp baking powder

½ – ¾ cup milk

2 cups blueberries

Topping

½ cup sugar

⅓ cup unbleached flour

½ tsp cinnamon

¼ cup melted butter

Preheat oven to 350°F (175°C).

For the batter: cream the sugar and butter. Beat in the egg, then add the sifted dry ingredients alternately with the milk, to make a fairly stiff batter. Gently mix the blueberries into it.

For the topping: in a small bowl, combine the sugar, flour, and cinnamon, then mix the melted butter in with a fork. When the butter is well integrated, set the topping aside. Spoon the batter into a greased and floured 9" x 9" pan and sprinkle the topping mixture evenly over the surface. Bake in the oven for 45 minutes.

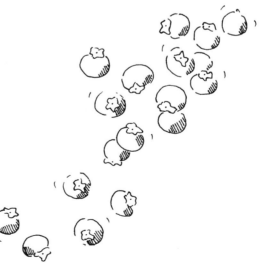

BROWNIES

These are sweet and darkly chocolatey, and the addition of chocolate chips to the batter produces a pleasantly complex texture when the brownies are completely cooled. It is important to use high quality chips rather than the baking chips sold in supermarkets, which tend to be waxier in texture and less richly flavored than Belgian or Swiss chocolate chips.

MAKES 24

1 cup butter

1 cup sugar

1 cup brown sugar

¾ cup cocoa

3 eggs

1 cup all-purpose flour

2 tsp baking powder

2 tsp vanilla extract

¾ cup chocolate chips (good quality)

1 cup walnuts, chopped

Preheat oven to 350°F (175°C).

In a pot over medium heat, melt the butter, then add the sugar and cocoa, stirring until smooth and warm. Remove from heat and add the eggs one at a time, stirring vigorously.

Sift the flour and baking powder into the mixture all at once, mix well, and add the vanilla, chocolate chips, and nuts.

Pour the mixture into a buttered 9" x 13" pan. Bake in the oven for approximately 35 minutes or until crust is firm and resistant when gently pressed. Because this is a very sweet mixture, watch the baking carefully after 30 minutes to avoid burning.

BUTTERFLY CUPCAKES

Adapted long ago from a little recipe book of vegetarian recipes from India, this cake recipe has become a tried-and-true favorite in our family. The condensed milk provides the sweetening and some of the fat, making for a very quick and easy recipe that is completely reliable for layer cakes or cupcakes. To turn plain cupcakes into butterfly cakes is easier than it sounds, and children always enjoy their charm and novelty as well as their sweet gentle flavors.

MAKES 20

1 10-oz (300-ml) tin sweetened condensed milk

1 cup water

¼ cup melted butter

2 cups flour

2 tsp baking powder

½ tsp soda

pinch salt

1½ – 2 cups whipped cream

icing sugar (garnish)

Preheat oven to 350°F (175°C).

In a bowl, beat the condensed milk, water, and butter together.

In a larger bowl, sift the dry ingredients, then make a well in the center and add the milk mixture. The batter may need to be beaten briefly to get it smooth.

Divide it evenly into 20 cupcake papers, placed in muffin pans to ensure an even shape for each cake. Bake the cupcakes in the oven for approximately 20 minutes or until the center of a cupcake springs back when gently pressed, and the cakes are beginning to brown slightly. Let the cakes cool for a few minutes, then lift them out of the muffin pans and cool them on a rack. Once cool, they may be stored in a sealed container for a day if necessary.

Shortly before picnic time, cut a circle, 1 to 1½ inches (2½ to 4 cm) in diameter out of each cake in the middle of the top, cutting down and in with the knife blade to remove a cone shaped piece of cake. Be careful not to cut right down to the bottom of the cakes! Carefully place each cone next to its own cake. In the hole left by each cone, place a good dollop of whipped cream, so that it overflows the hole without reaching the edge of the cake. When all the cakes are filled, cut each cone in half from its circular top down to the point. Place the two halves on top of the whipped cream to look like the wings of a butterfly. When all the cakes are assembled this way, place them on a cake rack and dust them generously with icing sugar, using a fine sifter. The cakes should be kept cool once they are cream-filled.

Note: To make the batter into a layer cake, pour it into two 8" round pans, greased and floured, and bake at 350°F (175°C) for 30 minutes then test for doneness. Cool on a rack before filling with raspberry jam and frosting with lemon frosting (See Lemon Chocolate Fudge Squares, p. 304).

BUTTERSCOTCH ALMOND COOKIES

Our afternoon tea menu is graced by these delicately tasty little biscuits, but they are good any time, and they keep for days, if they get the opportunity.

MAKES 60 TO 65 SMALL COOKIES

1¼ cups (packed) brown sugar

½ cup butter

I egg

1¼ cups unbleached flour

¼ tsp salt

1½ tsp baking powder

I cup ground almonds (sometimes sold as almond meal)

Preheat oven to 375°F (190°C).

In a large bowl, cream the butter, add the sugar, and beat. Add the egg, beat well, then mix in the rest of the ingredients.

Place the mixture in teaspoonfuls on a greased oven tray, allowing room for spreading. Flatten slightly with a fork or the back of a spoon. Bake in the oven for about 12 minutes. Cookies are done when they are delicately brown. Cool on a rack.

Note: Substitute I cup of rolled oats and 2 tbsp of wheatgerm for the almonds, and make no other changes, and voilà, you have equally nutritious and good-tasting Butterscotch Oatmeal Cookies.

CHILLED CARAMELIZED ORANGES WITH GREEK YOGURT

Just reading this recipe from the creative kitchen of the renowned Nigella Lawson will make you salivate, so be warned. The cardamom adds its sophisticated note to the sweetness of the caramel and the tang of the oranges, and you have a dessert that is elegant in its very simplicity. You can make it well ahead but no longer than a day, or the caramelized sugar will dissolve.

SERVES 6 TO 8

6 navel oranges or any small, thin-skinned variety

I lb I½ oz (500 g) caster sugar (fine sugar, sometimes called "berry sugar"; not icing sugar)

I cup water

8 cardamom pods, crushed

Greek yogurt, approximately I lb I½ oz (500 g)

Using a small sharp knife, cut a thin slice off the top and bottom of the oranges, and then slice off the skin vertically, turning the oranges as you go, being careful to keep as much flesh as possible but removing all the pith. Slice each orange into ¼-inch (5-mm) rounds, trying to reserve as much juice as you can. Just plonk the slices, pouring the juices, into a bowl as you cut them. Or just cut them straight into something like a lasagne dish.

For the caramel: combine the sugar, water, and cardamom pods into a large saucepan over low heat and swirl (not stir) a little to dissolve the sugar, then slowly bring to the boil without stirring, until the syrup becomes a dark amber color.

Take the saucepan off the heat and tip in the oranges and any juice that has collected. Quickly coat the orange slices in the caramel and pour onto a flat plate; act with speed otherwise the caramel will set before you can get it out of the saucepan. If you can pick out the cardamom pods without burning your fingers, good, but there's no need to get too exercised about it; let those eating do a little work as well.

Let the oranges cool, and then put them in the fridge to chill for a little while. Put the Greek yogurt in a bowl on the table for people to eat it with.

CARROT COCONUT CAKE WITH CREAM CHEESE/WHITE CHOCOLATE ICING

If you can't get to Audrey Alsterberg and Wanda Urbanowicz's Rebar Restaurant, in Victoria, B.C., where this moist, spicy cake is made regularly, well ... you'll just have to make it yourself! It's a beauty — the ultimate carrot cake!

SERVES 8

1¼ cups carrots, grated

¾ cup crushed pineapple

¾ cup unsweetened coconut

¾ cup walnuts, chopped

½ cup dates, chopped

¾ cup vegetable oil

¾ cup brown sugar

⅓ cup white sugar

3 eggs

2 tsp vanilla extract

1½ cups unbleached flour

1½ tsp cinnamon

2 tsp baking powder

1 tsp baking soda

¼ tsp salt

1½ tsp ground ginger

Preheat oven to 350°F (175°C).

Butter and flour two 8" round cake pans and set aside. In a large bowl, combine grated carrot, pineapple, coconut, and walnuts. In another large bowl, beat the sugars with the eggs. Stir in the vanilla and whip on High until the volume has tripled. On Low, pour the oil in slowly to blend in.

In another bowl, combine the remaining dry ingredients and gently stir into the egg mix. Fold in the carrot mixture. Divide the batter between the cake pans and smooth the tops. Bake in the oven for 30 minutes, until an inserted toothpick comes out clean.

While the cakes cool, prepare the icing. Beat cream cheese on High until smooth and fluffy. Lightly blend in vanilla and butter. Melt white chocolate in a double boiler over medium heat. Add hot melted chocolate to the cream cheese mixture. Scrape down the sides of the bowl and mix on High again until smooth and fluffy. Slowly add icing sugar, stopping to scrape down the sides now and then. Beat on High, until all the sugar is well incorporated and the icing is light and fluffy, about 3 minutes.

½ tsp nutmeg, freshly grated

½ tsp allspice

Icing

9 oz (270 g) Philadelphia-brand cream cheese (firm block, not spreadable)

¼ cup unsalted butter, softened

1 tsp vanilla extract

3 oz (90 g) white chocolate

3 cups icing sugar, sifted

Spread bottom layer with one-third of the icing, smoothing it evenly to the edges. Chill for 10 minutes. Place the top cake layer on and frost the top and sides as you like. Garnish with toasted coconut, walnuts, and/or a decorative piped border. Store refrigerated where it will keep well for up to 4 days.

CHOCOLATE CHIP SEED COOKIES

High in calories, these cookies are great for hikes or for the kind of vigorous picnic where people are swimming, throwing balls about, and expending lots of energy. (Did someone mention kids?) The seeds in the recipe add a lovely complexity of flavor and texture, and render these cookies very nutritious, but they certainly don't taste "eat-it-up-it's-good-for-you."

MAKES ABOUT 40 COOKIES

½ cup butter

¾ cup brown sugar, packed

I egg

I tbsp water

I tsp vanilla extract

½ cup whole-wheat flour

¼ cup unbleached flour

¼ cup wheat germ

½ tsp baking soda

½ tsp salt

I tbsp ground flax seeds

¾ cup quick oats

I½ cups finely processed seeds (I cup sunflower, ½ cup pumpkin)

½ cup chocolate chips

Preheat oven to 375°F (190°C).

In a mixing bowl, cream the butter and sugar, then beat in the egg, water, and vanilla. In another bowl, combine all the dry ingredients and incorporate them into the creamed mixture. Place tablespoonsful on greased cookie sheets, and flatten a little, leaving ½ to I inch (1.5 to 2.5 cm) for spreading. Bake in the oven for 15 to 18 minutes. (Exact time depends on your sheet thickness, and oven heat.) Remove to cool on racks.

CHOCOLATE-DIPPED STRAWBERRIES

Although Chocolate-Dipped Strawberries aren't the ideal dessert on a very hot day, they are so delicious that no one will mind a bit of melted chocolate on their fingers if the thermometer rises unexpectedly.

SERVES 4

3 – 5 large strawberries per person

4 oz (just over 100 g) dark chocolate will cover 12 to 14 strawberries

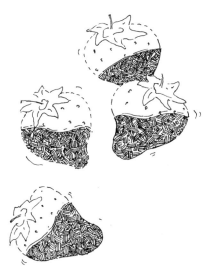

Wash and dry the strawberries but leave the stems on, and chill them in the refrigerator for half an hour just before you are ready to dip them.

Place a sheet of tinfoil on a metal baking dish and put the dish in the freezer or refrigerator.

Into a small deep bowl, break the chocolate into small pieces, then stand the bowl in hot (not boiling) water, making sure not a drop of water gets into the chocolate. Move the chocolate gently to and fro as it melts, and replace the water to keep it hot, until the chocolate is melted and smooth.

When the chocolate is ready, take the pan and the strawberries from the refrigerator, and dip the bottom two-thirds of each strawberry in the chocolate then shake off the excess and place the strawberry on its side on the chilled tinfoil.

When all the berries are dipped, place the pan in the refrigerator until the chocolate is completely firm. The dipped berries will keep for a few hours if they remain cool.

DEVIL'S FOOD CAKE

In famous American chef James McNair's beautiful book of cakes, he gives many helpful instructions for cake preparation, baking, and finishing. He says he likes to finish this dark, delicious chocolate cake by slicing each layer horizontally in half and making a double recipe of the ganache (see next page). Since our afternoon tea menu demands a completely splendid cake, and we can't imagine anything more splendid than four layers loaded with chocolate ganache, we've included the ganache recipe.

SERVES 10

¾ cup unsweetened natural cocoa (not Dutch-processed)

1½ cups boiling water or hot strong brewed coffee

¾ cup whole milk

3 cups all-purpose flour

1 tsp baking soda

¾ tsp salt

¾ cup (1½ sticks) unsalted butter, at room temperature

2¼ cups sugar

3 eggs at room temperature, lightly beaten

1½ tsp pure vanilla extract

ganache (recipe follows)

seedless raspberry jam (a favorite recipe or high-quality commercial product) for spreading (optional)

Position racks so that the cake layers will bake in the middle of the oven and preheat the oven to 350°F (175°C). Grease and line two 9" round cake pans.

In a heatproof bowl or glass measuring cup, place the cocoa, then slowly add the boiling water or hot coffee, and stir until smooth. Stir in the milk and set aside to cool to room temperature.

In a strainer or sifter, place the flour, baking soda, and salt together, and sift into a bowl. Repeat the process 2 more times. Whisk to mix well and set aside.

In the bowl of a stand mixer fitted with a flat beater, or in a bowl with a hand mixer, beat the butter at medium speed until soft and creamy, about 45 seconds. With the mixer still running, slowly add the sugar, then stop the mixer and scrape the mixture that clings to the sides of the bowl into the center. Continue beating at medium speed until the mixture is very light and fluffy, about 5 minutes. Slowly drizzle in the eggs and beat well; stop at least once to scrape the sides of the bowl. Add the vanilla and blend well.

Using the mixer on low speed or a rubber spatula, fold in about one-third of the flour mixture, then half of the cocoa mixture, scraping the sides of the bowl and folding just until the ingredients are incorporated. In the same manner, fold in half of the remaining flour mixture, then the remaining cocoa mixture, and finally the remaining flour mixture.

Divide the batter evenly between the prepared pans and smooth the tops with a rubber spatula. Bake until each cake layer springs back when lightly touched in the center with your fingertip and a wooden skewer inserted into the center of each layer comes out clean, about 35 minutes.

Remove the pans to cool on a wire rack for 5 to 10 minutes, then turn the layers out onto the rack to cool completely.

Prepare the ganache as directed below, spreading each layer with a thin layer of jam (if using) before spreading with the ganache.

CHOCOLATE GANACHE

James McNair recommends using the finest quality chocolate — Callebaut, Guittard, Lindt, Scharffen Berger, or Valrhona — for this rich filling. For those who prefer a less darkly chocolatey ganache, he suggests using milk chocolate, or white chocolate (as long as it's made with cocoa butter), or blending some white chocolate in with the bittersweet that he likes to use. European gianduja, a mix of ground nuts and chocolate, can also be used.

MAKES ABOUT 4 CUPS

1½ lb (700 g) finest-quality bittersweet (not unsweetened), semisweet, milk, or white chocolate containing cocoa butter, finely chopped

In a bowl or food processor, place the chocolate and butter. In a saucepan over medium heat, combine the cream and corn syrup and bring just to a boil. Pour over the chocolate and butter and stir or process until the chocolate is melted and the mixture is smooth. If using a food processor, transfer the mixture to a bowl. Stir in the vanilla, brandy, or liqueur.

6 tbsp unsalted butter, at room
temperature, cut into small pieces

1½ cups heavy (whipping) cream

3 tbsp light corn syrup

1 tbsp vanilla extract, brandy, or coffee-
or fruit-flavored liqueur

If using as a glaze, quickly pour or spoon the ganache over the cake.

If using as an icing, set the bowl in a larger bowl of iced water and stir the ganache frequently until cool, or cover and refrigerate until cool and set to the touch, at least 2 hours or for up to overnight. If refrigerated, return to room temperature. Beat briefly with a hand mixer to smooth and lighten to a spreadable consistency; avoid overbeating. If the ganache becomes too stiff during spreading, dip the spatula into hot water and wipe dry.

MOCHA GANACHE

Use semisweet chocolate. Stir 4 to 5 tsp instant espresso into the hot cream mixture.

NUT GANACHE

Use gianduja made with almonds, hazelnuts (filberts), or other nuts in place of the chocolate.

PEPPERMINT GANACHE

Use semisweet chocolate. Add 1 tsp pure peppermint extract or 4 drops peppermint oil in place of the vanilla or spirit.

TRUFFLE GANACHE

Use semisweet or bittersweet chocolate. Increase the amount of cream to 2 cups and reduce the butter to 3 tbsp.

DOUBLE CHOCOLATE RASPBERRY TARTS

Highly regarded American cookbook author Trish Deseine has combined chocolate and raspberries, always the perfect couple, in a scrumptious and simple-to-make dessert just right for sophisticated picnicking.

SERVES 6

9 oz (250 g) Double Chocolate Raspberry Tart Pastry (see recipe p. 294)

7 oz (200 g) good quality white chocolate

1⅔ cups light cream

9 oz (250 g) raspberries, gently washed

Roll out the pastry, and cut out 6 circles to fit tartlet pans roughly 4 inches (10 cm) in diameter. Bake blind (see note below). Set aside in a cool place.

In a bowl, melt the white chocolate and add the cream, stirring constantly. Leave to cool slightly, but not too much, as the cream must still be fluid enough to pour into the tartlet shells.

Fill the shells with the mixture and place the raspberries evenly on top, allowing them to sink in slightly. Keep in a cool place.

Note: Baking "blind" means cooking a pastry shell without any filling. To prevent it from puffing up, the base needs to be filled with dried beans or baking beans. The advantage of the latter is that they diffuse the heat, thus cooking the pastry base as well as the sides exposed to the heat of the oven. Whether you use dried beans or proper baking beans, you need to make sure you remove them before adding the filling if your guests are to retain their beautiful and expensive crowns!

DOUBLE CHOCOLATE RASPBERRY TART PASTRY

This pastry, which you need to prepare Trish Deseine's insanely good Double Chocolate Raspberry Tarts, may well become a staple of your kitchen, to be used when you want to whip up an impressive dessert without spending all day in the kitchen.

TO FILL A PASTRY SHELL ABOUT 11" IN DIAMETER

2 cups all-purpose flour

1¾ sticks (7/8 cup) unsalted butter

1 cup confectioners sugar (icing sugar)

7 tbsp cocoa powder

1 egg yolk

1 tbsp cold water

In a bowl, pour in the flour, make a well in the center, and add all the remaining ingredients.

Combine well, using a fork. Knead to form a smooth dough. Shape into a ball, wrap in plastic wrap, and leave to rest in a refrigerator for 2 hours.

DRIED FIGS CARAMELIZED WITH KUMQUATS, MASCARPONE, AND GINGER

Nadine Abensur, of the British vegetarian restaurant group, Cranks, and author of The Cranks Bible, *says she has been making this sophisticated but simple dessert for many years. She uses it with cake, sweet tarts, or ice cream, and suggests putting it inside a crepe and flambéing it in brandy. But, the truth is, it's exquisite all on its own, as a star act. Her recipe serves 4 to 6, but two people can easily eat the lot.*

SERVES 4 TO 6

8 oz (225 g) kumquats

8 oz (225 g) very good dried Turkish figs

3 tbsp warm water

1 tsp orange-flower water (optional)

2 tbsp orange juice

2 tbsp brandy

2 tsp soft brown sugar

To serve

8 oz (225 g) mascarpone cheese

1 – 2 pieces crystallized ginger, finely chopped

a pinch of ground cinnamon (optional)

Cut the kumquats in half. If they are inordinately stuffed full with pips, scoop them out, taking care not to discard the flesh too.

Remove the tough stalk from the figs and soak in the warm water, orange-flower water, orange juice, and brandy for about 10 minutes until the figs are a little softened and plumped up.

Transfer the soaked figs, soaking liquid and all, to a saucepan and add the kumquats and sugar. Over medium high heat bring to a boil, reduce heat to low, and simmer gently for 7 to 8 minutes until the kumquats are soft but still their own pretty shape and luminous orange, with their topsy-turvy tastes — the sweet skins and the sour insides — fully brought out. Add a little water or extra orange juice to prevent drying out and sticking during cooking.

Mix the crystallized ginger with the mascarpone, dust lightly with a little cinnamon, and serve with the kumquats.

FRESH FRUIT SALAD

Fruit salad served in small cups or bowls is a great dessert for a summer picnic. Since some fresh fruits turn brown quite quickly after being cut up, follow this recipe to keep your fruit salad fresh-looking and attractive for several hours. You may use whatever fruit you have and enjoy, but the principle is the same, and the fresh lemon juice is crucial.

SERVES 6 TO 8

juice of 2 lemons

4 (or more) tbsp sugar

2 bananas

I large tart apple

2 large, fully ripe peaches

I orange, peeled and cut into small pieces

2 kiwi fruit, peeled and cut

I cup seedless grapes

I cup pineapple chunks

4 cups fresh berries (strawberries, raspberries, blueberries, etc as available)

In a large bowl, add the lemon juice and stir in the sugar until dissolved. Slice the bananas directly into the bowl and toss them to coat with juice. Peel the apple and cut it into small chunks, add to the bananas, and gently toss again.

Peel the peaches by simmering them in boiling water for 25 seconds. If they are ripe the skin will slip off easily. Make a well in the center of the salad and slice the peaches into the juice.

With each addition of fruit to this point, the salad needs to be gently stirred to distribute the lemon juice over the cut surfaces of the fruit. When the peaches are incorporated, add the rest of the fruit and mix well again. Taste and add more sugar if desired.

Cover and chill until ready to eat. Serve with heavy cream, whipped cream, or vanilla yogurt.

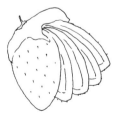

GINGER CRUNCH SQUARES

The pleasant bite of ginger makes these rich sweet morsels a little out of the ordinary, and a perfect treat for already well-fed picnickers.

MAKES 18 TO 20 PIECES

½ cup butter

¾ cup brown sugar, firmly packed

1½ cups flour

1½ tsp baking powder

1 tsp ground ginger

Icing

¼ cup butter

2 – 3 tsp ground ginger, divided

3 tbsp golden syrup

1 cup icing sugar

1 – 2 tsp ground ginger

Preheat oven to 375°F (190°C).

In a bowl, cream ½ cup butter with the sugar until light and creamy. Add the sifted flour and baking powder and 1 tsp of ground ginger, and work into the butter mixture to make a loose, crumbly dough. Press the dough evenly into a greased baking tin (9" square), and bake in the oven for 20 to 25 minutes, until golden brown.

For the icing, which is poured on the baked dough while it is still hot from the oven: in a small saucepan, melt the ¼ cup butter. Add the golden syrup and then blend in the icing sugar and ginger, according to taste. Remove from the heat and stir until smooth.

Allow the baked dough to cool for a few minutes, pour the warm icing over it, and cut into squares when the icing solidifies somewhat but before the squares are completely cool.

GINGERBREAD BUTTERFLY CUPCAKES

They look light-hearted enough to take flight, so eat them up quickly before they get away. To see how to turn your gingerbread cupcakes into butterflies, please see the recipe for Butterfly Cupcakes (p. 283).

MAKES 20 CUPCAKES

½ cup melted butter

⅔ cup brown sugar

1 large egg, beaten

2½ cups flour

1½ tsp baking soda

1½ tsp cinnamon

1½ tsp ground ginger

¼ tsp ground cloves

½ tsp salt

1 cup molasses

1 cup hot water

1½ – 2 cups whipped cream (¾ – 1 cup whipping cream)

Preheat oven to 350°F (175°C).

In a large bowl, beat the melted butter, brown sugar, and egg. Sift the dry ingredients together. In another bowl, combine the molasses and hot water. Add the dry ingredients and the molasses mixture alternately to the butter mixture, in 2 portions each, stirring just enough to blend.

Divide into 20 cupcake papers sitting in muffin pans. Bake in the oven for 20 minutes, or until the center of a cupcake springs back when gently pressed, or a cake tester comes out clean. Let the cakes cool on a rack before turning them into butterflies.

GOOSEBERRY (OR APPLE) CREAME

This delicious creamy dessert appears in contemporary recipe books as Gooseberry Fool. Unfortunately, gooseberries are increasingly rare these days, so if you cannot find a source for them, use tart cooking apples instead. You may cut down on the quantity of cream if you wish, since the recipe modified here suggests you "make of it what thicknes you please, and soe serve it up."

SERVES 6 TO 8

1¾ lb (800 g) ripe gooseberries or cooking apples

1 cup water

½ – 1 cup sugar

2 tbsp rosewater (optional)

3 cups whipped cream (1½ cups whipping cream, whipped stiff)

Wash and top and tail the gooseberries. If using apples, peel and core them, then chop them as for applesauce.

Place the fruit in a deep pot with the water over medium low heat, and slowly bring the water to the boil, turning the fruit with a spoon.

When the water is boiling and some of the fruit is softening enough to produce some juice, cover the pot, and gently simmer the fruit, stirring it frequently, until it is completely soft and cooked through. The gooseberries should split open as they cook.

Remove the pot from the heat and mash or food process the fruit and juice until smooth. (Rubbing it through a fine strainer is more authentic but oh so time-consuming!)

Add the sugar, testing for sweetness after ½ cup. Chill the fruit mixture thoroughly.

Stir in the rosewater if desired, and gently fold in the whipped cream, until the fool is smooth. Pour the dessert into a serving bowl and keep it well-chilled until serving time.

HOKEY POKEY BISCUITS

If you have friends who have lived in or visited Down Under, they will recognize these crunchy cookies. (Golden syrup is like a pale gold, delicately flavored molasses, and although it seldom appears in North American recipes, it is available in most supermarkets in cans or bottles. It's also good with pancakes or crumpets.)

MAKES ABOUT 40 COOKIES

½ cup butter

¾ cup brown sugar

I tbsp golden syrup

I tsp soda

I cup all-purpose flour

I tsp baking powder

Preheat oven to 375°F (190°C).

In a medium saucepan, melt the butter, sugar, and golden syrup. Remove from the heat when the mixture is warm but not yet hot, add the baking soda, and mix well. The mixture will become frothy. Add the sifted flour and baking powder, and blend the dough until smooth.

Place teaspoonsfuls of the mixture on greased cookie sheets, leaving room for a little spreading to take place. Bake in the oven for 10 to 12 minutes. Watch for burning after the first 10 minutes.

LAZY SHERRY TRIFLE

While it is laudable to make a trifle from scratch, it is possible to make a splendid dessert with some help from prepared ingredients.

SERVES 8

1 pound cake or plain sponge layer cake (about 1¼ lb [550 g])

1 14-oz (398-ml) can prepared egg custard

1 14-oz (398-ml) can crushed pineapple

1 10-oz (300-g) pkg frozen raspberries, thawed

5 tbsp sherry (rum is good too)

1½ cups whipping cream

Cut the cake into thin slices.

Drain the pineapple and raspberries and set the juice aside. Combine the fruit. Add the sherry to a quarter of a cup of the reserved juice.

Place a layer of sliced cake in a serving bowl. Drizzle about one-third of the liquid over the cake and spread one-third of the fruit mixture over it. Spread one-third of the custard over this layer, then repeat the layers in the same order. Cover the trifle and chill it for several hours or overnight.

Whip the cream in a cold bowl, spread it over the surface of the trifle, and keep the dessert cool until ready to eat.

Note: If you like a sweeter dessert, use rum rather than sherry and add ¼ cup fruit sugar to the raspberries.

LEMON CHEESECAKE WITH SOUR CREAM TOPPING

Cheesecake has been enjoyed in different guises and in different cultures for a very long time. By providing a lighter version of his scrumptious cheesecake, as well as the richer one given first, How to Cook Everything *author Mark Bittman stays in tune with our times in his presentation of a timeless favorite.*

SERVES 12

unsalted butter for greasing the pan

1 double recipe graham cracker crust

4 eggs, separated

24 oz (3 8-oz [225-g] packages) cream cheese

grated zest and juice of 1 lemon

1 cup sugar, plus 1 tbsp (optional)

1 tbsp all-purpose flour

2 cups sour cream (optional)

1 tsp vanilla extract (optional)

Prepare a double recipe of the graham cracker crust recipe as detailed on the box. Liberally butter a 9" or 10" springform pan, then press the crust into its bottom. Preheat the oven to 325°F (160°C).

In a large bowl, use an electric mixer to beat the egg yolks until light; add the cheese, lemon zest, and juice, and 1 cup of the sugar and beat until smooth. Stir in the flour.

In another bowl, beat the egg whites until they hold soft peaks; use a rubber spatula or your hand to fold them into the yolk-cheese mixture gently but thoroughly. Turn the batter into the prepared pan and place the pan in a baking pan large enough to hold it comfortably. Add warm water to the baking pan, so that it comes to within 1 inch (2.5 cm) of the top of the springform pan.

Transfer carefully to the oven and bake until the cake is just set and very lightly browned, about an hour. Turn the oven up to 450°F (230°C) if you're making the sour cream topping.

Remove the cake from the oven and cool completely if not adding the sour cream topping. If you're making the topping, combine the sour cream with the vanilla and the optional 1 tbsp sugar and spread on the top of the cake. Return it to the oven for 10 minutes, without the water bath; turn off the oven and let the cake cool for 30 minutes before removing it. Cool on a rack, cover with plastic wrap, then refrigerate until well chilled before slicing and serving. This will keep in good shape for several days.

RICOTTA CHEESECAKE

This is somewhat lighter (and far lower in calories, especially if you use part-skim ricotta): Substitute 1½ lbs (675 g) fresh ricotta for the cream cheese. Beat it in an electric mixer until lightened, then add the yolks. Increase the sugar to 1¼ cups; the flour remains the same. Substitute 1 tsp orange zest for the lemon zest, and use 1 additional tsp vanilla in place of the lemon juice. You can omit or include the sour cream topping, as you like. Bake as above.

LEMON CHOCOLATE
FUDGE SQUARES

This recipe needs to be made at least a day ahead of the picnic, and you will be hard pressed to make sure there's enough left for the feast itself if you start to nibble too soon. It's a no-bake dessert, with a lively combination of chocolate, lemon, and, if you choose, walnuts.

MAKES 32 SMALL PIECES

1 12-oz (350-g) package of arrowroot biscuits

½ cup butter

½ cup white sugar

2 tbsp cocoa

1 large egg

1 tsp vanilla extract

¼ cup fresh walnuts, chopped small

Icing

1½ cups icing sugar

2 tbsp soft butter

juice of a lemon

½ tsp lemon zest

dried cranberries or shreds of lemon zest (for decoration)

Crush the biscuits, a few at a time, in your hands, to make pieces no larger than 1 inch by ½ inch (2½ cm by 1 cm). You will end up with lots of crumbs too. That's good.

Melt the butter, sugar, and cocoa in a pot over low heat. Blend thoroughly, remove from the heat, and beat in the egg and vanilla. Add the broken biscuits (and ¼ cup of chopped walnuts if you desire).

Mix well and press firmly into a greased 8" pan. Cool and refrigerate overnight. Next day, frost with:

For the icing: blend the sugar, butter, and zest, adding just enough lemon juice to make a soft but not runny icing. Spread it over the chilled chocolate base, scoring it lightly with a fork.

Cut into rectangles, 1 inch (2½ cm) by 2 inches (5 cm). Place a "craisin" or a tiny shred of lemon zest in the center of each square. Chill well before removing from pan.

MACKROONS

No Elizabethan feast would be complete without almonds, here in a sweet setting, but often part of meat dishes too. To be authentic you should blanch your almonds and beat them in a mortar, but we are suggesting ground almonds instead. Rosewater and muske, both very popular in Elizabethan recipes, have been replaced in this contemporary version by the tart sweetness of baking cherries.

MAKES 24 COOKIES

1 cup (or ¼ lb [100g] pack) ground almonds

½ cup chopped walnuts or hazelnuts

¾ cup icing sugar

½ tsp baking powder

pinch salt

beaten white of one egg

12 baking cherries

Preheat oven to 325°F (160°C).

In a bowl, mix all ingredients except the cherries to a stiff paste. Form into small balls (about 24) and flatten slightly on parchment paper, or, if not available, on a well-greased oven tray. Press half a cherry, cut side down, lightly into each cookie.

Bake in the oven for about 20 minutes until cookies just begin to color. Cool on a rack.

MARINATED PEACHES

The first time I enjoyed this simple summer treat was in France, at the table of Monique and Pierre Leon, my amazingly patient French teachers. Since I had watched them prepare it, I could make it myself later, and have done so on countless summer afternoons in the decades since that time.

SERVES 6

1 cup white wine (dry Riesling or a fruity Southern Hemisphere Sauvignon Blanc would work well)

½ cup freshly squeezed lemon or lime juice

⅔ cup sugar (you can vary this amount depending on individual preference)

8 large fully ripe peaches

In a bowl, combine the wine, juice, and sugar until the sugar is dissolved. Set this syrup aside.

Bring a large pot of water to a boil, add half the peaches, and simmer for 25 seconds. Remove the peaches with a slotted spoon and put them in a colander. Cool them a little with cold water. Repeat with the rest of the peaches. Slide the skins off them, then slice them into the prepared syrup. Turn the pieces gently for a minute or two then taste the syrup and add a little more sugar as desired.

Leave the fruit to marinate for at least a couple of hours. Serve at room temperature in bowls or cups, with plenty of syrup for each serving.

MERINGUES

Oh what sensuous pleasure, to scoop up some whipped cream with your crisp, melt-in-the-mouth meringue, top it with a strawberry, a raspberry or two, or a slice of peach or nectarine, and let the flavors and textures explode in your mouth. Can be messy but what the heck! It's a picnic!

MAKES 20 TO 25 PIECES, OR 1 LARGE ONE

3 egg whites

¼ tsp salt

¼ tsp cream of tartar

1 cup fruit sugar or other superfine sugar

½ tsp vanilla or other flavoring

Preheat oven to 250°F (120°C).

Make sure egg whites contain no trace of yolk after separation and that the bowl used is completely dry. Beat the egg whites with salt and cream of tartar until they form a soft foam. Add a tbsp of the sugar and beat thoroughly. Continue to add sugar one spoonful at a time, beating well after each addition. The meringue should hold its shape in stiff peaks.

Cover a baking sheet with parchment paper, and use a spoon or an icing bag with a large nozzle to shape small meringues (they will spread a little during cooking, so allow ½ inch [1 cm] between each). Or shape a single round meringue on the parchment paper, allowing ½ inch [1 cm] of spread during cooking to achieve the size needed.

Bake the meringues in the oven until they are crisp: 1½ to 2 hours.

Cool them completely and store them in a container with a lid in a cool dry place and they will keep for several weeks. Serve them with plenty of whipped cream and fresh fruit.

MINT JULEP PEACHES

Nigella Lawson has the knack for elegant entertaining, as her gorgeous Forever Summer *makes abundantly clear. This recipe for Mint Julep Peaches emphasizes the splendor of the fruit in both taste and visual appeal. That every summer day should be so picture-perfect!*

SERVES 6 TO 8

3 cups (700 ml) water

1½ lbs (700 g) caster sugar (fine sugar, sometimes called "berry sugar"; not icing sugar)

1 cup (250 ml) bourbon

8 white-fleshed peaches

small bunch fresh mint (garnish)

In a wide-bottomed saucepan, combine water, sugar, and ⅘ cup (200 ml) of the bourbon. Swirl about to help the sugar start dissolving a bit, then put on the hob over medium heat and bring to a boil. Let it boil for 5 minutes or so and then turn the heat down so that the syrup simmers; you want pronounced but not fierce bubbles.

Cut the peaches in half and remove the stones then lower these halves so that they fit snugly, cut side down, in the pan and poach for a couple of minutes before turning them over and poaching for another 2 to 3 minutes cut side up; obviously, the ripeness of the peach should determine exactly how long they need cooking. (And if the peaches are very unripe, it will be much easier to remove the stones after cooking.) The best way of testing the peaches is to prod the cut sides with a fork; you'll be seeing the fruit hump side up later, and don't want any fork marks to mar the pink-cheeked beauty of these pale-fleshed peaches. When they feel tender but not flabbily soft, remove with a slotted spoon to a dish and continue till you've cooked all the peaches.

Pour the juices that have collected in the plate — pink from the color of the skins — back into the poaching liquid, itself blush-deepened from cooking the fruit, then measure 200 mls of the liquid into a small saucepan. Add the remaining ⅕ cup (50 ml) of bourbon to this pan, put on the heat, and boil till reduced by about half.

While this is happening, carefully peel off the skins; this should be easy enough. And in cooking, you'll see that the rosy fuzz leaves behind its marks on the white fruit so that each peach half is tenderly colored with an uneven pink. (You can freeze the remaining poaching liquid — just add a little water and a dash more bourbon when you reheat it.)

You can leave the peach halves, cut side down, covered with clingwrap, on a plate till you need them. Should the peaches start turning brown on standing, spritz with lime.

Let the reduced syrup cool in a jug. Before serving, pour some of the thick pink-bronze syrup over the peaches and scatter the torn-off mint leaves, some left whole, some roughly chopped, on top.

PEANUT BUTTER SQUARES

Rich, sweet, ideal for a picnic involving some vigorous exercise, but irresistible anytime anywhere, these nutty squares are another recipe contribution from Mark B., who reckons there might be 5,000 calories in a single panful! Don't tell anyone!

MAKES 32

Base

½ cup corn syrup

½ cup brown sugar

2 tbsp butter

I cup peanut butter

I cup crisp rice cereal

2 cups corn flakes

Icing

¼ cup butter

½ cup brown sugar

2 tbsp milk

I cup icing sugar

For the base: in a pot over medium heat, bring the corn syrup, brown sugar, and butter to a boil, remove from the heat, and add the peanut butter and the two cereals. Mix well, then press the mixture into an 8" x 8" pan.

For the icing: in a small pot, heat the butter and sugar until bubbling, and continue to heat and stir for 2 minutes. Remove from the heat and add the milk. Bring the mixture to the boil again, then remove from the heat and add the icing sugar. Beat the icing until smooth, and spread it evenly over the base mixture.

Chill until firm. Cut into small rectangles I by 2 inches (2½ by 5 cm).

PRUNES IN PORT

Dried plums, which is how we are to address prunes in order to be politically correct, have been much maligned under their old name. This recipe proves once and for all that they do not deserve their bad reputation. Eaten at leisure on a summer's night, with perhaps a dollop of crème fraîche or sour cream, Prunes in Port makes an idyllic dessert.

MAKES LOTS

1 lb (455 g) large prunes (not pitted ones, which will lose their shape too easily)

4 cups good quality port wine, or enough to cover the prunes in a large jar

Select a glass container that you can cover, and that will accommodate all the prunes. Pour enough port wine over the prunes in the jar to cover them and 1 inch (2½ cm) more. Place the lid on the container, and leave it in a cool place.

In the first few days, check the level of the port in the jar and top it up to just cover the fruit. After that, let the prunes macerate for a couple of months. (No sneaking any!)

Serve the prunes in small dishes with a spoonful or two of the juice, and crème fraîche, sour cream, or pressed yogurt.

prunes

PURPLE GRAPE JELLY

Agar agar is a thickening, or gelling, agent used in Asian cultures over the centuries, and it has a number of things over its cousin, gelatin. For one thing, it's not made from animal by-products (it's even nutritious!), and for another, it keeps its shape even in very hot weather. Its texture is not exactly the same as gelatin's but once you've tried it you won't want to switch back. Buy agar agar in flake form from Asian markets and health food stores, and be sure to follow the directions below for its use.

SERVES 6 TO 8

I lb (455 g) deep purple–colored grapes (Concord or Coronation grapes are very suitable)

I cup water

¼ – ½ cup sugar

2 – 3 tbsp agar agar flakes

Wash the grapes and remove them from the stems. Place them in a pot with the water and slowly bring them to a boil. Let them simmer for about 7 to 10 minutes, covered, or until they are soft and pulpy. Push them through a strainer, mashing the grapes to push as much pulp as possible through. Discard the skins and seeds.

Measure the grape juice and pulp and add to it ¼ cup of the sugar. Stir to dissolve the sugar, taste for sweetness, then allow the syrup to cool.

When it is completely cool, add the agar agar flakes in the proportion of I tbsp of agar agar for each cup of liquid (¼ cup of liquid would need I tsp of agar agar). Stir well for a couple of minutes.

Set aside for 15 minutes to soak, then stir well again and bring the mixture slowly to the boil, stirring and whisking it to help the agar agar flakes soften completely. Simmer it for a couple of minutes then whisk it again and remove it from the heat. The flakes should be invisible now, but if there are some clear gelatinous-looking bubbles, you can strain them out.

Pour the mixture into a square pan or casserole and allow it to cool, then refrigerate it until it is completely set. It should set firmly enough for you to cut it into small cubes, which look very pretty spooned into a small bowl and topped with a dab of whipped cream or I tbsp of crème fraîche.

RASPBERRY MOUSSE

Because it seems sacrilegious to cook fresh raspberries in their all-too-short season, this recipe is best made with frozen fruit. Fortunately, last year's harvest is sometimes on sale in June as the supermarkets empty their freezers in readiness for the new crop. If you are using commercially frozen raspberries they may already be in syrup, and in that case you may not need to add any sugar to this recipe, formulated for loose pack frozen raspberries. To serve the mousse, decorate it with some fresh raspberries and maybe a drizzle of melted chocolate, or add fresh raspberries to each serving.

SERVES 4 TO 6

2 cups frozen raspberries

½ cup sugar

2 tbsp cornstarch

¼ cup water

I cup whipping cream

fresh raspberries (garnish)

In a pot over medium heat, heat the thawed raspberries in their own juice until nearly boiling. Add the sugar and dissolve. In a small bowl or cup, mix the cornstarch and water until smooth, then add it to the hot fruit and stir well. Continue stirring as the mixture heats and thickens.

Remove the pot from the heat as soon as the mixture starts to boil. Cool it, stirring it gently from time to time so that a skin does not develop on the surface. Then refrigerate the mixture.

When it is completely chilled, whip the cream until it is stiff, and fold it into the fruit mixture until it is smoothly incorporated.

Spoon it into a serving container with a lid. Keep the mousse chilled until serving time. Sprinkle fresh raspberries over top before serving.

RHUBARB AND STRAWBERRY PIE

Mark B. and his family make great fruit pies as a family tradition. The pastry, his Aunt Sally's recipe, makes a tender crust, and the combination of rhubarb and strawberries is perfect for it.

SERVES 6

1 cup sugar

¼ cup flour

¼ tsp salt

½ tsp nutmeg

2 cups rhubarb, chopped

2 cups strawberries, sliced, or blackberries

Preheat oven to 400°F (200°C).

In a bowl, combine all the ingredients and allow to stand for 20 minutes, to start the juices running.

Roll out the pastry (see recipe below), and cut a circle to fit a 10" pie plate. The top crust can be another circle or a lattice made of pastry strips.

Place the fruit mixture in the pan, then top with the second circle or lattice, moistening the edges of the circle with a wet pastry brush to make sure the two crusts adhere. Bake in the oven for about 40 to 45 minutes. Serve slightly warm.

Pastry for fruit pie

1 cup shortening

¼ cup soft butter

3 cups flour

1 tsp salt

½ cup cold water

Cream the shortening and butter, then add the flour and salt (previously sifted together). Add the water all at once and mix until combined. Chill pastry for easier handling. Makes 3 crusts, enough for 2 pies with lattice topping.

RUSTIC APRICOT GALETTE

Regan Daley can sweet-talk you through anything, with the clarity of her instructions and the reassurance of her kindly voice! Pâte brisée is a breeze under her guidance and you can do it, too. She suggests serving this glorious galette with honeyed mascarpone, lightly sweetened whipped cream, or vanilla ice cream.

SERVES 6 TO 8

Pâte Brisée

1¼ cups all-purpose flour

½ tsp salt

I tsp granulated sugar

½ cup unsalted butter, cold, in small cubes

3 – 5 tbsp ice water

Filling

2 lbs (900 g) ripe but not mushy, fresh apricots, preferably local

½ cup granulated sugar (or more if the fruit is not very sweet)

3 tbsp cornstarch

2 tbsp unsalted butter, cold, cut into small bits

I large egg white, lightly beaten with I tbsp water

I tbsp granulated sugar, for sprinkling

Food processor method: place the flour, salt, and sugar in the bowl of a food processor fitted with a steel blade. Add the butter cubes and pulse using short bursts until the largest pieces of butter are about the size of large peas. Add the ice water through the open feed tube while using long pulses, until the dough comes together. Stop the machine and feel the dough. It should hold together well when squeezed. Add a little more water if the mixture is too dry and crumbly.

By-hand method: place the flour, salt, and sugar in a large bowl and stir to blend. Add the butter cubes and, using a pastry blender or two knives, cut them into the dry ingredients until the largest pieces of butter are about the size of large peas. Add the water, beginning with 3 tbsp all at once, and use the tips of your fingers to lightly and rapidly toss and rub the mixture until the dough holds together when squeezed. If necessary, add I or 2 more tbsp of the ice water until the desired consistency is achieved.

Turn the dough out onto a piece of plastic wrap and use the plastic to help form the dough into a flattish disk. Wrap tightly, pressing the dough to the edges of the plastic packet. Chill at least 2 hours, or up to 4 days. Dough may be frozen at this point, wrapped very well, for up to 2 months. Thaw overnight in the refrigerator before proceeding.

Preheat oven to 425°F (220°C). Lay a large rectangle of parchment paper on a surface large enough to roll out your pastry. Remove the pastry from the refrigerator and let it temper slightly, until it is soft enough to roll out.

Meanwhile, wipe the apricots with a damp towel and dry them well. Cut each apricot in half and discard the stone. Cut each half in half again and place the quarters in a large non-reactive bowl. Add the ½ cup sugar and the cornstarch, then toss to thoroughly coat.

Lightly dust the sheet of parchment paper with a little flour and place the disk of pastry in the centre. Roll the pastry out to a circle about 12 inches (30 cm) in diameter and ¼ inch (.6 cm) thick and brush away any excess flour. Make sure the pastry isn't sticking to the paper; periodically lift the edges and sprinkle the paper with a dash more flour if it does. (If the pastry is really sticking, slide the paper onto a cutting board or baking sheet and pop the whole thing in the refrigerator for a few minutes. Warm pastry will stick no matter what, and will absorb so much flour that it will become tough. Keep it cool and you'll have no troubles.) When you have a large enough circle, slide the paper and the pastry onto a large baking sheet.

Pile the apricots and their sugary syrup into the centre of the pastry circle, leaving 1½ to 2 inches (3.8 to 5 cm) around the outside free of filling or syrup. Pat the fruit together to make it as compact as possible, mounding it a little higher in the very centre. Dot the filling with the little pieces of butter, scattering them over the fruit. With clean fingers, fold up the outside edge of the pastry over the filling, gently pressing the folds together to secure the pastry. Brush the pastry with the egg white/water glaze, then sprinkle with the 1 tbsp sugar.

Place the baking sheet in the centre of the oven and bake at 425°F (220°C) for 20 minutes, then reduce the temperature to 375°F (190°C) and bake another 25 to 35 minutes, or until the pastry is crisp and golden and the filling is bubbling in the centre of the tart. Cool on the sheet set over a wire rack. The galette may be served warm or at room temperature. On its own, it makes a delicate and refreshing dessert for a summer lunch or light supper; paired with one of the accompaniments suggested above, it becomes a truly celebratory finale!

SHERRY BALLS

Easy to prepare and convenient because you need to make them well before the picnic (before the last minute rush is even thought about), they are also sensuously, satisfyingly sweet and rich. They will keep in the fridge for a week or more.

MAKES 4 DOZEN BITE-SIZE BALLS

¼ cup candied ginger

¼ cup baking cherries

½ cup raisins

¼ cup dried apricots

½ cup toasted almonds

½ cup filberts or pecans

½ cup melted butter

¾ cup icing sugar

1 cup graham crumbs

3 tbsp sherry

1 tsp orange or lemon zest (optional)

1¾ cups fine-shredded unsweetened coconut, divided

Chop or coarsely food-process the first 6 ingredients. Blend the butter, icing sugar, crumbs, and sherry and mix in the chopped fruit and 1 cup of the coconut.

Form the mixture into small balls and roll each in the remaining coconut. (Messy, but easier if you put the coconut in a small deep bowl. You can also chill the mixture a little first).

Place the balls in the fridge and do not even taste one for at least 24 hours! They need that time to develop flavor and texture.

STRAWBERRIES

Because of the season of their ripening, and because they are so irresistibly delicious, fresh strawberries need to be included in summer picnics, especially if you live in an area where strawberries are available locally. Of all the many ways to serve them, my favorite one is traditional Strawberry Shortcake (p. 319) with lashings of whipped cream. And of course, luxurious and sensual Chocolate-Dipped Strawberries (p. 289)! But there are other simpler presentations that are also very good.

Macerated Strawberries

SERVES 6 TO 8

12 cups strawberry slices

⅔ cup port wine or your favorite
  liqueur

Macerated Strawberries
Wash, dry, and slice the strawberries, then toss them in a bowl with the liquid, and leave at room temperature for an hour or more, turning them occasionally. Good with whipped cream, pressed yogurt and brown sugar, or sweetened ricotta cheese.

Strawberries with Yogurt Honey Dip
See recipe for Yogurt Honey Dip (p. 322)

STRAWBERRY SHORTCAKE

To be convinced that summer has truly arrived, you need to bake (and eat) a Strawberry Shortcake. As long as you whip the cream at the last minute, and keep it cool by sitting it over a bowl or plastic bag of ice cubes in a cooler, it is perfect fare for a picnic, delicious, colorful, and sensuous. The sweetness of this classic dessert comes mainly from the fruit and the sugar you add to it, but sweetening the whipped cream with a little sugar or honey will make the dessert more appealing to those with a sweet tooth.

SERVES 8

3 cups unbleached flour

2 tbsp baking powder

3 tbsp sugar

½ tsp salt

⅔ cup butter

1 large egg

milk, to make 1¼ cups in combination with the egg

4 – 6 cups ripe strawberries, washed, cored, and sliced

¼ cup fruit sugar

¼ cup sherry or liqueur (optional)

2 cups whipping cream

Preheat oven to 450°F (230°C).

Butter two 8"round cake pans. Sift the first 4 ingredients and cut the butter in to them (use well-chilled butter) as for pastry.

Beat the egg in a two-cup measure, add milk to 1¼ cups, and then beat again to blend. Make a well in the center of the flour mixture and pour in the liquid ingredients, then mix with a fork, working the mixture as little as possible in order to blend the ingredients.

Divide the dough into 2 portions and press and shape it gently into the two cake pans. Bake in the oven for 16 to 18 minutes. Turn out of the pans and set to cool on a rack.

Gently stir the fruit sugar and sherry into the sliced berries. Whip the cream into soft peaks and spoon it into a lidded bowl which can be fitted into a larger bowl of ice.

When the shortcakes are ready to be served, cut them into wedges, heap each with sliced berries, including some juice, and top with a spoonful of whipped cream.

TRADITIONAL COVERED APPLE PIE

Wanda Beaver of Wanda's Pie in the Sky fame, knows all about pies and how to make them fabulously good. Her recipe for this traditional pie includes a pie crust recipe too, with step-by-step instructions to make it easy. So why not give it a go, even if you haven't made a pie before? The aroma of apple pie baking, and especially this fragrantly spicy one, makes the work worthwhile even before you start eating!

SERVES 8

1 recipe Double Crust Pastry
   (see p. 321)

7 cups tart apples, peeled and cut into
   ¼-inch (.6-cm) slices

½ cup granulated sugar

2 tbsp cornstarch

2 tsp lemon juice

1 tsp ground cinnamon

½ tsp ground nutmeg

2 tbsp butter

1 egg beaten with 1 tbsp cold water

1 tbsp granulated sugar

Prepare the pastry as directed, setting aside the smaller disk. Preheat oven to 400°F (200°C).

In a large bowl mix together the apples, ½ cup sugar, cornstarch, lemon juice, cinnamon, and nutmeg. Turn into the prepared crust, leaving room at the edges for sealing and crimping the top crust. Dot with the butter. On a floured board roll out the remaining disk of dough into a circle ⅛-inch (0.3 cm) thick. Cut a circle the size of the pie plate. Cut vents in the dough to allow the steam to escape. Wet the edges of the pie crust, and place the pastry circle over the fruit. Seal and flute the edges. Brush with the egg wash and sprinkle with the 1 tbsp sugar. If time allows, refrigerate for 30 minutes.

Bake in the oven for 10 minutes, then reduce heat to 350°F (175°C). Bake for 50 to 60 minutes, or until the pastry is golden and the filling is bubbly. Serve warm or at room temperature. Store lightly covered at room temperature for up to 2 days.

apple pie

DOUBLE CRUST PASTRY

Here is the pastry you need to make Wanda Beaver's Traditional Covered Apple Pie. You'll surely find it useful for other pies, too.

MAKES PASTRY FOR ONE 10-INCH (25-CM) DOUBLE-CRUST PIE

2¼ cups all-purpose flour

¼ tsp salt

½ cup cold butter, cut into ½-inch (1-cm) pieces

½ cup shortening, cut into ½-inch (1-cm) pieces and frozen for 15 minutes

⅓ cup cold water

Make sure all the ingredients are as cold as possible. Using a food processor or a pastry cutter and a large bowl, combine the flour, salt, butter, and shortening. Process or cut in until the mixture resembles coarse meal and begins to clump together. Sprinkle with water, let rest for 30 seconds, and then either process very briefly or cut with about 15 strokes of the pastry cutter, just until the dough begins to stick together and come away from the sides of the bowl.

Turn onto a lightly floured work surface and press together to form a short cylinder. Divide into ⅔ and ⅓ and press into disks. Wrap in plastic and chill for at least 20 minutes.

Allow the dough to warm slightly at room temperature if it is too hard to roll. On a lightly floured board, roll the larger disk to a thickness of ⅛ inch (0.3 cm). Cut a circle about 1½ inches (3.8 cm) larger than the pie plate and transfer the pastry to the plate by folding it in half or by rolling it onto the rolling pin. Turn the pastry under, leaving an edge that hangs about ½ inch (1.2 cm) over the plate. Roll the second disk as directed by the recipe.

YOGURT HONEY DIP

Skim yogurt makes this a healthy alternative to whole-milk yogurt, but whatever yogurt you decide to use, the addition of a little honey transforms it into a dessert, served with fresh fruit chunks.

MAKES 1 CUP

1 cup plain yogurt

3 – 4 tsp liquid honey or more, as desired

Combine the two ingredients, stirring as little as possible, drizzling the honey over the surface of the yogurt and folding it in. The more you stir natural yogurt (i.e., no thickeners or stabilizers, simply milk and bacterial cultures), the thinner it becomes.

DRINKS

FRUIT PUNCH

This mild, fruity punch has a citrus base, with a little zing of ginger.

MAKES 12 1-CUP SERVINGS, PLUS ICE

1 cup strong tea (brewed for 4 to 5 minutes only, cooled)

¾ cup lemon juice

1½ cups pineapple juice

1½ cups orange juice

1 qt (1 litre) ginger ale

1 qt (1 litre) 7-Up

8 lemon wedges, frozen (garnish)

8 sprigs mint (garnish)

In a large container, combine tea and 3 juices. Chill, and just before serving add the ginger ale and 7-Up.

Serve over ice, in tall glasses, with a frozen lemon wedge and a mint sprig in each glass.

HIPPOCRAS

This is an ancient drink, sweet and spicy, credited to Hippocrates, who would have brewed it for its medicinal qualities. It was widely enjoyed by Elizabethans, as it had been by their ancestors for centuries. It survives in various forms in various cultures as mulled or spiced wine, glogg, and by other names. Sherry is used in our recipe as the equivalent of sack. Drink your Hippocras as a liqueur, after you've eaten well.

MAKES ABOUT 3 26-OZ (750-ML) BOTTLES

2 26-oz (750-ml) bottles dry white wine

1 26-oz (750-ml) bottle sweet sherry

½ – ⅔ (or more) cups sugar

2 tbsp freshly grated ginger root (or more)

6 cinnamon sticks

2 nutmegs, broken into several pieces

1 tsp cloves

In a 3 or 4 quart (3 or 4 litre) jar with a lid, mix all the ingredients until the sugar has dissolved. Let the mixture stand for 2 days, then strain it through a fine strainer or filter it with coffee filters, and pour it into bottles.

HOT BEVERAGES YOU CAN TAKE IN A VACUUM FLASK

COCOA

MAKES 4 CUPS

1 cup boiling water

¼ cup cocoa

pinch salt

2 – 4 tbsp sugar

3 cups milk

With a whisk, blend the water, cocoa, salt, and sugar in a saucepan, then bring to a boil over medium heat, stirring constantly. When it has boiled, whisk in the milk, and bring back up to the simmer point. Pour into a vacuum flask.

HOT LEMONADE

MAKES ABOUT 4½ CUPS

4 cups water

½ – 1 cup sugar

the skin of 1 lemon, cut into slices

8 tbsp of lemon juice (juice of 2 or 3 lemons)

Bring the water, sugar, and lemon skin to a boil, and boil for 2 minutes. Remove from heat and remove the lemon skin. Add the lemon juice, taste to adjust sweetness, and pour the hot drink into a vacuum flask.

HOT CRANBERRY JUICE

MAKES 4 CUPS

4 cups cranberry cocktail

1 lemon, sliced

6 cloves

fresh grated nutmeg

1 – 2 tsp honey

In a pot over medium high heat, bring the ingredients just to simmer point. Remove lemon slices before pouring drink into the flask.

ICED MINT SYRUP

Fragrant and pretty, this is also a great thirst quencher.

SERVES 8

4 cups mint leaves, packed firmly into a measuring cup

⅔ cup sugar

8 cups water

½ cup fresh lemon juice

lemon slices and sprigs of mint (garnish)

In a food processor or blender, process the mint leaves with half of the sugar until the mint is finely-chopped. Add the rest of the sugar to the water and stir until dissolved. Add the lemon juice and the processed mint. Stir and then allow to settle for half an hour.

To strain the liquid, use paper coffee filters, or cheesecloth lining a metal strainer. Chill the strained syrup and serve in tall glasses of ice with a mint sprig and a lemon slice.

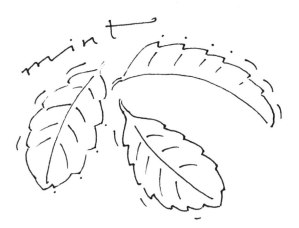

ICED TEA

This classic deserves to be made with good quality loose tea for clear, refreshing flavor. Try it with Assam tea leaves.

SERVES 10

3 tbsp loose tea

4 cups (1 litre) boiling water

2 cups cold water

ice cubes

1 lemon (optional)

sugar or honey (optional)

Place the loose tea in a teapot that you have heated with hot water and emptied. Pour the boiling water over the loose tea and leave to steep for 3 minutes. Strain the liquid into a glass or porcelain container and allow it to cool to room temperature.

Add 2 cups of cold water, and, if desired, a lemon cut into very thin slices, and a tbsp or two of sugar or honey. To serve the iced tea, fill glasses with ice cubes and pour the tea over. This recipe makes approximately 6 cups of strong tea, which, with ice cubes, makes 10 servings.

LEMONADE

A simple recipe for a refreshing drink, served over generous quantities of ice cubes. And try freezing thin lemon wedges to add to each glass at serving time.

MAKES 12 TO 14 ½-CUP SERVINGS, PLUS LOTS OF ICE

juice of 3 or 4 lemons (about 1 cup)

zest of 1 lemon

¾ – 1½ cups sugar

6 cups water

In a beverage container, combine all the ingredients and stir until the sugar is completely dissolved, then chill the lemonade until it is needed. It will keep well for several days if refrigerated.

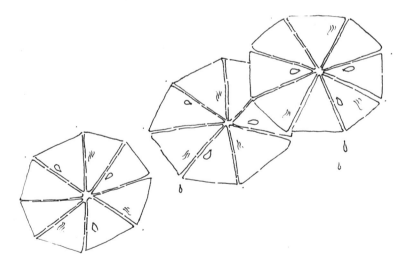

LEMONADE II

This is an old-time recipe for lemonade, and has the delicately bitter tang that lemon pith adds. For best flavor it should be made the day before it is needed, and it will keep in the fridge for several days.

MAKES ABOUT 12 1-CUP SERVINGS, PLUS ICE

4 or 5 lemons

10 cups water

1½ cups sugar

1 tsp salt

Scrape the zest from one of the lemons and put it in a large pot.

Cut the lemons, squeeze the juice and set it aside (should be 1 cup of juice).

Cut 4 of the squeezed lemon halves into two or three chunks, and place in the pot with the zest. Add water, sugar, and salt, and heat and stir the liquid until the sugar is dissolved. Bring to a boil, then simmer gently for 5 minutes.

Remove the pot from the heat and allow the syrup to cool completely, then remove the lemon skins, and add the lemon juice. Chill the lemonade before serving over ice. You will need to taste the lemonade to adjust the sweetness, either adding a little more lemon juice, or a little more sugar to taste.

MULLED WINE

A Shiraz (or Syrah) wine is good in this recipe, but other reds would no doubt be excellent too. Whatever your choice, your cold weather picnic will be the better for a mug or two, or three, of this mulled wine.

SERVES 6

Syrup

1 cup sugar

½ cup water

3 tsp whole cloves

2 sticks cinnamon, broken in pieces

1 nutmeg, crushed

zest of 1 lemon

peel of 2 mandarins or tangerines

1 cup lemon juice

½ cup lime juice

½ cup orange juice

2 bottles red wine

lemon, orange, and lime slices (garnish)

In a pot over high heat, combine the syrup ingredients and bring to a boil. Continue boiling for 5 minutes.

Strain syrup and add the lemon, lime, and orange juices.

In a large pot over medium heat, heat the mixture well and add the red wine. Heat again and serve very hot with a fruit slice as garnish.

SPICED FRUIT PUNCH

The delicately bitter undertone of tea is what characterizes many refreshing fruit punches, and this one, spicy and tangy with ginger, is particularly refreshing on a hot day.

MAKES ABOUT 24 GLASSES, WITH ICE AND GINGER ALE

8 cups apple juice

2 tbsp fresh ginger, grated

2 cups frozen raspberries in syrup, or 2 cups fresh raspberries, slightly crushed with ¼ cup fruit sugar

2 lemons, sliced thinly

2 cups strong tea

20 whole cloves

1 tsp cinnamon

½ tsp nutmeg, grated

3 1-quart (1-litre) bottles soda water or sparkling mineral water (for serving)

In a large beverage container, combine the apple juice, ginger, raspberries, and lemon slices and set aside.

Brew the tea for 4 minutes only, then remove the tea bags or teaball and add the cloves, cinnamon, and nutmeg. Allow the tea to cool completely.

Remove the cloves from the tea, then add it to the apple juice mixture and chill.

To serve, half fill glasses with Spiced Fruit Punch and top up with ice cubes and soda water.

WINE FRUIT PUNCH

To serve this colorful red punch, pour half a glass of the recipe below and add half a glass of wine and a small sprig of mint. If you prefer a less sweet punch, use 2 bottles of soda water instead of 1 each of soda water and ginger ale.

MAKES 36 ½-CUP SERVINGS

1 can frozen cranberry concentrate

1 can frozen raspberry concentrate

1 can frozen pineapple concentrate

3 cups strong tea, brewed for not more than 4 minutes

1 orange, sliced

1 lemon, sliced

2 trays of ice cubes

1 quart (1 litre) bottle ginger ale, well-chilled

1 quart (1 litre) bottle soda water, well-chilled

In a beverage container, combine the juice concentrates with the cooled tea, the sliced fruit, and the ice cubes. Keep refrigerated until just before serving, allowing the ice cubes time to melt somewhat, but not completely. Add the ginger ale and the soda. The punch is now ready to be combined with wine, preferably a dry, crisp white wine, but a light red would work well too.

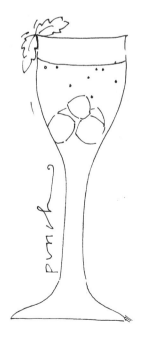

ENDNOTES

BIBLIOGRAPHY

"Advice to Picnic Parties." *Punchinello*, August 20, 1870, p. 325

Allen, Ida Bailey. *The Sunshine Book*, 3d ed. Loose-Wiles Biscuit Company, c. 1920s.

Atwood, E. "Hints for Outing Luncheons." *American Homes*, July 1913, pp. 262-63.

Austen, Jane. *Emma*. 1815. London: Oxford University Press, 1984.

Beard, D. "How to Have Fun at a Picnic." *Ladies' Home Journal*, July 1900, pp. 17-23.

Beard, James. *Treasury of Outdoor Cooking*. Illustrated by Helen Federico. New York: Golden Press, 1960.

Beeton, Mrs [Isabella Mary]. *Mrs Beeton's Book of Household Management, a Guide to Cookery in All Branches*. 1861. Rev ed. London: Ward, Lock, 1906.

Berg, H.O. "Picnics in Cleveland." *Playground*, August 1923, pp. 271-72.

Berton, Pierre, and Berton, Janet. *Pierre & Janet Berton's Canadian Food Guide*, 2d rev. ed. Toronto: McClelland & Stewart, 1974.

Botsford, H. "Picnics Give a Man a Chance!" *American Home*, July 1932, p. 42.

————— . "Remember When Picnics Were Fun?" *American Home*, July 1944, pp. 58-59.

Brownstone, Cecily. "Picnics: We Love You." *Parents' Magazine*, July 1946, p. 49.

"Building an Insulated Picnic Box." *Popular Science*, May 1952, pp. 202-03.

Carhart, A.H. "Picnic in Your Garden." *American Home*, July 1933, p. 55.

Colwin, Laurie. *Home Cooking*. New York: Knopf, 1988.

"Combination Food Hamper and Picnic Table." *Popular Mechanic*, June 1956, p. 189.

Cooke, Maud C. *Social Etiquette or, Manners and Customs of Polite Society. Containing Rules of Etiquette for All Occasions . . . Forming a Complete Guide to Self-Culture. The Art of Dressing Well, Conversation . . . Etc.* Boston: G.M. Smith, 1896.

"Dangerous: The Evils That Spring From Moonlight Picnics." *Brooklyn Eagle*, July 19, 1883, pp. 2 + ff.

David, Elizabeth. *An Omelette and a Glass of Wine*. New York: Viking, 1985.

De la Falaise, Maxime. *Seven Centuries of English Cooking*. 1973. New York: Grove Press, 1992.

Dewalt, Ernest R. "Working Time: Two Evenings." *Popular Science*, October 1943, pp. 292-94.

Douglas, Norman [Pilaff Bey]. *Venus in the Kitchen, Or, Love's Cookery Book*. London: Heinemann, 1952.

"Enjoyment: The Picnics and Excursions of Yesterday." *Brooklyn Eagle*, July 23, 1875, p. 4.

Fisher, M.F.K. *The Art of Eating*. New York: The World Publishing Company, 1954.

————— . *Here Let Us Feast: A Book of Banquets*. San Francisco: North Point Press, 1986.

Florence. "Picnics and Parties." *The Ladies' Repository: A Monthly Periodical Devoted to Literature, Arts, and Religion*, July 1848, p. 216.

Fox, Genevieve. "Mother's Kitchen in a City Park." *American City*, August 1925, p. 139.

Gallman, J. Matthew, ed. *The Civil War Chronicle: The Only Day-by-Day Portrait of America's Tragic Conflict as Told by Soldiers, Journalists, Politicians, Farmers, Nurses, Slaves, and Other Eyewitnesses.* New York: Crown Publishers, 2000.

"Give Me Ants, Lots of Ants." *American Home*, July 1964, p. 6.

Glass, M. "Picnics, Or What to Do Till the Dry Cleaner Comes." *Delineator*, August 1932, p. 91.

Hellman, Lillian, and Feibleman, Peter S. *Eating Together: Recipes and Recollections.* Boston: Little, Brown, 1984.

Hess, Karen. *Martha Washington's Book of Cookery.* New York: Columbia University Press, 1981.

Hewes, Lydia "Men on Picnics." *Good Housekeeping*, August 1940, p. 127.

"Homemade TV Meals Go to the Beach." *American Home*, August 1957, p. 56.

"Hot Dog Holocaust at Los Angeles Beach." *Life*, October 5, 1953, p. 53.

"How to Keep a Man Happy." *American Homes*, June 1958, p. 45-48.

Hunter, T. "Novel Ideas for Picnics." *Ladies' Home Journal*, July 1910, p. 29.

"I Hate Picnics." *Better Homes and Gardens*, July 1948, pp. 94-95.

Kirschbaum, Gabrielle. *Picnics for Lovers.* Illustrated by Frank Newfeld and Deana Richardson. Toronto: Van Nostrond Reinhold Ltd., 1980.

Liebling, A.J. *Liebling Abroad.* New York: Playboy Press, 1981.

Lyon, Jean. "Back Yard Picnics With Junior." *Parents' Magazine*, August 1953, p. 70.

MacFayden, B. "Making Men Pro-Picnic." *Good Housekeeping*, July 1930, pp. 86-87.

May, Robert. *The Accomplisht Cook, or, The Art & Mystery of Cookery: Wherein the Whole Art Is Revealed in a More Easie and Perfect Method Than Hath Been Publist in Any Language.* 1660. Facsimile of 1685 edition available online at *bib.ub.es/grewe/showbook.pl?gw025*.

McIntyre, Nancy Fair. *It's a Picnic.* Illustrated by Abner Graboff. New York: Viking, 1969.

Mellon, E.E. "Picnics Children Can Handle." *American Home*, August 1939, p. 45.

"A Mother's Day and Municipal Picnic." *The Outlook*, September 20, 1913, pp. 112-13.

"Municipal Picnic Areas and the Tourist." *Recreation*, June 1954, pp. 334-35.

Murray, Gladys. "Picnicking With a Baby." *Parents' Magazine*, July 1936, p. 21.

"Notes From Chicago." *Punchinello*, July 23, 1870, p. 269.

Normand, Jean-Michel. "Picnics Are Chic," *Le Monde.* May 28, 2003.

Phillips, H.I. "Book of Picnic Etiquette." *Collier's*, September 5, 1925, pp. 18-19.

"Picnic Excursions." *Appleton's Journal of Literature, Science, and Art*, August 14, 1669, p. 625.

"Picnic Parks and Gadgets Lure Public Outdoors." *Life*, June 9, 1941, pp. 74-77.

"Picnic Time." *Ladies' Home Journal*, July 1973, pp. 84-85.

Picnic Time. Lynn, Mass: Lydia E. Pinkham Medicine Co., c. 1920s.

"Plan of the Month: Suitcase Picnic Bench." *Popular Mechanic*, July 1952, pp. 164-65.

Post, Emily. *Etiquette: The Blue Book of Social Usage.* New York: Funk & Wagnalls, 1960.

"Recreation Facilities and Equipment." *Recreation*, October 1954, pp. 476-78.

"Renaissance of the Picnic." *Playground*, July 1923, p. 225.

"The Rise of the Picnic." *The Economist*, August 2, 2003, p. 49.

Simonds, M.G. "How Do You Handle Booyahs for Commercialized Picnics?" *American City*, February 1940, p. 77.

Smith, G.P. and Rile, K. "Are You a Picnic Pest?" *Good Housekeeping*, July 1938, p. 14.

"There's a New Era in Picnicking." *House Beautiful*, July 1946, pp. 92-93.

Thompson, E. P. *Customs in Common: Studies in Traditional Popular Culture.* New York: The New Press, 1991.

Trillin, Calvin. *Alice, Let's Eat.* New York: Smithmark Publishing, 1996.

————— . *American Fried: Adventures of a Happy Eater.* Garden City, NY: Doubleday, 1974.

United States. Department of Agriculture. "A Century of Change in America's Eating Habits." *FoodReview*, January-April 2000. Available online at *ers.usda.gov/publications/foodreview/jan2000*.

Villas, James. *American Taste: A Celebration of Gastronomy Coast-to-Coast.* Guilford, Conn: The Lyons Press, 1997.

Visser, Margaret. *The Rituals of Dinner: The Origins, Evolution, Eccentricities, and Meaning of Table Manners.* Toronto: HarperCollins, 1991.

"War Games Picnic." *Life*, September 14, 1942, pp. 122-25.

"Wartime Parties." *Life*, June 8, 1942, pp. 74-75.

"What to Wear to the Company Outing." *Glamour*, July 1988, p. 78.

Wheeler, Richard. *A Rising Thunder: From Lincoln's Election to the Battle of Bull Run: An Eyewitness History.* New York: HarperCollins, 1994.

Wine, Cynthia. *Eating for a Living: Notes From a Professional Diner.* Toronto: Viking, 1993.

Zyvatkauskas, Betty, and Zyvatkauskas, Sonia. *Eating Shakespeare: Recipes and More From the Bard's Kitchen.* Toronto: Prentice Hall Canada, 2000.

COPYRIGHT

Goldstein, Joyce
From *Enoteca*. Copyright © 2001 by Joyce Goldstein. Used with permission of Chronicle Books LLC, San Francisco. Visit *www.chroniclebooks.com.*

Jamal, Krishna
From *Flavors of India*. Copyright © 1998 by Krishna Jamal. Used with permission of Krishna Jamal.

Jones, Bill
From *Chef's Salad*. Copyright © 2003 by Bill Jones. Reprinted by permission of Whitecap Books.

Lawson, Nigella
From *Forever Summer* by Nigella Lawson. Copyright © 2003 by Nigella Lawson. Reprinted by permission of Hyperion.

Lindsay, Anne
From *The New Lighthearted Cookbook: Recipes for Heart Healthy Cooking* by Anne Lindsay. Copyright © 2003 by Anne Lindsay. Used with permission of Key Porter Books.

McIntosh, Barbara-jo.
From *The Tin Fish Gourmet: Great Seafood From Cupboard to Table* by Barbara-jo McIntosh. Copyright © 1998 by Barbara-jo McIntosh. Used with permission of Barbara-jo McIntosh.

McNair, James
From *James McNair's Cakes* © 1999 by James K. McNair, photographs by Andrew Moore. Used with permissions of Chronicle Books LLC, San Francisco. Visit *www.chroniclebooks.com.*

Menghi, Umberto
From *Toscana Mia: The Heart and Soul of Tuscan Cooking* by Umberto Menghi. Copyright © 2000. Used with permission of Douglas & McIntyre.

Peterson, James
From *Glorious French Food* by James Peterson. Copyright © 2002 by James Peterson. All rights reserved. Reproduced here by permission of Wiley Publishing, Inc.

Veljacic, David
From *The Fire Chef: Fast Grilling and Slow Cooking on the Barbecue* by David Veljacic. Copyright © 1999 by David Veljacic. Used with permission of Douglas & McIntyre.

INDEX

INDEX

INDEX

INDEX

INDEX

INDEX

INDEX

INDEX

INDEX

INDEX

INDEX

John Burns is a Vancouver-based journalist and editor at the *Georgia Straight*, Canada's largest alternative weekly, who writes frequently on food, trends, and publishing. He is a frequent contributor to the Canadian Broadcasting Corporation.

Elisabeth Caton is a long-time educator and food writer who lives in Vancouver.